Business Strategy and Competitive Advantage

Michael Porter is recognised as one of the top authorities on business strategy and competitive advantage. The historical review of strategic management clearly shows that Porter's research has bridged up two general paradigms (before and after the 1980s) thus helping both researchers and practitioners to better understand unanticipated global changes. His two generic strategies, cost leadership and diversification, the two interdependent strategic options, are key in the context of the competitiveness of orthodox microeconomic theory. This is where Porter went further, constructing a popular value chain concept that provides the ability to disaggregate the key activities of business process in creating products and services in terms of cost analysis and value creation.

This book is a collection of seven interconnected chapters that provides a coherent understanding of Michael Porter's contribution to the field of strategic management. It addresses key changes and challenges in the global business environment. The value chain concept has become highly applicable in both theory and practice. In this book, the authors offer an original interpretation of the Porters' research on strategic management in order to unravel or simplify his key theoretical concepts. It will be of interest to researchers, academics, practitioners and students in the fields of strategic management and international business.

Jovo Ateljević is a Professor of Economics and Business Studies in the Department of Economics at the University of Banja Luka, Bosnia and Herzegovina.

Dženan Kulović is an Associate Professor of Management and Organisation in the Department of Economics at the University of Zenica, Bosnia and Herzegovina.

Filip Đoković is an Associate Professor of Tourism and Business Studies in the Department of Tourism and Hotel Management at the Singidunum University, Serbia.

Mirza Bavčić is a Country Manager and Co-owner of Express Courier - Authorised Service Contractor for UPS in Sarajevo, Bosnia and Herzegovina.

Routledge Research in Strategic Management

This series explores, develops and critiques the numerous models and frameworks designed to assist in strategic decision-making in internal and external environments. It publishes scholarly research in all methodologies and perspectives that comprise the discipline, and welcomes diverse multi-disciplinary research methods, including qualitative and quantitative studies, and conceptual and computational models. It also welcomes the practical application of the strategic management process to a business world inspired by new economic paradigms.

Strategic Analysis: Processes and Tools
Andrea Beretta Zanoni

Strategic Management and the Circular Economy
Marcello Tonelli and Nicolò Cristoni

Strategic and Innovative Pricing: Price Models for a Digital Economy
Mathias Cöster, Einar Iveroth, Nils-Göran Olve, Carl-Johan Petri and Alf Westelius

Competitive International Strategy: Key Implementation Issues
Edited by Anders Pehrsson

Ambidextrous Strategy: Antecedents, Strategic Choices, and Performance
Agnieszka Zakrzewska-Bielawska

Strategic Management During a Pandemic
Edited by Vikas Kumar and Gaurav Gupta

Acquisitions and Corporate Strategy: Alliances, Performance, and Divestment
Edited by David R. King

Strategic Management and Myopia: Challenges and Implications
Wojciech Czakon

Business Strategy and Competitive Advantage: A Reinterpretation of Michael Porter's Work
Jovo Ateljević, Dženan Kulović, Filip Đoković and Mirza Bavčić

https://www.routledge.com/Routledge-Research-in-Strategic-Management/book-series/SE0470

Business Strategy and Competitive Advantage

A Reinterpretation of Michael Porter's Work

Jovo Ateljević, Dženan Kulović, Filip Đoković, and Mirza Bavčić

Routledge
Taylor & Francis Group
NEW YORK AND LONDON

First published 2023
by Routledge
605 Third Avenue, New York, NY 10158

and by Routledge
4 Park Square, Milton Park, Abingdon, Oxon, OX14 4RN

Routledge is an imprint of the Taylor & Francis Group, an informa business

ISBN: 978-1-032-41666-3 (hbk)
ISBN: 978-1-032-41668-7 (pbk)
ISBN: 978-1-003-35917-3 (ebk)

DOI: 10.4324/9781003359173

Typeset in Bembo
by MPS Limited, Dehradun

Contents

Tables

Figures

Preface

Paradigm change in the strategic management led to the emergence of the paradox of strategic thinking, according to which, on the one hand, there is an inadmissible vagueness of strategic management, and on the other hand, its strong expansion. However, it is unchanged that the creation and maintenance of competitive advantage remained at the heart of the business strategy. Undoubtedly, the most important contribution to the permanent removal, and permanent reshaping, of that very paradox was made by Harvard Business School Professor Michael Porter, generally recognised as the father of the modern business strategy. His works have shaped our basic understanding of competitive advantage and competitive strategy over the past three decades despite the fact that he has widely been contested and often criticised. The integration of these two, theoretically separated but practically deeply connected processes, is the essential topic of this book, which is primarily intended for academics and practitioners. Michael Porter's comprehensive view of strategic management significantly determined the content of the book, which consists of six interrelated chapters. They follow and clarify Michael Porter's concepts – how they were tentatively created deepened over time and supplemented by criticism. The ultimate aim of this book is to clarify Porter's contribution to strategic management based on the industrial organisation, on the basis of which he founded his, to date, it seems, unsurpassed conceptual concepts. The formation of a generic business strategy is conditioned by the analysis of the company (with the help of the conceptual framework of the value chain) and the analysis of the environment (with the help of the conceptual framework of the five competitive forces), on the basis of which it creates and maintains a competitive advantage through the lens of sources of competitive advantage (low costs or differentiation). Thanks to his unique ability to connect economic theory and managerial practice, Michael Porter helps us understand business strategy as an existential being of modern strategic management. This book not only brings together the influential works of Michael Porter but also contains his latest reflections on competitiveness in the world of global business. Despite the dramatic changes in the competitive environment, his concepts remain highly relevant.

Authors

1 Shifting Paradigms in Business Competition

Introduction and context

The competitiveness of companies is the key to their success and survival in a changing global market. In spite of numerous successes, companies, that is, corporations are increasingly facing problems, and academic circles emphasise that the way they are managed is not synchronised with changes in the business environment. Despite the fact that a small number of large companies dominate the global market, there are a significant number of those who are continuously fighting for mere survival, as well as those who are not in the system of related economic and political power. With the changes that have taken place in the economy, both globally and nationally, especially since the peak of the semi-global financial crisis, the so-called classic "hands off" capitalism is experiencing a rapid transformation in which political power comes to the fore. This was most felt by the financial sector, which according to research considers politics (political power) to be the biggest risk factor. This new approach to the economy aims to control global banks and fragment the banking sector (although we are witnessing the business success of large US banks), but its failure would not have a significant impact on the global market. The price of rescuing banks during the financial crisis is paid by market participants, the economy and ordinary people. The new interventionism implies greater fiscal control and more aggressive tax policy, even a reduction in the internationalisation of domestic companies. The active role of the state, on the one hand, and the demands of the public/consumers, on the other hand, impose new rules in the business environment and pose new challenges for businesses whose positioning requires an innovative approach to strategic decision-making. According to the results of a significant number of empirical studies, in changed circumstances, concern for company behaviour is evident in a wider range of interest groups, including employees, consumers, the local community and public sector representatives. This attitude changes the traditional approach of companies in creating values based on their own interests and the interests of owners and executive managers. Also, this attitude affects their defined business strategies. The influence of interest

DOI: 10.4324/9781003359173-1

groups on the strategic directions of companies also affects their social position. The purpose of the company is reflected in the process of making strategic decisions. The aim of this introductory chapter is to analyse changes in strategic management with a focus on the purpose of the company, a concept that is often understood in theory and practice as an abstract construct. In order to better understand the context and concept of new approaches in running companies, this chapter covers a relatively long period of time: From Alfred Marshall to the present – in the interaction of macro and micro aspects of economic trends. In that sense, the structure of work is defined, starting with the evolution of economic thought.

The evolution of economic thought: From cost control to the affirmation of the knowledge economy

In 1942, John Maynard Keynes used a biographical essay on his mentor, Alfred Marshall, to describe a good economist:

> ... he must be mathematician, historian, statesman, philosopher – in some degree. He must understand symbols and speak in words. He must contemplate the particular in terms of the general, and touch abstract and concrete in the same flight of thought. He must be purposeful and disinterested in a simultaneous mood; as aloof and incorruptible as an artist, yet sometimes as near the earth as a politician.
> (The Economist, 2017a:63)

Such perfection is almost impossible to meet, so Keynes thought: *God, even competent economists are rare birds*. It was at the Cambridge, the Department of Economics, which was founded by Marshall himself, the father of economics as a scientific discipline. At a time when the Cambridge School of Economics was the leading school of its kind, the best were educated there and earned the title of economist in order to be successful traders, able to provide advice to policy makers, impartially and professionally. Today exam questions, both at the Cambridge and at other universities, are different, technically more demanding, and the answers require solid knowledge of mathematical models. All this tells us how much economics as a scientific discipline has evolved.

Let us return to Alfred Marshall, the author of the popular textbook *Principles of Economics* (1890), in which he established the use of diagrams illustrating economic phenomena, including the supply and demand curve, the mantra of microeconomic analysis. As an economic neoclassicist, Marshall used a fictitious firm as a unit of analysis in optimising business costs (minimising costs) in his research. Focusing on the cost leadership of the observed company, he often did not take into account other aspects of its business, including innovation, technological progress, business decision-making and everything that is necessary today to manage the company. The central Marshall's problem, as well as the problem of the economist Leon Walras (Walras's law, the theory of general equilibrium,

$$\sum_{j=1}^{k} p_j \cdot D_j - \sum_{j=1}^{k} p_j \cdot S_j = 0 \tag{1.1}$$

where p_j is the price of goods, D_j is supply and S_j is demand, respectively),[1] is the role of prices in conditions of balanced supply and demand. Hence, the term marginality means the use of marginal concepts within the economics. Marginal concepts include marginal cost, marginal productivity and marginal utility, the law of reduction of the rate of replacement (substitution) and the law of reduction of marginal utility.

We must emphasise that Marshall, who studied history and philosophy in addition to economics, claims that fragmented statistical hypotheses are used as a temporary means of measuring dynamic economic concepts (principles), so economics should be understood as a living force or driver, and its main concern is human beings who need to be encouraged to think and make decisions: Good or bad, in order to create social change and progress.

Keynes and Pigou, both Marshall's students, transformed this discipline by giving it a new theoretical basis in terms of the functioning of the economic system, taking an active role in creating economic policies. Many well-known economists agree that the discipline at both the micro and macro levels is overloaded with numbers and facts whose sources are often questionable, and their analysis yields estimated results (predictions) of economic trends.

New economic paradigms

After more than a century, the circumstances in the global market are incomparably different. The increasingly dynamic global market and accelerated technological changes have called into question the sustainability of the company's competitive advantage, as well as the conventional approach to strategic planning. In such circumstances, the company's management uses various conceptual tools and techniques such as Total Quality Management (TQM), benchmarking, restructuring and the like to improve productivity and the quality of products and services. The results are excellent in terms of operating level but often unsustainable in terms of profitability. Why is it so?

More than 50 years ago, the competitiveness of companies was largely based on cost leadership, i.e. low production or operating costs. Lowering relative costs often results from the benefits of the curve of experience. With the rise of global competition, other approaches to creating competitive advantage were born, including diversification, which is characteristic for the period of the 1980s. Also, during this period, one of the most deserving scientists in the field of management, especially strategic, Michael Porter, worked and created. His works which related to *competitive advantage* at both micro and macro levels are still an indispensable reference in teaching and research in the field of economics. He defined and affirmed widely known generic strategies that take significant place in both theory and practice. Indeed, Porter's contribution to the field occupied the central stage as presented in Table 1.1. He developed some of the most applicable models in theory and practice including five forces and value chain frameworks. The historical review of strategic management clearly shows that Porter's research has bridged up two general paradigms (before and after the 1980s), thus helping both researchers and practitioners to better understand changes. Certainly, managers must comprehend the evolution of strategy to effectively facilitate decision-making process, closely following key changes in the business environment, most of all digital technology and digital transformation. However, the essence of strategic management remained unchanged that is matching business resources to market opportunities.

Now we return to the conventional way of business strategic thinking. Two generic strategies, costs and diversification, are keys in the context of the competitiveness of orthodox microeconomic theory whose analysis is largely based on market demand dynamics.[2] In the business world, there are two demand conditions that a company encounters in terms of supply: A flat demand curve[3] (Figure 1.1) and the downward curve[4] (negative downward slope, the law of diminishing demand; Figure 1.2) for most goods and services (not always the case for luxury goods/services).[5] Other factors that affect demand should be mentioned, such as those related to the amount of income – personal income, substitutes, complementarity, taste and consumer preferences, etc.

In the second case where the curve tends to fall,[6] the perception of customers in terms of the value that one company offers in relation to another means that prices are simply determined by the market mechanism,[7] regardless of the wishes of the company. In such circumstances, there is always only one type of generic strategy to create a competitive advantage for a company, and that is low production costs. Although there are a number of ways for a company to position itself at the bottom of the cost curve in the market, each approach should provide a competitive advantage of low costs. This is where Porter went further, constructing a popular *value chain* concept that provides the ability to disaggregate the key activities of business process in creating products and services in terms of cost analysis and value creation. Here we are talking about a new paradigm of cost management, i.e. the transition from the classic costing to the so-called *Activity-Based Costing* (ABC) method, which introduces radical changes in business management. The conventional approach to measuring effectiveness and efficiency is solely based on traditional accounting performance measures, while the Balance Scorecard (BSC) best reflects a modern approach that takes into account qualitative measures.

Table 1.1 Understanding strategic management over time

Period	*1960s*	*1970s*	*1980s*	*1990s*	*2000*	*2020s*
Label	Definition of Strategy	Conceptualising Strategic Management	Industrial Organisation Economics View of Strategy	Resource-Based View of Strategy	New Paradigm for Strategic Management	Digital Transformation
Selected authors	Andrews (1971)	Rumelt (1974), Mintzberg (1978)	Porter (1980), Porter (1986)	Bartlett (1979), Ghoshal (1986), Wernerfelt (1984), Barney (2001), Prahalad and Hamel (1990)	Nonaka (1991), Hammel (2000), Pfeffer and Sutton (2000), Everett Rogers (2000)	Kaufman and Horton (2015), McGrath (2013), Kotter (2012), Bolstorff (2003)
Dominant themes	Corporate strategy, planning growth	Strategic management content and planning	Competitive advantage development	Resources and capabilities development	Learning knowledge and innovation	Digital intrinsic agility, digital balance, digital frameworks
Rationale	Strategy as a rule for making decisions	Evaluation and implementation of critical aspects of formulated strategy	Five forces analysis of the industry attractiveness to develop competitive advantage through generic strategy	Valuable, rare and costly to imitate	Dynamic strategic model to obtain information, create knowledge and intangible capabilities	Exploitation of new business strategy opportunities Brand controls the channel; digital media create values Strategic role of customers

(Continued)

Table 1.1 (Continued)

Period	*1960s*	*1970s*	*1980s*	*1990s*	*2000*	*2020s*
Concepts and tools	Strengths, Weaknesses, Opportunities, and Threats (SWOT); value, rarity, imitability, and organization; experience; curve; Boston Consulting Group (BCG)	Value chain	Five forces model; strategic choice, value chain model	Core competence; value system; VRIO; game theory	New integrated information technology system	Digitally Integrated Organisation (DIO); Integrated Digital Marketing (IDM) Strategic Analyses; Customer Relationship Management (CRM); Social Customer Relationship Management (SCRM)

Source: Adopted from Mele and Guilen (2006) and extended by the authors.

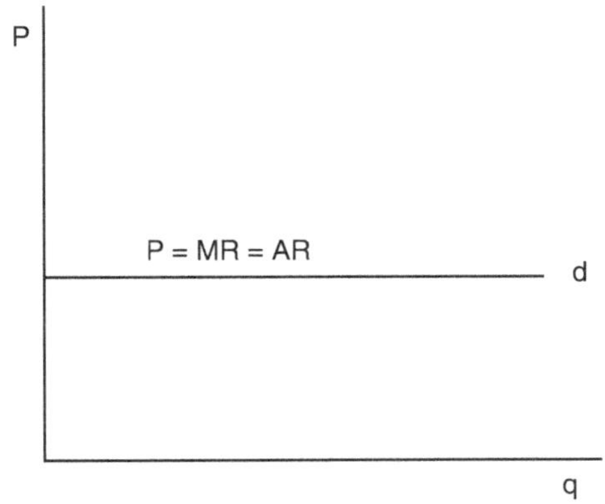

Figure 1.1 Flat demand curve.

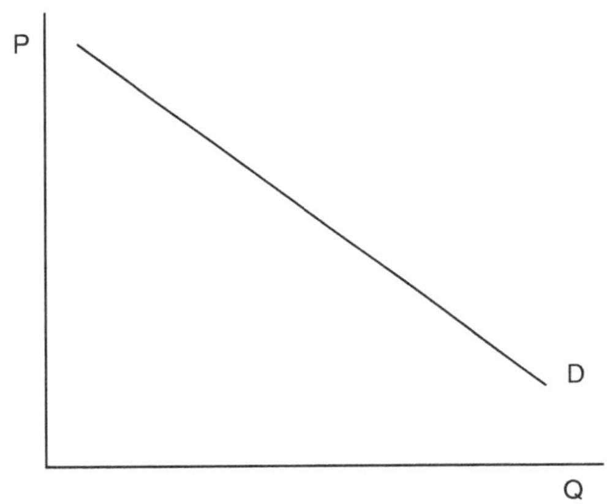

Figure 1.2 Curve of the law of diminishing (market) demand of a competing company.

Source: The authors.

One of the most popular business approaches of recent times related to cost management is *outsourcing* or relocation of certain business activities, which has significantly contributed to the change of market structures and cost management. The value chain has become extensible and does not end with the sale of goods and services, or monitoring of their use and customer satisfaction (e.g. post-service), just as it does not begin with the procurement of inputs for production. A good part of the value in the chain arises in the research and development (R&D) phase. Thus, the *value chain* has evolved: From production to market orientation. Thanks to this approach, companies create higher quality products at significantly lower costs.

In the context of the traditional model, i.e. the supply and demand curve, the question of customer preference in terms of decision-making in the buying process arises, where customers choose (*trade off*) between the perceived value (specificity) and price. Those who value the uniqueness of products and services more are willing to pay a higher price. Such a phenomenon on the market is a problem for microeconomists when modelling supply and demand. In circumstances where customers have a choice, the popularity of the diversification strategy grows, but under the conditions that the company keeps costs at more or less the same level, lower than the competition costs and convinces customers that the diversified product/service is better than competitors. There are several ways to achieve a diversification advantage, but only one is crucial in creating a competitive advantage.

From the previous discussion, it can be concluded that according to microeconomic theory, there are only two provable ways to achieve enterprise competitiveness. The question is whether something has been applied in theoretical settings in the last 30 years, and what characterises competitiveness today. Today, it is widely known that (positioned) companies do not have a ready response to defense against competition and can rely less and less on strategies of low costs and diversification. Global competitions, easier access to financial capital, erosion of entry barriers in the international market, significantly hinder the sustainability of competitive advantage. A large number of examples from practice support this claim. In practice, company managers are increasingly using a comprehensive and dynamic approach to management, often abandoning possible competitive positions. Why? Porter in his work *What Is Strategy* (HBR) claims that operational efficiency, although necessary for achieving superior performance, can be easily and quickly copied. In essence, strategy is the selection of a unique position built into a system of activities that is much harder to imitate. Using cases such as IKEA and Vanguard, Porter showed in his analysis that compromise and coherence between activities are necessary for strategic sustainability. However, these and other successful companies, in addition to their superior business models, have a clear mission in line with the expectations of the company's key stakeholders. In other words, they have a clearly defined purpose of the company. What has contributed to the fact that purpose as philosophy has again become a central link in the decision-making process?

Through investment, growth, development and innovation, companies have transformed the lives of many people around the world in the last 150 years, primarily in terms of quality of life. Unfortunately, when more company leadership is needed in the world, a large number of CEOs cannot argue why business is important for economic growth, development and social stability. Research shows that a small percentage (less than 20%) of managers pay attention to the purpose of the company (Craig and Snook, 2014). In many cases, there is a lack of understanding of the purpose itself, as well as a lack of its clear communication within the company. Researchers claim that global market disruptions, including the financial crisis and the scandals of large companies, have led to the situation in which the public, especially the younger ones, have less and less confidence in the business world – both in companies and CEOs. Companies are also blamed for the lack of care for the environment, as well as the deepening of social differences. Between 2004 and 2014, GDP per capita globally grew from $7,781 to $10,779 (Allianz, 2015:10). Despite the general increase in wealth, changes in the field are insignificant: Inequality is at its historical peak; 1% of the population controls over 50% of wealth (Allianz, 2015:12). The differences are growing even within companies, where the salaries of CEOs are up to 350 times higher than workers' salaries (Gretchen, 2014). It is worth identifying other reasons such as the erosion of brand control through more intensive use of social media and consumer influence; threats and opportunities of digitalisation and technology in general (rapid expansion of broadband Internet); thinking about changes of employees, the public, investors, local communities and other stakeholders. There are a growing number of practitioners and theorists who believe that leadership and how to motivate employees in complex times should be based on greater participation of employees and other stakeholders in the company's strategic decision-making process.

In the context of technological progress, the trend of reducing employees in production, especially in developed countries, is unstoppable. According to research by the United Nations Institute for Development and Organization (UNIDO), there was a significant drop in employment in the manufacturing sector, to just 63 million in 2014, while that number rose in developing countries from 234 million in 1991 to 304 million in 2014 (Figure 1.2; The Economist, 2017b:18). This is where the value of added value is hidden, which is much higher in technologically developed countries, where 1/6 of the workforce creates 2/3 of the final value of the product (The Economist, 2017b:18). Market leaders invest in R&D, innovation, business alliances, marketing and all those business model activities where the company capabilities play a key role in creating products and services, while activities that largely do not require this are relocated where there are low costs, proximity to the raw material base, lower taxes and other administrative burdens, proximity to the market, etc. The expansion of this way of doing business has influenced the modernisation of programmes at the faculties of economics and management. Subjects such as international business, supply chain management occupy a dominant place at leading global universities and business schools (Figure 1.3).

Conceptual and practical understanding of the purpose of the company

What is the *purpose*, and what is its essential meaning in the context of business activity? The term *purpose* itself has no universal definition and has different meanings in theory and practice. In the social sense, the purpose means the reason for existence and inspires the call to action. In a business context, this concept means acting in accordance with the purpose in order

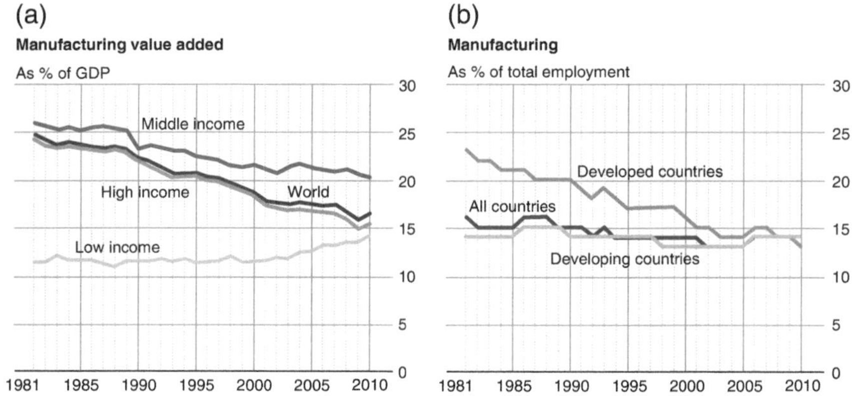

Figure 1.3 Decline of manufacturing jobs.

Source: The Economist (2017b:18).

to create added value for owners and society over time. In the management literature, the purpose of a company is defined as the central reason for its existence, a key goal of the company that connects all those who in one way or another depend on the company and vice versa. Purpose is an integral part of a company vision and mission and is directly influenced by four groups of factors: corporate governance (who the company should serve), business ethics (purpose priorities), interest groups – stakeholders (who the company serves) and cultural context (purpose priorities). The purpose of the company puts people and their expectations at the centre of the company. This approach to managing a company is necessary to understand the complex role of people inside and outside the company (Johnson et al., 2005).

Purpose and academic discourse

After losing its importance in the 1970s and 1980s, the purpose as a business guide became relevant again in the late 80s of the 20th century, in order to gain full affirmation in the business community and society today. Public discourse on the purpose of business companies has quadrupled since 1994, and is growing exponentially, even faster than the discourse of "sustainability" (EY Beacon Institute, 2015). It is obvious that companies that have realised the importance of business purpose timely have become leaders or are among the most successful in the market. According to the report by the EY Beacon Institute in just a few years, from 2013 to 2015, in over 100 research papers, the purpose of the company was the subject of analysis. Much of the literature focuses on several current aspects, including the role of leadership in affirming a company's purpose, the purpose as a tool for involving consumers and employees in the planning process, making strategic decisions and measuring commitment to purpose itself. There are a growing number of authors who argue that the role of leadership in affirming purpose is crucial in terms of its communication within and outside the company. Connecting the leader and the purpose of the company is important because of the authenticity of the purpose, necessary to build trust with stakeholders. Empirical research confirms that this approach to running a company, which focuses on its purpose, is imposed by the behaviour of employees and their aspirations to participate in the life of the company. Case studies show that the alignment of the understanding of the *core* (central) value of the company between management and employees is crucial for its success.

According to research, a positive correlation has been expressed between the purpose and engagement of consumers, especially in the part related to corporate social responsibility (CSR). In this regard, the engagement of consumers and their expectations that companies do more than just increase profits are emphasised. However, there is not enough research to answer the question of how consumers perceive companies whose purpose is to create social and financial value compared to those who are socially responsible in the traditional way in order to minimise negative effects and intentions to do what is considered good. Some works deal with measuring the relationship between purpose and trust, authenticity and brand value, which is in line with the claim that purpose has an impact on strengthening the relationship between consumers and other stakeholders.

In the case of consumers, the literature deals with the analysis of employee participation in business processes, including decision-making, or their impact on the management of the company. In this context, a clearly defined purpose of the company has a crucial role in motivating employees and shaping their sense of "belonging" to it. Practice shows that companies that have the ability to meet the expectations of employees and realise their full capacity record better results in terms of performance, and improve productivity and creativity of employees. This is important in terms of attracting and retaining talents, and this is positively related to trust and understanding of the purpose of the company. The question arises for companies that emphasise their purpose: To what extent will such demand cause changes in the existing structure of employees in terms of achieving their greater compliance? An unambiguous understanding of the purpose of the company by the employees is important for the full utilisation of all its capacities.

The purpose and success of the company

> I think everyone who starts a business does it for a purpose. Also, I think that the fact that you are in business means that your intention is to create something that will change people's lives. Otherwise, you will not have a successful business.
>
> (Branson, 2015)

Is Nestle Corporation operating and developing for a clear purpose? Nestle has been facing perhaps the biggest challenges in the company's 150-year history lately, despite the fact that in 2015 it achieved a gross turnover of $90 billion in 189 countries (www.nestle.com). In the USA alone, the company lost over 3% of the market in a relatively short period of time, which is worrying for this type of industry. Why? More and more consumers are avoiding packaged "unhealthy" foods, foods that contain sugar, salt and preservatives. Paradoxically, in addition to main competitors, Kraft and Heinz (one company since 2015), the biggest competitors of this giant are small companies that offer healthier food and are "closer" to the consumer – companies with a clear business vision and purpose, and greater responsibility towards society. Nestle had a massive programme of selling baby food to third world countries, which turned out to be unhealthy, and that it causes health problems and death. The company reacted only after 10 years: After an intensive boycott of the market and negative publicity (Ivypanda, 2021). Global markets also reacted.

The purpose in itself seems like a simple concept. In a broader sense, the purpose defines the role of an individual or company in society, and with the complexity of interpersonal relationships it helps to harness the energy and creativity of employees for the growth and development of the company. Drucker believes that experts cannot be controlled, but motivated, because for them, the purposefulness of business is more important than profit. If the whole game is turned in the direction of money, disparities and improper distribution are inevitable (Harvard Business Review, 2009). In an extensive analysis of the EY Beacon Institute from 2016, five ways were identified which explain how a clearly defined purpose significantly affects the success of the company (Table 1.1).

Measuring business success

When we talk about measuring the success of a company, it is important to distinguish the set goals from their realisation. In many cases, that is, companies, there is a big gap between the belief that purpose needs to be built into the company and the ability to make it happen, ideal in relation to the actual purpose, as shown in Table 1.2. In a large number of sectors (industries), the largest gap was recorded in leadership, development and training of human resources, performance and reward measurement matrix, and talent and knowledge management.

Outcomes of purpose-oriented strategy, decisions and action plans can be measured in a conventional way using variables such as revenue growth, market participation, customer loyalty and satisfaction, brand reputation, etc. However, there are a large number of researchers and practitioners, and other experts who believe that non-financial aspects (variables) should be included in the metrics of measurement in order to answer the following question: How do company actually create value?

Table 1.2 Purpose as a generator of success and defining an action plan

1 Purpose as the basis of strategic clarity	• Purpose serves as a guide for short-term and long-term decision-making, especially in times of transformation and growing expectations; • Application of purpose as a guide for doing business, what should/should not be done; • The purpose serves as a magnifying glass to see the overall picture of the company as a system.
2 Purpose channels innovation	• Purpose provides a framework that helps the company understand the bigger picture in terms of product and service improvement; • Purpose helps employees see themselves in the role of problem solving and value creation; • Purpose prevents short-termness and broadens horizons for employees.
3 Purpose as a force for transformation and response to challenges	• Motivation by purpose not by fear in challenging times; • Purpose as a driver of change, help in understanding the long-term context of short-term changes; • Purpose as a force to help the company resist external pressures and create value in a different way.
4 Purpose and understanding of universal needs	• Purpose helps us to understand better people's "hidden" needs and contributes to defining broader goals; a strong driver of behaviour; • The purpose helps to bring together global differences – teams, in an innovative way.
5 Purpose helps business connection	• Using the purpose as a guide and strength for better business cooperation; • Using the purpose for finding a common ground for questions about why and how business cooperation works; • Using the purpose within the company to help individuals understand in each part of the company the common goal and act in that direction.

Source: EY Beacon Institute (2017).

When we talk about the very purpose of the company, we cannot help but emphasise the contribution of Peter Drucker, one of the leading, if not the main founders of modern management. In his long career as a consultant, writer and advisor, Drucker has made significant contribution to addressing pragmatic solutions in local communities around the world; he regained confidence in companies (and businesses) shortly before the major corporate and accounting scandals and the global financial crisis; he motivated talents who do not expect an unrealistic monetary reward; he addressed the problems that today's society is facing, including climate change, health care, education, etc. (Harvard Business Review, 2009).

In his work, Drucker emphasises the importance of the wider business environment and very rarely blames individuals for failure. He believes that it is necessary to look at the system as a whole, as well as the design of the company and its organisation, processes, norms and routine, and above all the purpose of the company. In a number of consulting projects, Drucker's key question is: What is your mission?

Balancing business models and company strategy

Despite arguments based on empirical research enough to change the business philosophy, Davos (2017) seems to have shown that there are no significant changes, at least when it comes to multinational companies. True, there is concern among CEOs as a result of the revolt of a growing number of people against corporatism. The question faced by managers of large companies is: Who is more important, shareholders or people/consumers? Masses of concerned citizens and politicians (the example of the new US President Donald Trump) are asking companies to be more socially responsible, to invest more "at home," pay higher taxes, increase salaries and employ more people, and support politicians who will realise these demands (Navarro, 2017). Davos highlighted the key arguments of the paper which argues that economic theory is slow to detect changes in the market. Marshall's contribution, as well as the contribution of his successors, is unquestionable, but it is necessary to respect the context of the time more. Marshall defined the principles of supply and demand in the context of perfect competition, where market participants do not have a significant impact on prices, and in such circumstances, business efficiency, whatever that means, is the dominant factor in the company's success. In changing market circumstances, the competitiveness of a company is based on internal capabilities (Barney, 2001) and special competencies (Hamel and Prahalad, 1994) which further denies the principle of the supply and demand curve. Efficiency will certainly remain an important aspect of strategic decision-making. However, in the architecture of modern business models, effectiveness is central. Efficiency in business means doing the right things, where the difference between the actual and the desired output is determined during the measurement. In order to achieve better efficiency, discipline and rigor are needed, which introduces certain inflexibility into the business system. However, effectiveness helps to correct long-term strategic directions in accordance with changes in the environment.

This chapter addressed several important issues and opened a debate in the field of economic theory in the context of a dynamic business environment. The question that arises is "How can it be explained that microeconomic analysis knows only two ways in which individual participants play a strategy game at the branch level?" The answer to the question posed arises from the assumption of microeconomic analysis that a price is formed in the intersection of the demand curve and the supply curve. Competitive positioning of companies in branches takes place through a strategic game as a set of market-related choices. Originally, the term market referred to the area where buyers and sellers gathered to exchange goods. In micro-economic analysis, sellers represent the industry and buyers represent the market. Each individual customer has its own demand curve as a function of price and quantity, and each individual company has its own supply curve as a function of price and quantity.

While this chapter provides a broader context of the changing business environment, the following chapters focus on Porter's contribution to this important subject.

Notes

1 Walras's law is a principle in general equilibrium theory which states that budget constraints mean that the values of excess demand (or, conversely, excess in the materials market) must give a result of zero.
2 A market is a set of buyers and sellers who, through their actual or potential interactions, determine the price of products and services. It is also a process in which the decisions of buyers and sellers for certain goods or services are harmonised through prices and competition.
3 The market of full (perfect) competition … is reflected in the form of a short-term supply curve of a competing company when the part of the marginal cost curve is above the average variable costs.
4 The demand curve represents the relationship of prices and quantities of goods purchased or for which there is demand on the market; in other words, the demand curve is a graph showing the relationship between the price of goods and the quantity demanded.
5 In microeconomics, the cost curve graphically represents production costs as a function of total quantity produced. In free market conditions, efficient firms use this curve to optimise production (cost minimisation).
6 Rational buyers will buy more of those goods or services whose price tends to fall since they can buy more goods and services for their income.
7 The law of supply and demand motivates and rewards economic entities that are more efficient and productive, and punishes those that are economically inefficient and insufficiently productive.

References

Allianz, S. E. (2015): Global Wealth Report, Munich, September 29. Available at Allianz Global Wealth Report 2015 (20 April 2021).

Barney, J. B. (2001): "Is the Resource-Based Theory a Useful Perspective for Strategic Management Research? Yes." *Academy of Management Review*, vol. 26, no. 1, pp. 41–56.

Branson, R. (2015): "Purpose Transformation" Keynote Address, Purpose Power: Driving Innovation and Growth, EY-Sponsored Event. Available at https://kiteinsights.com/wp-content/uploads/2022/04/EY-the-state-of-the-debate-on-purpose-in-business-.

Craig, N., Snook, S. (2014): "From Purpose to Impact: Figure Out Your Passion and Put It to Work." *Harvard Business Review*, vol. 92, no. 5, 105–111.

EY Beacon Institute (2015): "Standardized Article Count on Corporate Purpose and Sustainability," An Analysis of How and Why Top Leaders of Global Organizations Leverage Purpose to Transform.

Gretchen, G. (September 23, 2014): "CEOs Get Paid Too Much, According to Pretty Much Everyone in the World." *Harvard Business Review*, 13–16.

Hamel G., Prahalad C. K. (1994): *Competing for the Future*, Boston: Harvard University Press.

Harvard Business Review (2009): The Drucker Centennial: What Would Peter Do. *Drucker Today*.

Ivypanda (2021): "Nestle's Baby Formula and Third World Countries." Available at www.ivypanda.com (15 August 2021).

Johnson, G., Scholes, K., Whittington, R. (2005): *Exploring Corporate Strategy, Text and Cases*, UK: Pearson Education Limited.

Kaufman, I., Horton, C. (2015): *Digital Marketing: Integrating Strategy and Tactics with Values*, New York and London: Routledge Taylor & Francis Group.

Mele, D., Guillén M. P. (2006): "Intellectual Evolution of Strategic Management and Its Relationship with Ethics and Social Responsibility." *SSRN Electronic Journal*. doi:10.2139/ssrn.960663.

Navarro, P. (2017): "Free-Trader Turned Game-Changer." *The Economist*, January 21–27, pp. 17–18.

Nestle.com (2015): Annnual Report. Available at www.nestle.com (15 October 2015).

The Economist (2017a): *Cambridge Economista*, December 24, 2016–January 6, 2017.

The Economist (2017b): *Briefing: Manufacturing*, January 14–20.

2 Porter's Contribution to Strategic Management

The paradoxical foundation of strategic management

Proper understanding of strategic management is needed to observe strategic management while acknowledging all the influential factors at the same time. If such an approach of understanding strategic management is achieved, a far more complex understanding of the strategic management theory and practice is developed: *Theory and practice that comprise not only a simple either/or choice between stability and instability, but rather a complex both/and choice between stability and instability.*

This leads to the creation of a paradox. According to Ralph Stacey (1993), a paradox can denote a clear contrast, a state simultaneously influenced by two clearly conflicting elements. Japanese companies, for example, have to cope with a paradox of simultaneously combining business operations with below average costs with business operations with above average quality. Instead of simply accepting the fact that quality costs more, companies are in search of cost reduction while increasing investment in quality at the same time (Liker and Franz, 2011).

However, American companies, for example, have to deal with a paradox of aspiring towards a state of harmony, while simultaneously aspiring towards a state of discrepancy. The power of discrepancy forces produces an atmosphere of creative tension within the company resulting in the creation and generation of new perspectives through a conflict of contrasts, changing the company and leading it into a new constellation of harmony and discrepancy (Pascale, 2005).

The principal and practical existence of strategic management leads to a paradox: On the one side, theoretically speaking, there is the unacceptable inexactness of strategic management, whereas on the other side, practically speaking, there is a strong expansion of strategic management.

The unacceptable inexactness of strategic management is characterised by the following characteristics (Nag et al., 2007):

1 Common object of interest between strategic management and several other disciplines (economics, marketing, sociology) related to it by the

DOI: 10.4324/9781003359173-2

research subject. Following that principle, the identity of the discipline is insufficiently clear by its nature and relatively disputable.

2 Today, it is possible to find a vast number of published and formally recognised definitions of strategic management, but their content varies to a high degree. Each attempt at defining strategic management as a discipline raises a host of questions with only a handful of answers.
3 A small number of papers and research cover the topic (the basic and fundamental issues) of strategic management. It is the result of a decreasing interest of the scholar and research public to focus on these questions essential in today's research practice.
4 It is evident that there is not a clearly stated agreement over the meaning of the term strategic management. Hence, there are different interpretations of this term causing a semantical confusion that reduces the credibility and scientific verification of many papers covering this topic.

The strong expansion of strategic management is characterised by the following:

1 The *new age* with its variability was a powerful factor at highlighting the strategic aspect of management encouraging a strong development of the discipline. Following this principle, we can discuss a continuous historical development and evolution of strategic management as a discipline.
2 Over 80% of all scientific contributions to the discipline aimed at special and specific content within the discipline have been created in the last two decades. Hence, the substantial development of the discipline is vast and intense with a tendency of constant development.
3 Strategic management has a highly valued magazine (publishes hundreds of articles annually), association (gathers hundreds of people annually) that discuss the discipline. This can be seen as an institutional support to the development of the discipline.
4 Today, strategic management as a regular academic discipline is present at all higher education institutions and at all course levels. Practically, the discipline is researched in all educational institutions at all study cycles.

The aforementioned characteristics confirm the real paradox that has engulfed scientists and scholars (Rasche, 2007): There is not anyone who can clearly define what strategic management is, but everyone can recognise strategic management in its essential form. The best way to understand the paradox of strategic management is to review certain paradoxes of the modern world identified by Charles Handy (1995):

- *The paradox of intelligence*: In today's conditions, intelligence is becoming a form of intangible property (asset) of successful company. The paradox of intelligence is that it is a specific form of property that depends on people and their competences. It can be easily transferred to others; it cannot be passed on; it sometimes remains hidden and undetected.

- *The paradox of work*: Work makes the world spin. It presents one of the most important backbones of human development. The paradox is that people work to create certain material assets that make life easier. To create more, people have to work more; by working more, there is less time to enjoy in life, i.e. in what they are creating.
- *The paradox of productivity*: The aspiration towards an increased productivity and reduction in the number of employees leads to an increased unemployment rate and a need to create small and medium size company (note: that is one of the changes and characteristics of the modern business world), which, then, are faced with relatively low productivity.
- *The paradox of time*: Aspiration towards efficiency increase should cut the time needed to perform various operations. That way, people would have more time. However, an increasing number of people are complaining they have less free time, which directly reflects the functioning of their business and private life.
- *The paradox of riches*: It is very complex and complicated. It actually consists of several paradoxes which are manifested in social layers within the boundaries of national economies (the rich are getting richer, the poor are getting poorer), as well as in the global world. The general idea is that around 20% people currently own around 80% of the overall riches.
- *The paradox of organisations*: It is directly related with the growth and creation of global company. The paradox is that many questions and problems imposed by globalisation have not been properly answered. Having that in mind, it is evident that some of the basic characteristics of strategic management, strategic thinking in particular, are receiving increased significance.
- *The paradox of age*: A group of several paradoxes related to the extension of the life cycle. Health service enhancement, retirement plans, high percentage of divorces, the extension of work life and similar are just some forms of its manifestation. In addition, people are continually seeking ways of ensuring a sustainable living during their lifetime.
- *The paradox of individual*: It is increasingly recognised that the individualism that dominates within Western organisations (such as those in the USA) needs to be slowly replaced by the teamwork that dominates within non-Western organisations (such as those in Japan). A common spirit should be the basis of teamwork. In this sense, people need others to be more truly themselves.
- *The paradox of justice*: A dilemma that has always existed and will probably exist forever. The paradox is that, although legal systems have developed over time, there is still a discrepancy between justice and fairness. Such a discrepancy is reflected in the business world and the way its participants function inside it.

The way which we perceive a paradox says a lot about the way we understand the theory and practice of strategic management.

The idea that the paradoxical situation which the scientific and scholar public have found themselves in can be solved defines strategic management by the following: Stability, regularity and predictability.

The idea that the paradoxical situation which the scientific and scholar public have found themselves in cannot be solved defines strategic management by the following: Instability, irregularity and unpredictability.

In the first scenario, the paradox is solved by a *permanent removal*, whereas in the second scenario, the paradox is solved by a *permanent reshaping* (Stacey, 1993).

Theoretical framework of strategic management

If we were to make an insight into the discipline's current state, it can be noticed that strategic management is being developed both as a heterogeneous and a scattered discipline (Tipurić, 2013). Without getting into details on the formation of the theoretical framework for studying strategic management, it can be undoubtedly stated that the increased focus on strategic management and its formation was strongly influenced by the observation of the concept of strategic management: *Either as a group of people or as a permanent process.*

Strategic management is not just the task or privilege of the managerial elite or a group of managers within the field of strategic management. Strategic management must be perceived as a specific philosophy and competence that embodies the entire company in order to achieve the formulated goals.

Strategic management is not just a process or a cycle, despite the fact that different authors try to represent different phases of the process by different schemes and charts. Strategic management must be recognised as a process connected with the flow of information between mutually connected phases of analysis with a purpose of achieving set goals.

Such a phenomenon often leads to the creation of a semantic disorder and inability to adequately interpret strategic management. An observation of different recently published papers leads to the conclusion that many authors, in an attempt to contribute, create, usually inconsistently, certain logical and methodological distinctions which result in different observations and different names of certain parts of strategic management. That is undoubtedly the result of selecting a certain approach to strategic management observation. Such a differentiation means a lot for the theoretical framework of strategic management, whereas it has little significance for the practical framework of strategic management since it does not, essentially, change or move anything.

The entire framework of strategic management study must consider all approaches to strategic management together: *Either as a group or as a permanent process*. This enables the creation of a theoretical framework for strategic management study whose understanding and application require forming its parts which we call constructs. Following such logic, there are groups of theoretical and practical literature categorised in several basic elements creating the theoretical framework of strategic management.

Some approaches are more widely spread and influential, whereas others have less of these features. Accordingly, the elements of the theoretical framework of strategic management can be roughly classified by scale and purpose as follows: (1) Strategic management schools, (2) strategic management perspectives, (3) strategic management tools and (4) strategic management portfolio.

Strategic management schools are conceptual frameworks used accordingly as basic theoretical instruments. For analytical purposes, the following nine strategic management schools are (Mintzberg, Ahlstrand, Lampel, 2005)

1 The design school refers to the observation of the business strategy process as an imagining process, i.e. a process of informal design.
2 The planning school refers to the observation of the business strategy process as a formal process of systematic planning.
3 The positioning school refers to the observation of the business strategy process as an analytical process aimed at business strategy content.
4 The entrepreneurial school refers to the observation of the business strategy process as a process of conceptualisation, a feature found in great leaders.
5 The cognitive school refers to the observation of the business strategy process as a mental process with an accentuated role of cognition.
6 The learning school refers to the observation of the business strategy process as a process of emerging beyond the supervision of top managers.
7 The power school refers to the observation of the business strategy process as negotiation between latently and affectively opposed sides.
8 The cultural school refers to the observation of the business strategy process as a collective process and a cooperative dimension in the process of strategy creation.
9 The environmental school refers to the observation of the business strategy process as a reactive process whose resources can be found in the extern surrounding.

The aforementioned strategic management schools are a conceptual model of investigating the process of strategic management, i.e. the role, significance and influence of formed business strategy concerning business. The basis for forming strategic management schools is mutual connections concerning the attitude and opinion of individuals which lead to the formation of logical and substantial units. Authors seek to place strategic management schools into a single unit.

Strategic management perspectives are a conditional category referring to wider and more comprehensive conceptual frameworks. For analytical purposes, the following three strategic management perspectives are highlighted (DeWit and Myer, 2014):

1 Strategy process refers to the formation of business strategy, the way to conceptualise the manner of creating a business strategy.
2 Strategy content refers to the result of business strategy, which inputs to consider to receive fixed final outputs.
3 Strategy context refers to strategic management surrounding, which intern and extern situations are embedded into the previous two dimensions.

Each strategic problem is three-dimensional: It includes the features of the process, the content and the context. A comprehensive observation and investigation of the three dimensions is the only way to understand strategic problems. Their interaction is visible. For example, the organising manner of a strategic process significantly affects the way the future strategic process is conducted.

Strategic management tools refer to more narrow conceptual frameworks used as auxiliary instruments of strategic management. For analytical purposes, the following two strategic management tools are highlighted:

1 The SWOT tool refers to the combination of strengths and weaknesses with opportunities and threats of intern factors towards extern factors.
2 The TOWS tool refers to the combination of strengths and weaknesses with opportunities and threats of extern factors towards intern factors.

All the processes need to be used to ensure an overall perspective and a credible basis for helping the company to create competitive advantage.

It often happens that certain factors are misclassified; hence, extra caution must be taken when considering a list of potential factors for discussion. However, it is far more useful and practical to say that the weakness of a company is the management's unsuccessful product development or sales increase.

Strategic management portfolio refers to conceptual frameworks used as auxiliary instruments of strategic management. For analytical purposes, the following two strategic management portfolios are highlighted:

1 Boston Consulting Group (BCG) portfolio refers to the combination of the market growth share with relative market share, starting from lower towards higher participation.

2 The new BCG portfolio refers to the combination of the degree of achieved advantage with the way of achieving advantage, starting from small towards big.

General Electric, Shell Chemicals and other have given a great contribution to its pioneer development and application. In practice, the matrix portfolio is favoured due to its simplicity, clarity and simple use. All of them provide relatively simple, basically the same, core strategy guidelines and instructions related to the specific position of the strategic business unit on the matrix. The guidelines and instructions offer advice on developing and building, keeping or selectively investing, harvesting, i.e. extracting profit or retreating and shutting down.

The presented strategic management framework offers a wide basis for studying strategic management. To this day, great efforts have been made by authors to create works attempting to define the theoretical framework of strategic management. The creation of elements shaping the theoretical framework of strategic management can be found within the framework of the tradition of strategic management or such elements are borrowed from other disciplines in order to start considering the important questions of determining the theoretical framework of strategic management.

Porter's contribution to the development of the new paradigm

In order to understand the contribution of Michael Porter to the development of the paradigm of strategic management, we need to consider the philosophy of the Harvard Business School (HBS) and the course titled *business policy*. The core of this process is certainly dominated by the *case study* method which assumes every company to be different and that it is impossible to make generalisations. The inductive approach is accepted, whereas the deductive approach is declined in the classroom.

Michael Porter, a long-standing educator covering the subject business policy at HBS, has never accepted the long known attitude of his colleagues that unique company cannot be grouped by any means. However, due to his conceptual knowledge, he has sharply recognised that everything can be combined into a single unit, and he structured a complex, integrated and multidimensional problem using the big picture approach. Michael Porter, following the death of Peter Drucker, has become the most influential guru of business strategy (Kiechel, 2010). The work of Michael Porter closely resembles the work of Igor Ansoff from 1975 (Grundy, 2003).

It can be argued that the work of Michael Porter is genuine to a high degree and a result of his own investigation leading to the development of his key ideas. He was given the title *university professor* in 2000, the highest degree there is at HBS in its, back then, 93 years of existence (Milisavljević, 2012). The importance of this title is highlighted by the fact that he is only the fourth person ever to receive it. The title exposition describes him as a pioneer in the application of the principles of economics to solve the important problems of company competitiveness and national economy. He is one of the most influential, if not the most influential, individuals in his field (business strategy and company competitiveness).

Truly, he has become the most cited author in the *Strategic Management Journal* magazine in the 1980–2000 period. His book *Competitive Strategy* is the most cited book (quoted 266 times), whereas his book *Competitive Advantage* is the third most cited book (quoted 135 times). Similarly, an old bibliometric study recognises Michael Porter as a key hub in strategic management research alongside Oliver Williams, Jeffrey Pfeffer and Henry Mintzberg (Huggins and Izushi, 2012). He founded the Strategy and Competitiveness Institute at HBS in June 2001. As the Institute's director, he is constantly conducting interdisciplinary research that enhances the intellectual capital of HBS. He usually presents his findings at the World Economic Forum where he functions as a moderator. His presence as a moderator has been noticed by politicians which can be seen through a seemingly irrelevant anecdote during the introduction of Bill Clinton at one meeting:

> … as I have never attended such a meeting, I asked president Clinton to stop by and attend the introductory part and I wanted to congratulate him and his team for founding this (The Clinton Global Initiative). President Clinton and I had a tradition of playing golf on New Year's. I can say, without a doubt, that he is a mediocre golfer. He is fun, energetic, but you know, his results, are, well, fair to middling. However, I need to point out that he is a world class organizer and motivator and this thing (The Clinton Global Initiative) is simply amazing. So president Clinton, I would like to congratulate you on your overall effort.

The work on *The Institute* is focused on three key areas:

1 Company competitiveness study and its implications for strategy;
2 The study of competitiveness of nations and its implications for strategy;
3 Interrelationships (competition and competitiveness).

After everything said, it is hard to deny that Michael Porter is not a dominant author in the field of strategic management with the highest influence on managers in and beyond the USA. Michael Porter has published two of the most influential books: *Competitive Strategy* and *Competitive Advantage*. The *Financial Times* has declared these two books *as the most influential managerial books in the last quarter of this century*.

The book *Competitive Strategy* has been published 63 times and translated into 19 languages, whereas the book *Competitive Advantage* has been published

38 times and translated into 25 languages. As highlighted earlier, Porter's educational background is characterised by interdisciplinary orientation.

He acquired his academic background in industrial organisation (doctorate in business economy in 1971). His interdisciplinary orientation is clearly visible in his books *Competitive Advantage* and *Competitive Strategy*, where he connected industrial organisation and business policy. For example, *Competitive Advantage* and *Competitive Strategy* cover a wide variety of disciplines including marketing, finance and operations while making connections with business policy and industrial organisation (Huggins and Izushi, 2012). He accentuates that it is impossible to completely comprehend competitive advantage and competitive strategy without combining all of these disciplines to form a complete picture of an overall company.

After publishing these two books, Michael Porter has, in a way, become a virtual professor, since his video presentations are used today as basic material at 56 universities worldwide. It can be freely argued that, after the publication of these two books, nothing is the same anymore in the rising scientific field of strategic management. Before these two books were published, the field of strategic management was a loosely connected set of unstructured ideas and limited theoretical realm with inconclusive implications for economic practice. After his two books appeared, strategic management has become an academic discipline formed on well-articulated theories created by answering a host of questions highly beneficial to company management. Many company located around the world and operating at different industries, such as Caterpillar, DuPont, Procter & Gamble, Royal Dutch Shell, Sysco and Taiwan Semiconductor Manufacturing Company and many others, follow the advice of Michael Porter on competitive advantage (Huggins and Izushi, 2012).

Namely, Michael Porter has proposed and created a special program at HBS for top managers (with an annual income of over one billion dollars) who represented a focus group for his future research. Michael Porter has developed a large number of concepts in his two books which have been studied by theoreticians and practitioners for over 30 years. Value chain, five forces analysis and generic strategy are only some of his key ideas.

He continually highlights the particularity of each company in his works. That is why he *dismisses the word model* and replaces it with the *word framework*. All of his works are embedded with the thesis that the essence of business strategy is the relationship between the company and its environment. Accordingly, he believes that the organisation has its analytical frame, and the surrounding has its industry frame.

The transition of the course business policy into the course business strategy

Following the recommendations of *Gordon-Howell's and Pierson's* report from 1959, a vast number of business schools introduced a course titled business policy[1] in its curriculum in the 1970s. Michael Porter has taught similar course for many years in the past. The aim of *business policy* was to integrate knowledge previously acquired in other courses in order to develop student competencies on using the acquired knowledge. The focus, from day 1, was on the case study method, a practice taken from HBS. For example, instead of having students participate in solving business problems needed for a financial or marketing analysis, business policy focuses on the development of competencies for identifying and solving real problems from a broader field of mutually independent areas.

A process of reconceptualisation of the content of business policy has occurred in the 1970s in which the course has been expanded, whereas the focus has shifted from relatively intern orientation to relatively extern orientation. The accumulation of acquired knowledge and the increase of research papers created ground for a new academic discipline: Strategic management. Such an expanded approach has led to the change of the course name from business policy to strategic management (Wheelen and Hunger, 2008).

After that, Michael Porter has taught Industry and Competitive Analysis as well as Competition and Strategy course for many years in the past.

The aim of strategic management is for students to make a connection between theory and practice by developing a comprehension of strategic tools and their limitations. In addition, an application of such comprehension is required in solving individual situation problems by identifying business strategies that fit each different situation.

Porter's theoretical ground for developing this discipline

Based on different definitions, we can conclude that the determination of business strategy is based on two key strategic dimensions:

1 Business strategy as a manner of company *behaviour at a certain period*;
2 Business strategy as a manner of company *development in the desired direction.*

Modern literature (Brnjas, 2000) tends to link these two concepts closer and integrate them. One of the best attempts at doing so was made Michael Porter himself; he used the concept of industrial organisation as the starting point. Based on his many years of work and published research on this subject, Michael Porter introduced concepts which were developed for years into the area of business strategy. Due to the dynamics of teaching which relies on the case study practice, Michael Porter was able to explain the behaviour of an individual company and the behaviour of the corporation surrounding and the way the company and the surrounding interact by means of business strategy.

He founded a rigorous theoretical framework for the industrial organisations with, back then, a still developing field of strategic management and elevated it to its current status of an academic discipline (Huggins and Izushi, 2012).

Industrial organisation is a discipline founded on microeconomic analysis. The methodology used in industrial organisation has been taken from methodologies of other theoretical disciplines and was used as a means of developing empirical research, i.e. insisting that each theoretical hypothesis is to be tested and checked through empirical research. That fact positions industrial organisation on a somewhat lower level of abstraction – it acknowledges empirical facts such as the imperfection of competitive relationships and changes in the ownership hierarchy and the corresponding changes in function of the goal.

The standard approach to studying industrial organisation according to Joe Benin (Shy, 1995) is to decompose the market to its structure, conduct and performance.

Although it is a highly developed discipline with a host of literature processing and developing in detail the theoretical concepts created from a wide variety of highly complex research, its overall theoretical, methodological and empirical literature can be placed within a simple concept known as the structure conduct performance paradigm. The relations between the three elements indicate their cause and effect character and the direction of their operation is strictly rectilinear. The specific economic theory used by Michael Porter is now well known: *The SCP* paradigm. However, when *Competitive Strategy* and *Competitive Advantage* were published, the relation between economic theory – any economic theory – and strategic management research and practice was yet to be thoroughly taken into account. This paradigm was initially created to help governments identify divisions without developed aspects of, for example, maximised social welfare and perfect competition dynamics. The two books have turned this theory upside down and identified in detail the fields needed for corporations to achieve above the average profitability (Huggins 2012).

The company is treated, in the model, as a passive object transforming the characteristics of the market structure (perfect competition, oligopoly and monopoly) into certain achieved profitability. It is no surprise that the subjects of *industrial organisation* and *microeconomic analysis* are found at the very core. Due to that fact, critics are constantly pointing out that the subject of industrial organisation is not the company, but the industry.

Considering the said, a logical question is placed: *How to explain the fact that microeconomic analysis recognises only two ways in which individual participants play the strategic game at industry level?*

The answer to this question can be found in the assumption of microeconomic analysis that *balanced price* is formed at the cross section of *the offer curve and demand curve.* Winning aspirations of company within industries are conducted via a strategic game functioning as a set of market-related ideas. Based on such an approach, Philip Kotler (2012) defines market as a set of existing and potential buyers of particular products. Initially, the term

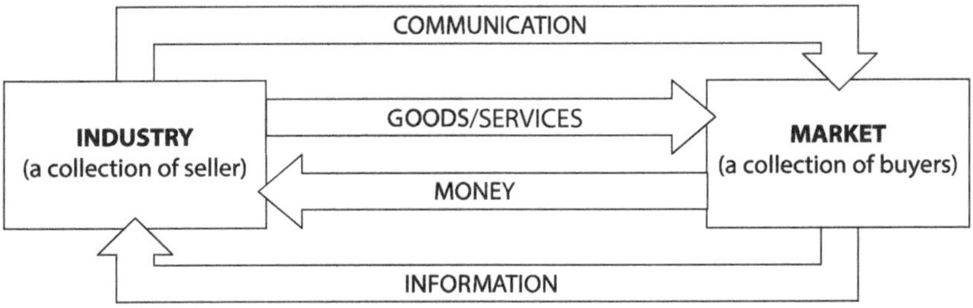

Figure 2.1 Simple relationship: industry-market.

Source: Adapted from Kotler (2000:43).

market referred to the location where buyers and sellers would meet to exchange goods. In microeconomic analysis, the seller represents the industry, whereas the buyers represent the market. Figure 2.1 illustrates the relation between the industry and the market.

Figure 2.1 shows that industry and market are bonded by four processes. The industry sends products and establishes communication with the market, whereas the market sends money and provides the industry with information. The inner lines display the exchange of money and products, whereas the outer lines display the exchange of information and communication. Market size depends on the number of buyers interested in a certain product. Hence, we have the following (Kotler et al., 1999):

a Potential market;
b Available market;
c Qualified market.

Potential market is a group of buyers interested (displaying a certain amount of interest) in buying a certain product. The sole interest of buyers is not sufficient enough to define a market. *Available market* is a group of buyers with an interest, income and availability for buying a particular product. The company or country can limit product sales to particular buyers in certain markets. Limiting the sales implies that the potential buyer has to be qualified. *Qualified market* is a group of buyers with interest, income, availability and qualifications for buying a particular product (Kotler, 2000).

The company can focus on the entire market or a particular segment. The *aimed (or covered) market* is the part of the market which the company plans to conquer. *Penetrated (or conquered) market* is the part of market already conquered by the company.

Figure 2.2 displays previously analysed definitions together with certain suggested numbers. The left part of the figure represents the percentage of potential market compared with the overall number of population, which is 10% in our case. The right side of the figure represents the percentage of available market compared with the potential market, which is 40% in our

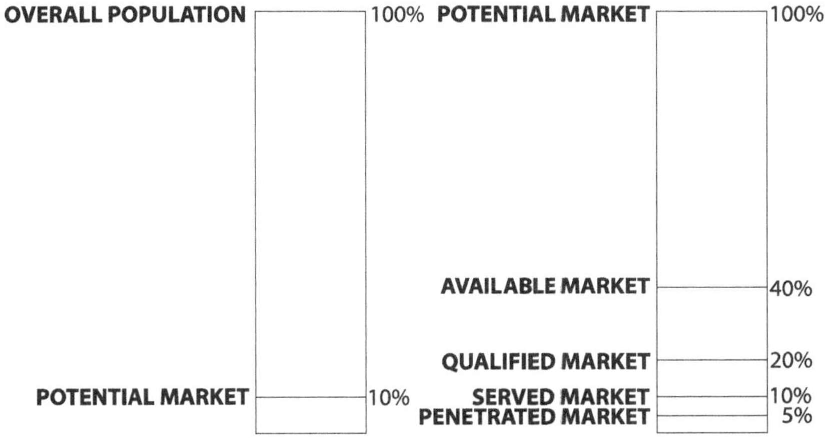

Figure 2.2 Market definition levels.

Source: Kotler et al. (1999).

case, qualified accessible market compared with potential market, which is 20% in our case, served market, which is 10% in our case compared with potential market and penetrated market, which is 5% in our case compared with potential market.

Typical market-related strategic choices include the following (Đuričin et al., 2015):

1 The growth of *core* business with a special focus on key products, market segments and geographical areas;
2 Achieving the leading position in *non-core* businesses with above the average structural attractiveness;
3 Constant preoccupation with the tendency of entering and expanding markets with above the average demographic growth.

Demand and supply operate within a market. Demand is the scale of customer determination to buy a product presented by the offer. Market selection depends on competition aspirations. It is far more important for a company to acquire competitive advantage on a market other than the one where it is positioned as a leader. However, it sometimes simply impossible not to have a clash with competition and achieve victory when the competition displays weaknesses (Đuričin et al., 2015).

Each *individual customer* has his/her *demand curve* as a *function of price* and *quantity*, and every individual company has its *supply curve* as a function of *price* and *quantity*. All mutual relations are displayed in Figure 2.3.

The curve of industry demand is a cumulate of individual customer demand curves as shown in Figure 2.3. The curve of industry demand, created in such a manner, is characterised by a negative slope. The function

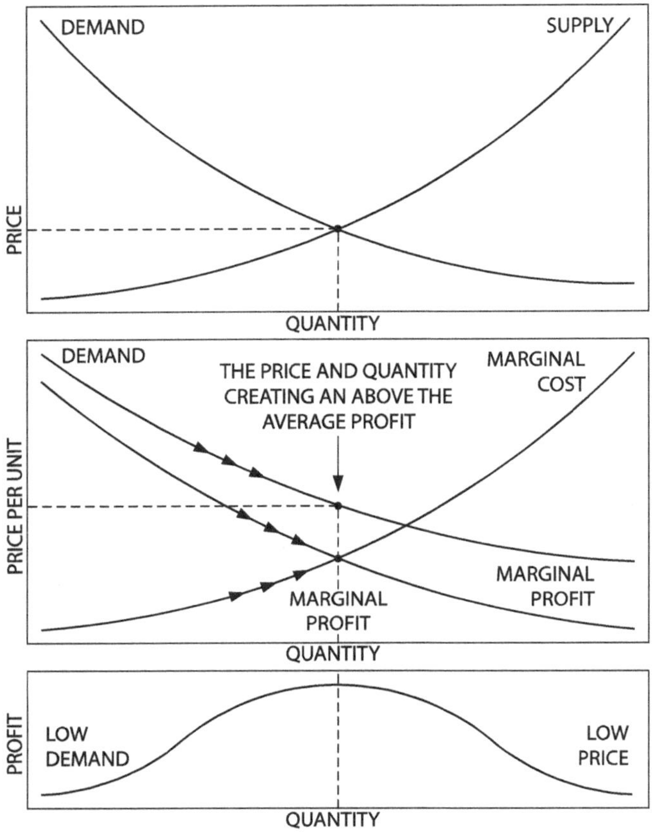

Figure 2.3 Supply, demand and balanced price in the function of profit.

Source: Adapted from Hagedoorn (1993:236).

of demand depicts the legality of buying a lesser amount of products at higher prices and vice versa by the customer. The curve of industry supply is the cumulate of individual company offers as displayed in Figure 2.3.

Looking from the aspect of *relative cost position*, higher or lower product prices *do not affect* the increase or fall of the demand for the product; hence, the *relative cost position* is the fundamental determinant of competitiveness and profitability. The price fluctuates over time, *but not as a consequence* of individual company actions. Looking from the aspect of *uniqueness*, when a balanced price is formed *as a cross-section of marginal cost and marginal income* on industry level, each company achieves different profitability (above or under its marginal cost) depending on its *uniqueness*, as shown in Figure 2.3. A microeconomic analysis results in a *slanted curve of demand* (the demand curve is less slanted than marginal income curve). Looking from the aspect of *uniqueness*, high or low product prices affect the growth or fall of product demand; hence, uniqueness is the fundamental determinant of competitiveness and profitability. The price fluctuates over time, but *as a consequence* of individual company actions.

These theoretical basics were a starting point of Michael Porter's work. Namely, his five competitive forces framework introduced in *Competitive Strategy* and company value chain framework introduced in *Competitive Advantage* are, today, standard analytical tools in industries and company, i.e. studied in detail by business school students and applied by top managers worldwide. His influence on practitioners is enormous, particularly due to his consulting activities as well as due to the application of his frameworks by others (Huggins and Izushi, 2012).

Criticism of Porter's contribution to strategic management

Michael Porter is considered one of the most influential theoreticians of strategic management today. Such a position was achieved in part due to numerous published works including two of the most noted books, *Competitive Advantage* and *Competitive Strategy*, later integrated in the book *Competitive Advantage of Nations*.

His popularity, spanning over a period of 30 continuous years, has exposed him to fierce criticism. Most critics argue that Michael Porter's attitude encourages an aspiration towards a monopoly system due to his claims that a company can achieve a higher degree of profit if the intensity of the competition is proportionally lower at a particular market segment.

Michael Porter skilfully utilised and connected all of his acquired knowledge and transferred it into concepts which have become a must in theory and practice of strategic management. He based his works vastly on existing concepts which he significantly modified, modernised and completed with his original insights which are largely a result of his experience from teaching at HBS.

The 2015 Thinkers50, in an overview of Michael Porter's contribution to strategic management, places him at the most influential management thinker in the world, whereas the popular business magazines places him at the high ranked place of thinkers who gave a vast contribution to strategic management in the last century.

Throughout his work, Michael Porter has developed a vast number of concepts which have been the focus of theoreticians and practitioners of strategic management in the last 30 years. Due to that fact, it is very hard to deny that Michael Porter is a dominant author in the field of strategic management today. However, despite that, there are a lot of critics.

Hence, *one group of critics* does not like the distinction of business strategies (cost leadership and differentiation) as generic strategies. They believe that the attainment of above the average profitability requires a combination of two generic strategies.

The *second group of critics* does not like his focus on a strategic business unit, and not organisation, which has led to fierce criticism. They believe that the portfolio concept has been discarded too early in strategic management.

The *third group of critics* does not like the fact that he does not separate the components of planning and action in his works, i.e. that he does not deal more with the shaping of business strategy. They believe that is the reason why the economic dimension, rather than the political dimension, dominates in business strategy.

Overviewing different perspectives of criticism towards Michael Porter's concepts, it can be concluded that they are faced with numerous limitations and oversights. However, this has helped many researchers to further explore both analytically and synthetically the aforementioned concepts, contributing both to their applicative and conceptual comprehension.

Without denying the benefits of such concepts as a way of strategic thinking in the process of opportunity and threat identification, all criticism can be displayed as follows:

1 All concepts (the concepts of value chain analysis and five competitive forces in particular) present a static image of competition in an industry, i.e. a strategic group – the organisation is faced with revolutionary changes altering the industry structure and strategic groups on a daily basis by reducing entry barriers into to the industry, i.e. strategic group.
2 All concepts (the concepts of value chain analysis and five competitive forces in particular) highlight the structure of competition in an industry, i.e. strategic group – the organisation can be profitable only due to its affiliation to an attractive industry and strategic group undermining the importance of diversity among organisation within a same industry, i.e. strategic group.

The fact is that the concepts proclaimed by Michael Porter do not have the same influence they had 30 years ago. The contemporary business concept, often interpreted by the phrase *New Age*, actualises new market validity that imposes new factors and demands an alignment of the organisation with its surrounding.

However, it, by no means, entails that the concepts proclaimed by Michael Porter are no longer usable. Modern conditions, without a doubt, require the consideration of concepts with all of their advantages and flaws, but within the framework of other contemporary tools of strategic management such as *Total Quality Management* – TQM and *Business Process Reengineering* – BPR.

Since he entered the stage, there have been many critics which he strongly refuted and rejected with sound arguments. Some of the most significant critics of Michael Porter who have written extensively on this topic include Henry Mintzberg, Gary Hamel and Larry Downes.

The concepts developed by Michael Porter have not been altered to this day in the sense of adding or taking away certain parts. That is the best example of their value and strength. If we were to examine Porter's recent work, we can conclude that he himself does not alter his concepts. Although we can state that the development of industries and companies was stable and simple compared with today's dynamics and complexity, the concepts fail to anticipate specific modern trends such as strategic alliances that have intertwined the relations between industries and organisation in such a way that it is impossible to give a simple explanation of the changes that have occurred on the market.

A sum up of the aforementioned criticism entails the following:

1 *The concepts represent a classic contemporary market.* Generically speaking, the concepts are intensified in regulated markets, i.e. diminished in deregulated markets.
2 *The concepts are best applicable in analysing simple market structures.* The description of concept analysis is becoming very profound in complex industries characterised by numerous interconnections.
3 *The concepts presume relatively stable market structures.* However, inertness is not an exception, but rather a rule in today's dynamic market realities significantly altering business conduction.
4 *The concepts are based on the idea of competition among* companies. They presume that companies seek to achieve competitive advantage over competition within the industry, suppliers, middlemen and buyers.

The fact is that the new modern conditions can completely change the existing business models and relationships within the value chain in a short time span. Hence, these concepts can be useful in a newly created situation and useless when dealing with predictions.

Such a focus discourages the concepts from considering the possibility of strategic alliances, electronic connection, information systems and other similar activities within the value chain. Three new forces upgrading Michael Porter's concept, exemplified by information technology, can be differentiated as follows: (1) Digitalisation which represents a wider approach to information; (2) globalisation which represents wider global cooperation; and (3) deregulation which represents the reduction in state protection.

The world of new strengths survives by feeding among itself. Information technology utilises the management of a larger number of suppliers, middlemen and customers which, in turn, accelerates globalisation.

National economies are increasingly turning into global economies; hence, there is a need for regulation in order to protect national economies. Due to an increasing pressure following a conducted regulation, only as a consequence of strategic alliances among individual national economies, with an aim of expanding the market to fit its products on the one side and an easier flow of critical information on the other side, deregulation is a process occurring with an increasing frequency. Companies, protected until now, have all of a sudden became vulnerable by realising the importance of information technologies as a vital component of companies success (Lagumdžija et al., 2008).

The number of competitors in the field of information technology was narrowed down to two: SAP and Oracle. The development of SAP and Oracle systems is completely compatible with the demands of contemporary strategic management. Keep in mind that Michael Porter tied the essence of generic strategy to value chain activities and forces within the structure of the industry focusing on the information for the planned and action component, essential for business strategy and operative efficiency.

Utilising the aforementioned information technologies provides a better understanding of the industry and company based on other and more versatile information. A better understanding of the activity leads to a more comprehensive overview of the preparation and conduction of decisions concerning cost reduction in a company and value enhancement for the customer.

The fundamental difference between the world of the so-called *Porter's powers* and the world of the so-called *contemporary powers* is, above all, the increased accentuation of the significance of information technologies. Whereas information technology was a tool for conducting change in the world of Porter's powers, it becomes a foundation for compromising the market in the world of contemporary powers.

Different approaches have led to the creation of the paradoxical foundation of strategic management, introducing a certain type of confusion into the studying and understanding of this uncompleted discipline by theoreticians and practitioners.

The contribution of Michael Porter to the development of the new paradigm imposes a need for a different understanding of strategic management. To what extent can we justify the current position of this guru on the list of the most influential theoreticians of strategic management after the death of Peter Drucker?

Analyse the contribution of Michael Porter to the development of strategic management in the context of the contemporary paradigm by comparing it with the definitions of strategic management by earlier authors such as Chandler, Ansoff and Andrews.

Note

1 Business policy received its full affirmation and popularisation in the 1950s and 1960s. The 1951 formulating and administering business policy textbook published by Christiansen, Berg, Salter and Stevenson stands out by defining business policy in its wider sense. After this publication, the business policy textbook published by Learned, Christiansen, Andrews and Guth appears in 1965 and many authors state that this book is the first significant step towards representing business policy as a form of strategic management.

References

Ansoff, I. (2007): *Strategic Management*, London: Palgrave Macmillan.

Brnjas, Z. (2000): *Strategijski menadžment: teorijske osnove sa primjerima iz praske*, Beograd: Grmeč.

DeWit, B., Myer, R. (2014): *Strategy: An International Perspective*, London: Andrew Ashwin.

Đuričin, D., Janošević, S., Kaličanin, Đ. (2015): *Menadžment i strategija*, Beograd: Ekonomski fakultet.

Grundy, T. (2003): *Gurus on Business Strategy*, London: Thorogood.

Hagedoorn, J. (1993): "Understanding the Rational of Strategic Technology Partnering, Interorganizational Modes of Cooperation and Sectorial Differences." *Strategic Management Journal*, vol. 14, no. 5, 371–385.

Handy, C. (1995): *The Age of Unreason*, London: Hutchinson.

Huggins, R., Izushi, H. (ur.) (2012): *Competition, Competitive Advantage and Clusters: The Ideas of Michael Porter*, London: Oxford.

Kiechel, W. (2010): *The Lords of Strategy: The Secret Intellectual History of the New Corporate World*, Boston: Harvard Business Review Press.

Kotler, P. (2000): *Marketing Management*, New Jersey: Prentice International, Inc.

Kotler, P. (2012): *Kotler o Marketingu*, Zagreb: Masmedia.

Kotler, P. et al. (1999): *Principles of Marketing*, London: Prentice Hall.

Lagumdžija, Z. (Ed.) (2008): *Menadžment informacioni sistemi: kompetitivnost i informacione tehnologije*, Sarajevo: Ekonomski fakultet.

Liker, J., Franz, J. (2011): *The Toyota Way to Continuous Improvement*, New York: McGraw-Hill.

Magretta, J. (2012): *Understanding Michael Porter: The Essential Guide to Competition and Strategy*, Boston: Harvard Business Review Press.

Mintzberg, H., Ostrand, L., Lampald, K. (2005): Strategic Safari: A Guided Tour Through the Wilds of Strategic Management, New York: The Free Press.

Mintzberg, H., Ostrand, L., & Lampald, K. (2005). Strategic Safari: A Guided Tour Through the Wilds of Strategic Management.

Milisavljević, M. (2012): *Strategijski menadžment: analiza, izbor, promena*, Beograd: Ekonomski fakultet.

Nag, R., Hambrick, D., Chen M. (2007): "What Is Strategic Management Realy?" *Strategic Management Journal*, vol. 28, no. 9: 935–955.

Pascale, R. (2005): *Your Company's Secret Change Agents*, Harvard Business Review.

Rasche, A. (2007): *The Paradoxical Foundation of Strategic Management*, Hamburg: Springer.

Shy, O. (1995): *Industrial Organization: Theory and Applications*, London: MITCovers, Williamson.

Stacey, R. (1993): *Strategy as Order Emerging from Chaos*, Hertfordshire: Long Range Planning.

Tipurić, D. (2014): *Iluzija strategije: Razotkrivanje socijalno konstruirane zbilje poduzeća*, Zagreb: Sinergija.

Wheelen, T., Hunger, D. (2008): *Strategic Management and Business Policy*, Englewood Cliffs, NJ: Prentice Hall.

3 Competitive Advantage

Creating sustainable competitive advantage

The fundamental question of strategic management emphasised in Michael Porter's works is (Rumelt et al., 1994): How does a company create and sustain competitive advantage?

It is evident that a company has competitive advantage if it is embedded with the ability of pleasing the customers better than its competition. The essence of a competitive position is no longer comparative advantage as a consequence of mass production and market marketing, but competitive advantage as a consequence of flexible production and collaborative marketing. In the past, it was deemed that the decrease in corporation size had to be followed by a transfer of activities to others. It was recognised as a downfall of company vitality. Today, it is believed that a decrease in company has to be followed by a creation of strategic alliances. It is recognised as an increase of competitive advantage of a company (Todorović et al., 2000). As Nataša Renko (2009) states, competitive advantage is a special feature differentiating the company from its competitors and it is particularly valued by customers. Competitive advantage is not just a question of success, since a company with competitive advantage achieves above the average profitability.[1]

Strategic competition can be viewed as a principle of working out new positions to detach buyers from their established positions or attract new buyers to the market. Hence, competitive advantage presents the decisive issue of company survival. Competitive advantage is a function of at least two groups of variables (Raguž-Vrdoljak et al., 2013): (1) Favourable national, local and industry conditions; and (2) the result of effort, people and knowledge to achieve better profitability than competition. Hence, the sources of competitive advantage can be traced down both to the environment and the company. New companies can prosper by taking the position formerly occupied by the competitor, but give it up due to its practice of being indecisive or imitating others for years. New companies arising from other industries can create new positions due to their activities

DOI: 10.4324/9781003359173-3

conducted in the previous industry. However, new positions are more often created due to changes.

Then main idea of competitive advantage is creating advantages of a company to:

1 Overpower the strengths of competition;
2 Utilise the market potential.

There are several ways for a company to handle competition. The first way is to use standard factors (e.g. delivery time); the second way is through forming unions (e.g. forming alliances); and the third way is via guerilla warfare (e.g. marketing campaigns). In any case, it is possible to change the game rules and find an alternative. Competitive advantage embodies the total system of values. The value system represents an entire chain of activities included in the process of creating and using a product. Close co-operation and constant exchange with suppliers, middlemen and buyers is involved in the process of creating and maintaining the value system.

The only way to sustain competitive advantage is to constantly upgrade. There are only a few competitive advantages that cannot be copied. That is the vital importance of constant upgrading. In some cases, the acquired competitive advantage can be sustained for decades due to an established value system (Raguž-Vrdoljak et al., 2013).

If a company has a huge advantage over its competitors, then we have absolute competitive advantage on one side, whereas if a company has small advantage over its competitors, then we have relative competitive advantage, on the other side. Most strategic-related problems in the 1960s and 1970s were solved using methods created for dealing only with individual problems (Rahimić, 2006). Accordingly, the concept of the experience curve was focused on the digression of expenses based on the economy of scale and the concept of production portfolio was focused on blunt simplification based on general conclusions. Unfortunately, the application of such concepts was not suitable for solving strategic problems. Igor Ansoff[2] is recognised as a pioneer in creating grounds for contemporary understanding of competitive advantage, stating that it is a result of seeking for a unique chance … which will enable the company to achieve competitive advantage (Ansoff, 1965).

Peter Drucker (1992), for example, highlights that business strategy is the theory on how to gain competitive advantage. If a company wants to determine whether it has achieved its ultimate goal – creating economic added value, it has to create a profit for its generation. Petraph and Barney (2003) state that a company has competitive advantage when its competent to create more economic added value than its competitors. Economic added value is the difference between the value perceived by buyers when buying products from the company and all economic expenses of those products.

Business strategy and operational effectiveness

Michael Porter (1996) states that business strategy means conducting activities that are different from those of the competition or conducting similar activities in different ways. That is the reason why he highlights the fact that company need help in achieving and sustaining above the average profitability (Porter, 2007). Companies need to be flexible to react quickly to competitive and market changes. In addition, companies need to take care of several basic competencies to maintain advantage over competition.

That is why he published an interesting article titled "What Is Strategy?" in which he literally confronted all the authors denying that positioning is at the heart of business strategy and that it is static rather than dynamic in its nature. However, he argues that it is a consequence of the fact that there is no distinction between operational effectiveness and business strategy. More worryingly, most strategic management concepts have been created as a consequence of not recognising the difference between operational effectiveness and business strategy. Operational effectiveness means conducting similar activities better than the competition. Contrary, business strategy means conducting activities that are different from the activities of the competition, or they are conducted in a different manner (Porter, 1998).

Some companies have the capacity of a better utilisation of their production factors than others due to the elimination of needless tasks, the use of modern technology, better employee motivation or a better insight of the management of certain activities. Such differences in operational effectiveness represent an important source of differences in competition profitability because they are a direct influence on the positions of relative expenses and the degree of differentiation. The difference in operational effectiveness was a source of competitive advantage in the 1980s. As competitors mutually imitate their quality enhancement, cycle time or partnership with suppliers, their business strategies become more similar, and competitiveness is turned into a race in the same track where nobody can win. Competition based solely on operational effectiveness is destructive for the competitors themselves since it causes extinction wars which can be stopped only by limiting the competition. Business strategy is creating a trade-off and competition. In addition to trade-off, it is recommended to harmonise activities conducted by the company, because such a practice reduces the expenses on one side and increases differentiation on the other side. Namely, competitive advantage is the result of a system of directed activities of a company, rather than a single activity which can be imitated by competitors. It is difficult, even for a highly capable competitor, to successfully imitate an entire system of activities.

While shaping business strategy, it is vital to research deeper and analyse each of the five competitive forces individually while acquiring knowledge on opportunities and dangers in the process. All the five competitive forces mutually form the intensity of competitiveness and profitability, and the strongest force is the decisive one when shaping the business strategy. The ultimate goal of this analysis is to explain the above the average profitability. Profitability is seen as one of the biggest indicators of company success. However, a company seeks to achieve above the average profitability which creates room for investment enhancement influencing the reduction of operating risk.

Michael Porter (Magretta, 2012) argues that the desired profitability has to be above industry average to ensure the growth and development of the company. The average industry profitability depends on the price flexibility of the product and production technology (exogenous variable) and industry structure and business strategy (endogenous variable) adopted by companies within the industry (Tipurić et al., 1999).

Michael Porter (2008) located the basis of above the average characteristics of a company in sustainable competitive advantage. It is powerful and unique enough to contribute to the above the average profitability and sufficiently adequate for further corporation development. The concept of sustainable competitive advantage is based on the long-term prospect, i.e. above the average competitive advantage sustainable over a long period of time. In other words, sustainable competitive advantage is not easily achieved nor imitated by competitors.

Michael Porter warns about the danger of demands for constant profitability. A created competitive position needs to be reinforced. However, such beliefs present dangerous semi truths which are increasingly leading companies into mutually destructive competitiveness. It is true that, as the regulatory rules are becoming more flexible and the markets are becoming more liberal, some obstacles are disappearing. The root of the problem should be sought after in the failure to make a distinction between operational effectiveness and business strategy. Operational effectiveness and business strategy are important for achieving above the average profitability which is the main goal of every company.

However, operational effectiveness and business strategy operate in very different ways. The company can deliver higher or same value to its customers with lower cost, or both. This entails the following calculation: *Providing higher value enables the company to charge more than the average unit price, whereas higher efficiency enables lower cost compared with the average unit.* The first component is associated with effectiveness (doing the right things) (Drucker, 1974) the second one is proportionally associated with efficiency (doing things right) (Figure 3.1; Drucker, 1974).

According to Aziz Šunje (2002), the following can be concluded when considering effectiveness and efficiency as two ambivalent orientations: *There is one (effectiveness) that is completely turned outwards and one (efficiency) that is completely turned inwards.*

The balancing process between efficiency and effectiveness is seen through *profit as a difference between total revenue (in that case, effectiveness is displayed as*

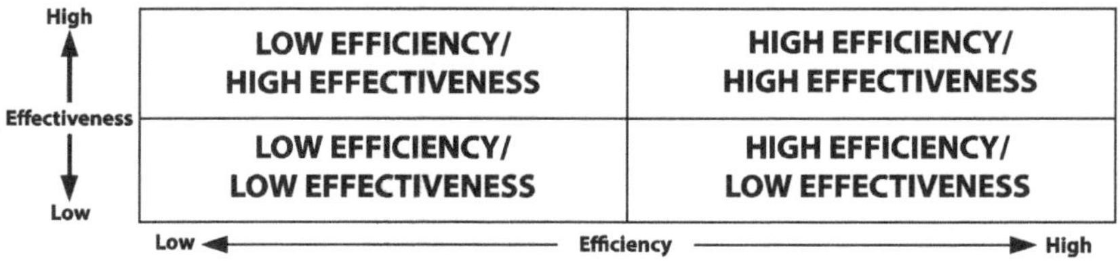

Figure 3.1 Effectiveness and efficiency ratio.

Source: Adapted from Hill and Jones (1998:6).

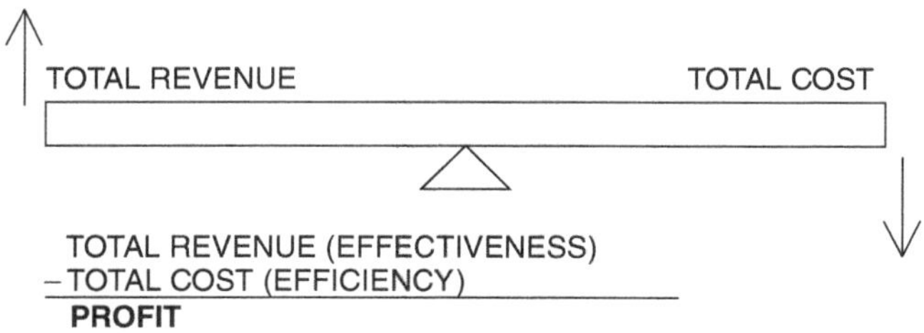

Figure 3.2 Profit as a measure of total income and total cost balancing.

Source: Šunje (2002:29).

operational effectiveness) and total costs (in that case, efficiency is displayed as operational efficiency). The stated existence of profit, in that case, confirms that the effective (total revenue) and efficient (total cost) orientation have been balanced. The goal is to make sure the total revenue (operational effectiveness) is higher than total cost (operational efficiency) (Figure 3.2).

Considering the context of operational effectiveness and operational efficiency, it can be concluded that it is quite an undertaking to keep these two ambivalent orientations balanced, i.e. to demand for both higher operational effectiveness and operational efficiency (to do the right thing in the right way). It is certain that each misbalance between operational effectiveness and operational efficiency reduces the level of success all the way to the level of failure.

Strategic positioning, once at the heart of business strategy, has been discarded as too static for today's dynamic markets and changing technology. Today, competitors can quickly copy each market position, hence competitive advantage is, at best, temporary. Positioning is one of the essences of business strategy. In the era of fast technological changes and changes of surroundings, there is an understanding that positioning has been discarded as being too static, due to the fact that a formed set of activities of a company could be easily and quickly copied by another company. In order to survive in such conditions, companies have to reorient their strategic positioning to some other possibilities. Some of these possibilities include outsourcing, benchmarking, alliances, partnerships, licensing and similar.

Michael Porter (1985) highlights the key structural industry features determining the strength of five competitive forces and industry profitability as well. The purpose is to find a position in the industry where the company can partially defend itself from five competitive forces and partially influence them to its own advantage. If there were such a single good position, there would be no need for business strategy on the market. Strategic positioning can be traced back to the positioning – analytical school of strategic management.

The school is titled as positioning due to the position inherited by the company or the position limiting and shaping its selection without defining it. *The school is additionally labelled as analytical* due to the calculations and data processing often conducted by consulting companies which effects their generic strategy proposal (Mintzberg et al., 2005).

Strategic positioning consists of three parts (Tošović-Stevanović, 2009):

1 Positioning based on the production of substituted products (Michael Porter labels it as positioning based on varieties);
2 Positioning based on needs (Michael Porter labels it as positioning based on diversity);
3 Positioning based on consumer segmentation (Michael Porter labels it as positioning based on approach).

Positioning based on variety, needs or approach or a combination requires a specific set of activities to be established. A smartly created and established set of activities can be a basis for a company for ensuring an appropriate position at the market in relation to its competitors.

There are six approaches to strategic positioning, according to Michael Porter (2001).

The first approach is to start with the right aim of achieving above the average profitability. Real economic added value can be created only if a business strategy based on sustainable profitability is used. Economic added value is created if the buyers are prepared to pay the price of a product which is higher than the costs of its production. If the goals are defined to focus on the scale of sales or market leadership with the key premise of following profit, there is usually a formation of a bad business strategy. The same scenario occurs if business strategies are created as a response to demands previously set by the investor.

In the second approach, the business strategy of the company has a task of creating a value offer or a set of benefits different from the one offered by the competition. Business strategy does not entail the best universal way for being a competitor and working hard to offer all the assets to customers. It defines the manner in which competition delivers superior value for a special set of application and a special set of customers. Value offer is an element of business strategy oriented externally in relation to the market, whereas value chain is an element of business strategy oriented towards the market. It is a somewhat limitation of activity adaptation for value delivery.

In the third approach, business strategy needs to be reflected in the reconfigured distinctive company value chain to establish new competitive advantage of a company. The company needs to configure the way of conducting primary and support activities in such a manner that it differs from competition to offer value at the market. If a company focuses on adopting the best practices, it will conduct most of its activities similarly as competition creating difficulties in forming and sustaining competitive advantage. Competitive advantage is a consequence of activities resulting in low cost or differentiation.

In the fourth approach, strong business strategies include balancing the selection of forces to be abandoned or forgotten by the company with an aim of reaching uniqueness. Such balances achieved in value chain activities are the one thing that make a company really different from others. When value chain enhancement does not require balancing, it quickly becomes the best practice which can be imitated by competitors without sacrificing their competitiveness. Trying to please all customers is an almost certain guarantee that the company will fail in achieving competitive advantage. Balancing is a choice which makes business strategy sustainable because some things are not easily balanced or neutralised.

The fifth approach entails the harmony of all elements at the disposal of a company. Business strategy includes the formation of a selection of mutually harmonised activities present within primary and support activities in a value chain. All company activities must be reinforced. In addition to reinforcing competitive advantage, such harmonisation is hard to imitate. Harmonisation implies that the values or expenses of an activity are influenced by the conduction manner of other activities. Harmonisation can be viewed as a result of the attitude that the unit is more important than individual parts, i.e. that value lies in quantity, not in several isolated parts.

The sixth approach implies that business strategy includes a continuity of directing. A company needs to define a unique value offer which will be sustained even if some variants have been overlooked. Continuous advancement is a requirement, but it always has to be strategically directed. It enhances the advancements in activities and their coordination to ensure the company forms unique competencies. Continuity does not mean inadaptability. When a company has stability at the heart of its value, it should aim at innovations. It is a paradox that the continuity of business strategy actually enhances the ability of a company to adapt to changes or innovations.

As Momčilo Milisavljević (2014) states, competitive advantage is not a static item present or absent in a company. It is more like a changing cycle process (shaped as the letter S). A company should use competitive advantage as a basis for selecting a field where it excels, instead of a field where it would like to be present. This means that it is more important for a company to establish already existing distinctive competences rather than to create new ones, which requires a longer time span. Constantly highlighting that business strategy is successful if more than one thing is done properly in a company, Michael Porter (1996) suggests a series of actions for achieving certain competitive advantages: (a) First, the company needs to create a unique competitive position; (b) second, all activities should be adapted to business strategy; (c) third, clear balance and choice compared with competition; (d) fourth, competitive advantages are rooted in the coordination of activities; (e) fifth, sustainability of competitive advantage is the result of having a set of activities; (f) sixth, operational effectiveness is a default category. That is the reason why Michael Porter (2006) argues that strategic positioning is not narrowing everything down to the question of *what shall be done, but rather a selection of things that will not be done.* A designed sustainable competitive advantage which is the heart, basis, base and driving force of business strategy is a company tool for ensuring above the average profitability – profitability above industry average.

Economic and social benefits

Michael Porter and Mark Kramer (1999) argue that a company needs to be socially responsible when generating above the average profitability by ensuring that it is possible to find convergence (approximation) between purely economic and purely social benefits. That hypothesis[3] is presented in Figure 3.3. Porter and Kramer believe that convergence is meaningful if it can meet the following two conditions: (1) It is a part of common good; and (2) it is a part of the competitive context. They highlight that social responsibility should not be discussed generally, but rather in a way suitable for the business strategy of a company.

A closer connection between social issues and company[4] operations means a higher possibility for the organisation to use its resources for useful social purposes. A transformation of activities in the value chain is suggested to make it useful for society and simultaneously reinforce the business strategy of the company. The believe that philanthropy which reinforces the ability of a company to enhance competitive conditions in the environment is useful. Integrating economic and social benefit require more than just good intentions (Milisavljević, 2014).

Creating a certain level of convergence has a double effect on the corporation: (1) It creates added social value; and (2) it reinforces the acquired competitive advantage. The authors believe that a meticulous analysis can locate areas which are embedded with pure economic and pure social benefits. Namely, without competitive advantage, a company will fall into below the average profitability which usually leads to the exhaustion of the company and its liquidation. Stronger competitive advantage leads to above the average profitability.

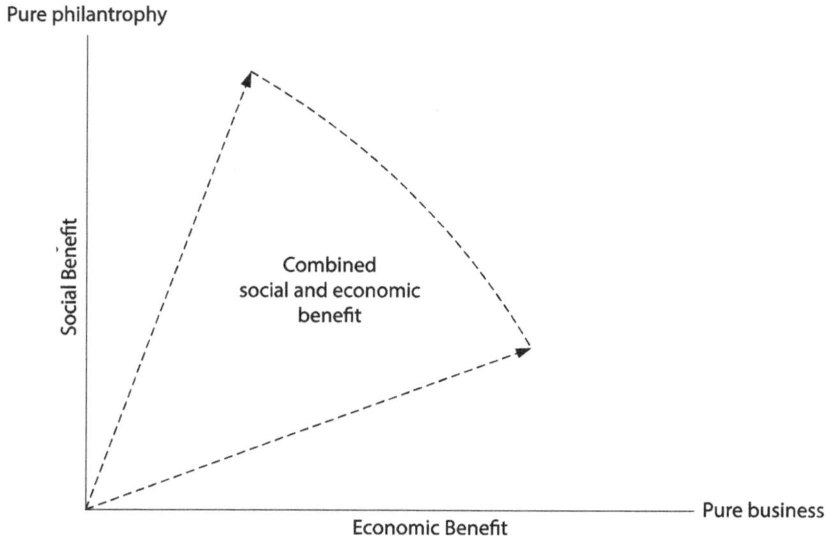

Figure 3.3 The relationship between economic and social benefit.
Source: Porter and Kramer (2002:5).

Profitability is an indicator measuring variables which can be classified into the following three categories:

1 Market conditions, such as *market growth rate, customer behaviour, distribution channels used and similar.*
2 Competitive position, such as *the scale of market share, the level of vertical integration, certain expenses of quality and similar.*
3 Business strategy such as *the price formation method, the costs of creating innovations, the way of determining competitors and similar.*

Hence, profitability depends on three variables: Market conditions, competitive position and business strategy. Many theoretical and practical ways of measuring the level of achieved profitability have been devised up to this day.[5]

However, it seems that the concept of economic value added (EVA) is most frequently used for such purpose. According to Charles Hill and Gareth Jones (Hill and Jones, 1998), the EVA concept consists of the following elements: (1) The estimated product value by the buyer (V); (2) product sale price by the company (P); and (3) production cost (C). The difference between V and P is called customer surplus, whereas the difference between P and C represents company profitability. The corporation is profitable as long as P is higher than C, although when working in an environment with stronger competition, the pressure on the sale price of the product by the company is higher in terms of reducing the price resulting in an increase of customer surplus (Figure 3.4).

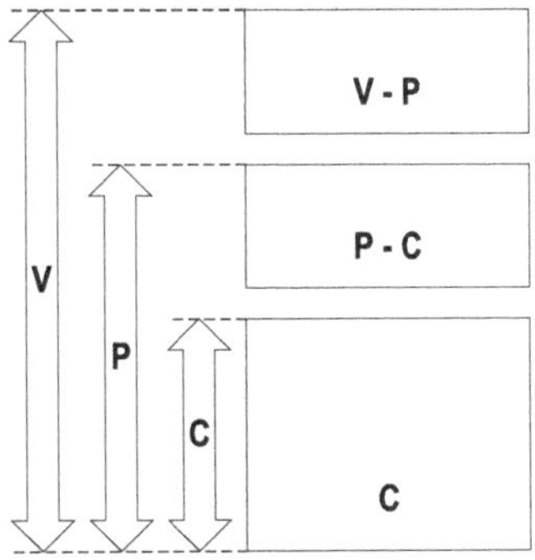

Figure 3.4 Creating economic added value.

Source: Adapted from Hill and Jones (1998:112).

The difference between V and C represents value created by the organisation, in the sense that a organisation uses its value chain, i.e. input logistics, operations and output logistics to convert inputs (input conversion leads to production cost – C) into outputs evaluated by customers at the V level. The company can create higher value either by lower production cost (C) or by distinctive features of products (V) with an expressed readiness of the buyers to pay a higher price for a product perceived in such a way. Following the aforementioned principle, the organisation, creates higher profitability by creating higher real value (V-C) compared to its competitors. Logically speaking, higher created values open up more space for a higher profit margin (P-C) as explicit profitability.

Considering the given context, Michael Porter (1985) states that it can be concluded that the concept of value creation truly lies at the heart of competitive advantage, in the sense that competitive advantage represents the basic tool for a company for generating created value (V-C). Michael Porter[6] believes that the best indicator of Return on Investment Capital (ROIC) is the one *measuring profit in relation to invested capital (operational expenses and total capital)*. It is the only indicator measuring the diversity in competition character: (a) Creating values for buyers; (b) the relationship with the competition; and (c) productive use of resources. ROIC integrates all of these three dimensions. It explains how a company utilises its resources. If it uses its resources in an appropriate way, it can cope with its competitors in a sustainable way. A company can permanently please its customers only if it realises the ROIC. Following such logic, i.e. the fact that created value (V-C) can be increased in two ways only by low production cost (C) or by differentiation of product features (V), Michael Porter differentiates two basic types of competitive advantage[7]:

1 Low production cost in tandem with acceptable quality create an advantage over competitors who cannot offer the same to their buyers

due to high cost of product production. Buyers will accept such an offer and buy more, increasing the producer's profitability in turn;
2 Differentiation of products based on creating product added values which often lead to higher price, but lead to higher quality too, which is often brand protected by the producer.

All the differences in companies in terms of cost or price originate from hundreds of activities needed to design, produce, sell and deliver their products or services such as customer service, final product installation or employee training. Conducting activities creates expenses, and cost advantage is created by conducting certain activities better than the competition. Hence, activities are the basic units of competitive advantage. The scale of competitive advantage is the difference between economic added value, possibly created by the ability of a company and economic added value created by the competitors' abilities. A successful company must be completely different from its competitors. Hence, company which excel at reducing expenses and differentiation create sustainable competitive advantage which is hard to reach by other competitors, especially in a short time span, as represented in Figure 3.5.

The concept of building competitive strategy is very subtle. Competitive advantage is created in a short period of time, but it also erodes quickly.

Competitive advantage is present when a company has a better position in terms of costs than its competitors, or it is embedded with an uniqueness sought after by the buyers (Tipurić, 2014).

Competitive advantage means producing an item at lower cost than your competitors or offering a product more valued by buyers than the product of the competitors. The sustainability of competitive advantage depends on several factors, some of the key ones include the following:

1 Property disposition – one of the fundamental factors determining sustainable competitive advantage. A company basing its competitive advantage on e.g. quality needs to have modern technology and educated employees at its disposal to achieve real competence for reaching high quality.
2 Information disposition – it is not enough just to have property at your disposal if the customers do not recognise the value of the product. Hence, a market research is needed to precisely determine the key preferences of customers, their expectations and needs which are not met appropriately.
3 Competition disposition – a company needs to analyse and determine the level of confrontation with competition in such a way that it brings forth benefits. The company can sometimes use the recognised weaknesses of its competitors to its advantage if it reacts quickly and seizes the opportunity by all means. The company undergoes several periods in the process of reaching sustainable competitive advantage.

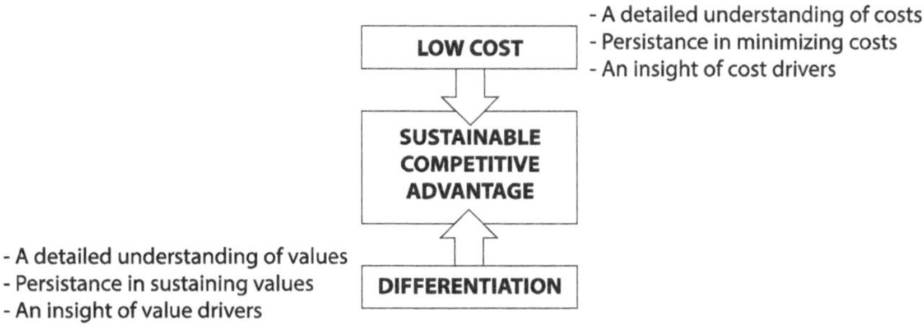

Figure 3.5 Sustainable competitive advantage.

Source: Adapted from Đuričin et al. (2015:136).

The company undergoes the following periods: (a) The period of sustainable competitive advantage where the actions of the company create competitive advantage; (b) the period of enjoying the benefits where a high level of achieved competitive advantage is created; and (c) the period of erosion of sustainable competitive advantage where the actions of competitors annul the competitive advantage, as shown in the image. Nataša Renko (2009) states that competitive advantage can be created only if it is:

1 Different, meaning that it is differently perceived by customers compared with other competitors;
2 Sustainable, meaning that competitors are not able to imitate it or reduce its advantages in a short time span;
3 Communicated, meaning that the buyers are informed on competitive advantages, making it visible.

Many competitive advantages do not have the features of sustainability, but rather the features of temporality. Instead of a frantic accentuation on a single competitive advantage, companies should develop several ones in order to a create their sustainability. The dynamics of changes in the surrounding are making it more difficult to achieve sustainable competitive advantage which is becoming an unrealistic fiction observed from a perspective of a longer period of time (D'Aveni, 1994).

The approaches to creating and sustaining competitive advantage

What are the approaches to creating and sustaining competitive advantage and how to achieve it? There are many different ways. Although mutually exclusive in literature, their nature can be recognised as complementary. Each, from their own angle, represents the items to be analysed and developed to create and sustain competitive advantage.

All the approaches can be narrowed down to two orientations:

1 External orientation (*external towards internal*) – an approach seeking success on the market and attaining it by external consonance, i.e. by creating roles *(structural approach)*;
2 Internal orientation (*internal towards external*) – an approach seeking success in the company and attaining it through internal consistency, i.e. by resource potential (*resource approach*).

Both approaches (the structural approach and the resource approach) have a lot of followers (internal orientation – Michael Porter; external orientation – Igor Ansoff) (Table 3.1).

The outset of the development of the so-called *structural approach* is tied to the 1930s, whereas the development of the so-called *resource approach* is tied to the 1990s. The structural approach is based on the *Structure Conduct Performance (SCP)* paradigm, whereas the resource approach is based on the *Resource-Based View (RBV)* paradigm. The common elements for both approaches are *is sustainable competitive advantage.*

Conduct is a specific activity of a company within an industry, whereas Performance has two meanings: The first meaning concerns the company performances as individual units, and the second one recognises industry performances as a whole. Although they are deemed mutually exclusive, we could argue that they are complementary and display everything that needs to be done to create sustainable competitive advantage.

The key difference between these two approaches is the definition of *Structure and Resource.* According to the structural approach, long-term success is determined by industry structure, whereas the resource approach determines long-term success by the structure of the resource. A corporation achieves sustainable competitive advantage by a structural approach on the basis of *positioning in an attractive structure of an industry*, whereas the same advantage is achieved by a resource approach on the basis of *advantages of core competence of a company.* A comparison of these two approaches is presented in Figure 3.6. In addition, some authors advocate both approaches (e.g. Robert Hoskisson), and some believe that neither of them is sufficient enough (e.g. Jeffrey Dyer). Hence, there is a need to integrate and revisit approaches and eventually combine and join them together.

The perspectives of the structural approach

Observing competitive advantage from a viewpoint of a structural approach, we can argue that strategic management is primarily interested in locating an attractive industry, discovering attractive market segments within it and alleviating the impact of competition by influencing the industry structure and the behaviour of competitors (Sikavica et al., 2008).

Table 3.1 The characteristics of the structural and the resource approach

Approaches	*Structural approach*	*Resource approach*
The object of consideration	Company as a portfolio of business units	Organisation as a resource reservoir
Competitors	SBU versus SBU	Company versus company
The character of strategic advantage	• Temporary • Eroding • Recognised	• Permanent • With a tendency • Hidden
Strategic focus	Tendency to be defensive: Building and defending existing jobs	Tendency to be offensive: Development and extension of new jobs
The horizon of planning	Highlights the short-term aspect	Highlights the long-term aspect
The role of strategic business unit	Pseudo-company	Centre of competence
The basis of competitiveness	Competing for products and markets	Competing for resources and competencies
Strategic goal	Defending the acquired market position	Creating sustainable competitive advantage
Main instruments and approaches	• Industry analysis • Strategy based on positioning and segmentation • Strategic planning	• Analysis of competencies • Strategy based on resources and competencies • Strategic networking
Key strategic resource	Financial capital	Company capability

Source: Adapted from Krueger and Homp (1997:63).

In literature, this approach is defined both broadly and narrowly, depending on its focus realm:

- Narrowly (Rasche, A., 2007), it focuses on the roles in the market game of the company;
- Broadly (De Wit and Mayer, 2005), it focuses on the fit between the company as a whole and its surrounding to achieve external consonance.

The roles found in the structural approach are defined as an expression of what needs to be done. They are formed as codified interpretations of activities founded by scientifically observed strategic practice. It is implied that the roles are free from any contextual meaning.

The perspectives of the resource approach

The resource approach to competitive advantage starts with the analysis of company resources in terms of competitive advantage and identifying those that can create competitive advantage, unlike those which cannot and

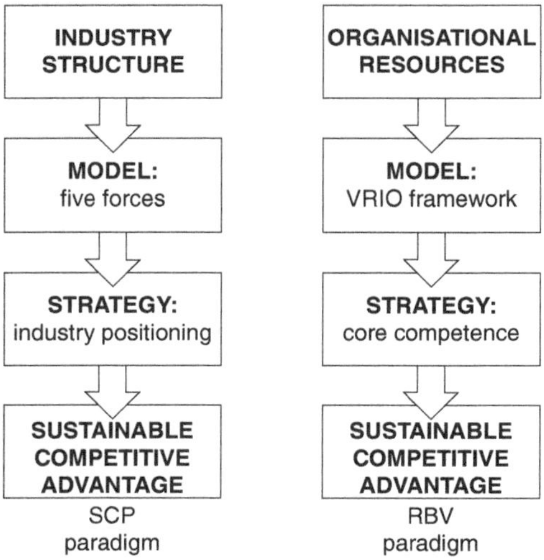

Figure 3.6 The comparison of structural and resource approach.

Source: Adapted from Tipurić (2014:177).

determining whether they are suitable for the conditions needed to achieve sustainable advantage (Sikavica et al., 2008).

In literature, the resource approach is defined both broadly and narrowly, depending on its focus realm:

- Narrowly (Rasche, 2007), it focuses on resources for reinforcing the competencies of a company,
- Broadly (De Wit and Mayer, 2005), it focuses on the fit between the variable parts within the corporation to achieve internal consonance.

Capabilities, in the terms of a resource approach, are defined as transformational capacities without an active role in the routine course of social interaction. They are created independent of the need for their application in a material or non-material form. It is implied that the resources need to be unique in their task of providing competitive advantage.

Porter's critic of the resource approach

Michael Porter, being a huge advocate of the structural approach, was notably critical in his works towards the advocates of the resource approach. The affirmation of the resource approach had led to a series of empirical research which have confirmed the founding assumptions of the approach relying on the research conducted by Richard Rumelt. The results reached through empirical research conducted by Richard Rumelt have placed a great challenge in front of Michael Porter. Gary Hamel and C. K. Prahalad started to seriously question his theories by counter-stating that a company needs to identify its key competences and use them as a basis for its choice of strategy. Michael Porter (1985) highlighted that the application of the mentioned approaches provides only operational effectiveness, rarely resulting in above the average profitability. He stated that they are very useful tools important for higher operational effectiveness in terms of short-term, and definitely not long-term, competitive advantage. That means that companies would have more operational effectiveness, but would certainly lack above the average profitability. *Operational effectiveness,* as Michael Porter (1996) states, means that *you are running on the same track but faster than others, whereas business strategy is a selection of a different strategy, a winning strategy.*

The common denominator of Michael Porter's works from the 1990s is that business strategy is equally important in an altering environment as it is in a stable one. It is a basis for competitive advantage in both cases. Michael Porter is particularly critical towards the resource approach highlighting that it is circular since the profitability of the company is based on having unique competences without broadly discussing the reasons which make resources and competences successful. He states that resources are significant because they are a precondition for conducting activities which create competence in particular markets. The importance of resources is visible in their role of conducting activities aimed at creating competences which will lead to the formation of competitive advantage.

Notes

1 For example, specialised stores offering a wide assortment of same category products take away market share from department stores with a wider concept offering a more limited assortment of products of different categories. Catalogue sale attracts buyers who like to be pleased. Generally speaking, both new and old companies are faced with the same challenges when searching for new strategic positions, although practically, new companies do have an advantage.

2 Igor Ansoff is considered the originator of the idea of creating and sustaining competitive advantage. He believes that there are three important conditions for creating and maintaining competitive advantage: (1) Customers must perceive a constant difference concerning important features between the product of the company and the product of competitors; (2) if this difference is a direct consequence of the competence gap between the products of the company and the competitor; and (3) if the difference and the gap can be expected in the future between the company's products and competitors. The competitive advantage created must be sustainable in the long run, which means it must be difficult to reach for competitors. The company must find a way to protect it for a certain period of time in a way that prevents competitors from imitating or mastering it.

3 Michael Porter's motivation to get more seriously involved in this phenomenon can be traced back to his statement from 2003: "My main criticism is that the area of social responsibility has become a religion served by many priests without the need for evidence and theory. Too many experts and managers are content with good intuition as an argument."

4 Research conducted by McKinsey consulting in 2005 suggests that worldwide managers believe that companies need to balance their duties to shareholders with explicit contributions for common good.
5 Porter believes that a sales yield ignores the capital invested in the business and that it is a bad criterion for evaluating the resource utilisation. Growth is the second popular criterion with market share. Just like sales yield it does not consider the capital needed to compete in an industry. Companies often use a non-profitable growth which does not lead to a superior yield on invested capital.
6 When trying to explain why only a small number of companies has successful business strategies, Michael Porter recognises inappropriate goals as the main culprit. Companies often use unprofitable growth which does not result in a superior yield of the invested part.
7 In the mid-1990s, authors Treacy and Wierseman offered three new approaches to creating competitive advantage, which are as follows: (1) Operational excellence activities is a source of competitive advantage by which a company focuses on improving operational activities and processes to achieve low cost in relation to competitors, with firms that have chosen this approach to competitive advantage achieving low cost and achieving profitability due to low cost. (2) Product leadership is a source of competitive advantage which focuses on technology and product development, with companies offering customers products and services that are technologically the most advanced and of highest quality and are always one step ahead of the competition. (3) Customer intimacy is a source of competitive advantage that is achieved by fully knowing the customer's needs better than the competition and complete by adapting to the specific needs of customers and establishing close relationships with customers.

References

Ansoff, I. (1965): *Corporate Strategy*, New York: McGraw-Hill.

D'Aveni, R. (1994): *Hypercompetition: Managing the Dynamics of Strategic Manuevering*, New York: The Free Press.

De Wit, B., Mayer, R. (2005): *Strategy Synthesis: Resolving Strategy Paradoxes to Create Competitive Advantage*, Hampshire: South-Western Cengage Learning.

Drucker, P. (1974): *Management: Task, Responsibilities, Practices*, Boston: Butterwort Heinemann.

Drucker, P. (1992): *Managing for the Future: The 1990's and Beyond*, New York: Truman Talley Books.

Đuričin, D., Janošević, S., Kaličanin, Đ. (2015): *Menadžment i strategija*, Beograd: Ekonomski fakultet.

Hill, C., Jones, G. (1998): *Strategic Management: An Integrated Approach*, Boston: Houghton Mifflin Company.

Magretta, J. (2012): *Understanding Michael Porter: The Essential Guide to Competition and Strategy*, Boston: Harvard Business Review Press.

Milisavljević, M. (2014): *Strategijski menadžment: analiza, izbor, promena*, Beograd: Ekonomski fakultet.

Mintzberg, H., Ostrand, L., Lampald, K. (2005): *Strategic Safari: A Guided Tour Through the Wilds of Strategic Management*, New York: The Free Press.

Petraph, M., Barney, J. (2003): "Unraveling the Resource-Based Tangle." *Managerial and Decision Economics*, vol. 24, no. 4: 309–323.

Porter, M. (1985): *Competitive Advantage: Creating and Sustaining Superior Performance*, Boston, The Free Press.

Porter, M. (1996): *What is Strategy?*, Harvard Business Review, vol. 74, no. 6, 61–78.

Porter, M. (1998): *On Competition*, Boston: Harvard Business School Press.

Porter, M. (2001): *Strategy and Internet*, Harvard Business Review, vol. 79, no. 3, 62–78.

Porter, M. (2006): *On Competition*, Boston: Harvard Business School Press.

Porter, M. (2007): "Konkurentska prednost - ostvarivanje i očuvanje vrhunskih poslovnih rezultata." *Fakultet za ekonomiju, finansije i administraciju.*

Porter, M. (2008): *On Competition: Updated and Expanded Edition*, Boston: Harvard Business Review Press.

Porter, M., Kramer, M. (1999): *Philanthropy's New Agenda: Creating Value*, Harvard Business Review, vol. 80, no 12, 57–68.

Porter, M., Kramer, M. (2002): *The Competitive Advantage of Corporate Philanthropy*, Harvard Business Review.

Rahimić, Z. (2006): *Izgradnja konkurentskih prednosti preduzéca kroz njegova strateška opredjeljenja*, Sarajevo: Ekonomski fakultet.

Raguž-Vrdoljak, I., Jelenc, L., Podrug, N. (2013): *Izvori konkurentske prednosti u XXI. stoljécu*, Dubrovnik: Sveučilište u Dubrovniku.

Rasche, A. (2007): *The Paradoxal Foundation of Strategic Management*, Hamburg: Springer.

Renko, N. (2009): *Strategije Marketinga*, Zagreb: Ljevak.

Rumelt, R., Schendel, D., Teece, D. (1994): *Fundamental Issues in Strategy*, Boston: Harvard Business School Press.

Sikavica, P., Bahtijarević-Šiber, F., Pološki Vokić, N. (2008): *Temelji menadžmenta*, Zagreb: Školska knjiga.

Šunje, A. (2002): *Top-menadžer: vizionar i strateg*, Sarajevo: Tirada.

Tipurić, D. (2014): *Iluzija strategije: razotkrivanje socijalno konstruisane zbilje poduzéca*, Zagreb: Sinergija.

Tipurić, D. (Ed.) (1999): *Konkurentska sposobnost poduzéca*, Zagreb: Sinergija.

Todorović, J., Đuričin, D., Janošević, S. (2000): *Strategijski menadžment*, Beograd: Institut za tržišna istraživanja.

Tošović-Stevanović, A. (2009): *Konkurentske prednosti i inovacije*, Beograd: Zadužbina Andrejević.

4 Environmental Analysis: *Porter's Five Competitive Forces Concept*

Strategic environmental analysis

Environmental strategic analysis presents an analysis of the *competitive forces of environment*. An industry should be the focal point of the analysis since overall changes in *competitive strengths* are seldom reflected in all industries equally. This is particularly related to diversified companies operating in several industries. After an industry is defined and determined, other factors reflecting competition need to be analysed. The reliability of industry analysis is highly dependent on the experiences of successful corporations on one side, and unsuccessful ones on the other side. Competitive strengths are active in the industry which is defined as a *group of companies producing products and selling them to customers*.

An industry (branch or company) is a group of companies offering a product or a type of product classified as an industry. Industries are classified according to the number of sellers, the level of differentiation, possible mobility, cost structure, degree of vertical integration and degree of globalisation.

The starting point in activity definition is defining the number of competitors and the degree of product differentiation.

Market and technology have a decisive effect on the formation of an industry. Industry borders are constantly expanding and reducing depending on the behaviour of its participants. According to Porter and van der Linde (1995a), the new paradigm of national economy competitiveness is dynamic and based on innovation.

He accentuates that a desirable goal should be a high life standard achieved through high competitiveness measured as the competence of a company to export a significant part of its final product while conducting business in a globally connected economy environment (Porter and van der Linde, 1995b).

Michael Porter (1990) advocates the idea that there is no success on an international market without success on the domestic market. That implies the creation of high standards and demands for business which can be placed in the context of four key groups of factors which correlate and interact to form competitive advantage of national economies. Michael Porter (1998) labelled those network-based relationships as clusters,

DOI: 10.4324/9781003359173-4

considering a cluster to be a manifestation of a diamond in practice. His analysis is based on case studies, rather than on economic analysis. Analysing clusters through the diamond model, he proved that their existence continuously aids the competitiveness of the market.

Clusters are a form of cooperation affecting the profitability positioned on a level between the sophistication of a company and the business climate. *Clusters are geographical concentrations of mutually connected companies, specialised suppliers, companies in associated industries and other organisations (universities, agencies, organisations) competing and cooperating together.* Michael Porter states several examples of clusters. He (Porter, 1990) believes that they influence national economies in three ways: First, by increasing the number of companies in that area; second, by accelerating the speed of company innovation in that area; third, by stimulating the foundation of new companies in that area.

Michael Porter (1980) believes that the sources of competitive advantage of a national economy can be found in the following[1]: (a) The conventional competitive advantage; (b) economy of scale or the curve of learning expanded above the cumulative realm that can be reached at an individual market of a national economy; (c) the advantages of product differentiation; and (d) public good or technological information coming from the market to be used at an individual market of a national economy. Such an aspect requires the formation of a strategy of business internationalisation, since Michael Porter recognises international market success as a primary indicator of the competitiveness of a national economy.

One of the analytical frameworks for success on the international market was actually developed by Michael Porter (1980) by identifying the following international business strategies:

1 Orientation towards global competitiveness by utilising the full capacity of industry product production and a tendency of competing at a global scale;
2 Global focus, in a sense of company orientation towards a particular segment of industry activities to be competed at globally;
3 Focus on the entire market with an idea that competitive advantage can be achieved through concentration on specific needs of a particular country;
4 Orientation on a protected segment, i.e. to enter the market of countries which have implemented a series of regulations to disable competition or make it difficult to achieve.

That fact, according to Michael Porter (1980), created a dilemma *whether to focus on a broad base strategy or a focused base strategy.*

The strategies of national economy growth rely on the competitive strategy of cost leadership or competitive strategy of differentiation. In order to find a different competitive position for different competitive strategies, competitiveness variables for different business strategies have been assigned a different degree of value. Therefore, it is highlighted that competitiveness and strategy need to be understood, designed and applied at different levels of classification of products, companies, industries and countries. This means that companies are transferring from a phase which Michael Porter (1991) labelled as factor-driven economy (where the most significant thing is the input price, i.e. the price of natural resources and workforce) to a phase Michael Porter (1991) labelled as innovation driven economy (where the most significant thing is the competency to produce innovative products using the most modern technology).

One of the most important innovations significantly affecting the paradigm change is the Internet.[2] Internet has radically changed the boundaries of business. A company can achieve success outside its national economy if it uses the Internet complementary, rather than separately, to its existing operations while simultaneously applying new combinations of virtual and physical activities which were impossible in the past.

Internet has finished the reconfiguration of industries and value chains facing high costs due to communication, information collection and the conduction of activities. Michael Porter (2001) believes that the relationship between the Internet and business strategy needs to be clarified. If companies wish to be competitive outside the borders of their national economy, they have to accept the Internet to improve their business strategy. Porter unambiguously confutes the argument that the Internet leads to the inertness of a business strategy. He argues that it does the opposite; it makes business strategy more important. Companies will fail to operate without it, but it will not be the source of their competitive advantage. The Internet technology can reinforce traditional resources of competitive advantage, simultaneously altering the activities of a company into a more personalised system, but without the capability to substitute them. Although the use of Internet can expand the market, it often results in the reduction of average profitability (Milisavljević, 2012).

The Internet has an influence on operative effectiveness and business strategy in a completely different manner. The Internet creates a situation where it is harder for companies to sustain advantage in terms of profitability, but it opens up a vast number of new possibilities for establishing or reinforcing an adequate strategic positioning.

An increase in profitability does not automatically ensure competitive advantage. Companies can achieve competitive advantage only if they are able to create and sustain profitability higher than that of their competitors. The nature of Internet application is to make it harder than ever to achieve advantage in terms of profitability. The advantages of using the Internet, according to Michael Porter (2001), are as follows:

1 The Internet reduces the negotiation factor of middlemen since information technology enables companies to access buyers in a completely different way which is significantly simplified than before.

2 The Internet can increase the average profitability of an industry in different ways: by increasing the overall size of the market and increasing its position in relation to markets with features such as the existence of traditional substitutes.

The disadvantages of using the Internet, according to Michael Porter (2001), are as follows:

1 The Internet technology has provided an easier access to information on products and suppliers for the buyers, increasing their negotiation power.
2 The Internet reduces the need for resources such as regular sales staff or access to existing middlemen, reducing barriers to potential entries.
3 It provides the fulfilment of needs in a new way, as well as the completion of certain functions in a different way by creating completely new substitutes.
4 Being an open system, companies are having increased difficulties in maintaining individual, limited offers, intensifying the rivalry among existing competitors.
5 The use of Internet leads to a geographical expansion of the market resulting in an increased number of companies competing among each other.
6 Internet technologies often lead to the reduction in variable expenses by shifting the focus towards the increase of fixed expenses creating a significantly higher pressure on companies to apply destructive price competitiveness.

The Internet affects generic strategies. The strategy of cost leadership shall become more relevant for some companies, although the use of Internet reduces the transaction costs and increases the efficiency of operations. It will become more difficult for many companies to follow the strategy of differentiation, since the Internet downgrades some of their most important assets. Internet creates an opportunity for an increased capability of mass adaptation of a higher number of competitors. The strategy of focus will receive increasing significance, since the Internet enables lower costs for aimed, narrow and specialised markets (Dess et al., 2007).

The Internet helps to reinforce the strategy of cost leadership and differentiation by using timely communication to programme production, manage warehouses, reduce stock and control costs. Unfortunately, all of the mentioned activities can be copied by other companies. Undoubtedly, the Internet enables all the companies to have an effect on the reduction of their costs and the enhancement of their differentiation (Lancolla and Suarez, 2012).

Several approaches for industry determination can be found in different literature. Derek Abell (1993) points out to the complexity where the problem of industry determination is approached through a strategic standpoint (Jarillo, 2003).

Derek Abell (1993) concluded that there is not a clear and doubtless definition of industry and the approach to its definition attempt depends on the aim of the analysis. Today, industry definition is becoming increasingly difficult since the borderlines between traditional industries are becoming vaguer, which is a consequence of the innovative approaches of company in creating competitive advantage and their transfer to other industries. Andrej Vizjak (2007) argues that such circumstances make it difficult to make a causable classification of the product of a company (e.g. whether it is a watch or piece of jewellery produced by Swatch, or whether it is coffee or pleasure offered by Illy), or to effectively determine the industry type of the company production (e.g. whether does Swatch operate in the industry of watches, fashion or trade).

Companies are constantly changing their production programme, whereas buyers are constantly changing their behaviour. The attractiveness of a particular industry is measured by average profitability. According to Michael Porter (1985), the profitability of the industry is influenced by the so-called competitive forces. Different intensity of competitive forces leads to different levels of profitability. The biggest profits are achieved in industries with a directed action of competitive forces, whereas industries with extremely high values of competitive forces suffer from profitability crisis.

Constructs of environmental strategic analysis

Environmental strategic analysis includes the following:

1 Industry analysis;
2 Strategic group analysis;
3 Competitors analysis from the environmental perspective.

Industry analysis

Michael Porter (2008) suggest the following procedure for industry analysis: (1) Define the relevant industry; (2) identify the participants and classify them according to corresponding criteria into strategic groups; (3) evaluate the background of every strategic strength to determine the strong and weak strategies; (4) determine the general industry structure and consider the strengths influencing the profitability; (5) analyse recent and possible changes in each of the five competitive forces individually, the positive ones, as well as the negative; (6) identify the aspects of industry structure which can be influenced by current competitors, new industry competitors or your own company.

Industry analysis is important for shaping the business strategy of individual competitors since it has a vital effect on the behaviour of the company. It is evident that industry factors influence all the companies within an industry, but each company, in its idiosyncratic way, reacts to them (Milisavljević, 2012). In order to be compared to others, a corporation needs to be highly informed on the *key success factors –KSF,*[3] which vastly influence the overall competitive position of a company within the industry. They are tied to each specific industry and differ from one industry to another.

Michael Porter (1980) differentiates four types of industries, which are as follows:

1 *Developing industries*: Developing industries are at the initial phase of their life cycle as an industry. Their basic feature is that they are completely new or completely altered industries.
2 *Mature industries*: Mature industries are at a critical phase of their life cycle as an industry. Their basic feature is that they have a wide spectre of possibilities for solutions ranging from cost leadership to differentiation or focusing.
3 *Falling industries*: Falling industries are at the final phase of their life cycle as an industry. Their basic feature is that they are completely atrophic or completely impotent industries.

After passing through the industry life cycle phases (from developing, though mature to falling), a company faces the following strategic alternatives (Figure 4.1; Harrigan and Porter, 1983): *(a) Harvest, (b) fast exit, (c) leadership and (d) niche guardian.* Disinvestment is the basis in case of strategic alternatives of harvest and fast exit and investment and disinvestment are the basis of strategic alternatives of leadership and niche guardian.

The strategic alternative of harvest or divest quickly includes the tendency to reduce market share to achieve the goal of maximising cash flows. Companies give up on investing and consider the option of liquidating some of its businesses. This strategic alternative can be implemented by companies which are able to survive more turbulent fluctuations on the market for a shorter or median period of time. *The strategic alternative of divest quickly* implies the achievement of the highest yield to invested capital in case of the sale of the company at the initial phase of a downfall in an industry. The biggest challenge for owners is to determine the right moment to sell, i.e. to timely react to industry trends. The essence is to create the highest possible sales price of the company. *The strategic alternative of leadership or niche* implies reaching the leader position in a falling industry. A leader can become dominant on the market, and it is often a company with rich experience in market operating. Mergers, i.e. external growth is sometimes practiced in order to achieve absolute and irrefutable dominance. *The strategic alternative of niche or harvest* implies the focus of attention towards the location of a niche without featured negative tendency in comparison with other niches. This strategy is actually the very final

	Has competitive strenghts for remaining demand pockets	Lacks competitive strenghts for remaining demand pockets
Favorable industry structure for decline	**LEADERSHIP OR NICHE**	**HARVEST OR DIVEST QUICKLY**
Unfavorable industry structure for decline	**NICHE OR HARVEST**	**DIVEST QUICKLY**

Figure 4.1 Strategic alternatives in a postindustrial cycle.

Source: Adapted from Harrigan and Porter (1983:118).

attempt at sustaining the life cycle of the company. Niche identification calls for investment which is expected to be recovered in the shortest possible period. The significance of selecting a strategic alternative in a falling industry is to determine whether it is more useful for a corporation to stay within an industry or to exit it in the shortest possible period. In addition, the understanding of the strategy by acknowledging the barriers of industry exit can be useful when determining the relative position of a company. Industry analysis is important for the selection of a strategic alternative of every industry participant (competitor) since the industry has a decisive effect on the behaviour of the company. Industry analysis is aimed at the analysis of the market structure which is used to determine the number and size of existing competitors.

According to Hill and Jones (1998), the industry structure can vary in terms of a higher or lower number of competitors which have to or do not have to be differentiated by their strength and market share.

Michael Porter (1980) labelled such an industry structure (a variable structure) as:

1 Fragmented;
2 Consolidated.

A *fragmented industry* is a form of industry with low concentration and a large number of small and medium companies without domination and influence on the shaping of events within the industry, whereas a *consolidated industry* is a form of a densely concentrated industry with a single or several big companies dominating and influencing the shaping of events within the industry.

Industry concentration is defined by the number and size distribution of companies within an industry. Such a classification opens up the possibility

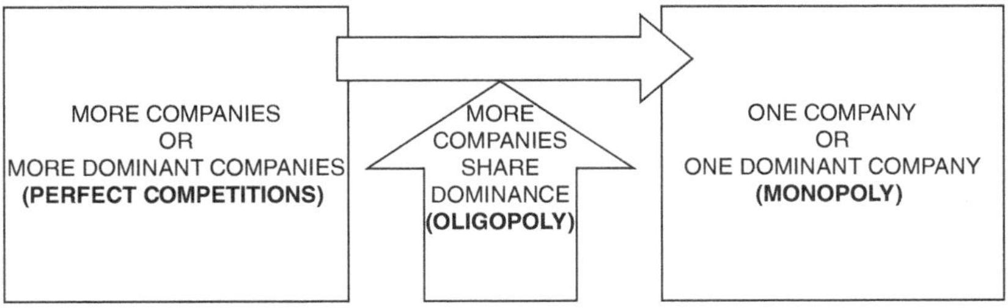

Figure 4.2 Market structure.

Adapted from Hill and Jones (1998:77).

of discussing *industries with a higher degree of concentration* with a small number of companies with a small share controlling a smaller part of the market and *industries with a lower degree of concentration* with a bigger number of companies with a smaller market share controlling a smaller part of the market. Michael Porter (1998) adapts the traditional neoclassical claim that the industry structure, i.e. multiple companies competing at the same market, demands technology advancement, cost minimisation, innovation development and similar.

He argues that a simple index of industry concentration is an insufficient gauge of the degree of rivalry among competitors. He thinks that the competitive structure of the industry does that job. Three basic forms of market structure are shown in Figure 4.2.[4]

a Perfect competition;
b Oligopoly;
c Monopoly.

Perfect competition describes an ideal competitive structure including a host of companies selling a product which cannot be differentiated at no other feature but price. The advantage of perfect competition is that all companies are in the same position, selling the same products and using the same middlemen. The disadvantage is that the lack of product differentiation keeps the profitability rate low for all participants.

Oligopoly describes the regular competitive structure where a small number of competitors control the market, particularly the price. In addition, the input barriers are so high that only a handful of companies can join in the competitive battle.

A small number of companies determine the price. The level of product differentiation is low and the market entry requirements are high. The key factor is the interdependence of the companies. Since a small number of companies share market control, each of them is always aware what the others are up to. The presence of few competitors forces the company to shape its business strategies to be aimed at achieving competitive advantage over others. Due to a small number of producers, price-based competition is not favourable since it leads to a decrease in profit for all producers.

Monopoly describes a common structure where a single company completely controls the product offer with no exact substitute. Since there is no competition, the company can form the price of the product on its own. The entrance of new competitors is made difficult. The advantage of monopoly is that a single company is in the same position as others, selling the same products at the same price using the same middlemen. The disadvantage is that the lack of product differentiation keeps the profitability rate low for all participants.

Ccompany core competence is attached to a particular industry which forms the surrounding. For example, a faculty, as an educational facility, belongs to the higher education business (industry), whereas a hospital, as a health facility, belongs to the business (industry) of health. Following this idea, it is necessary to have all the information on the respective industry of the business. Certo and Peter (1991) offer a very detailed manner of attaining the source of general information on an industry. An important source of information can often be found in the form of different headlines and regular content found in newspapers.[5] For example, *New York Times*, *Financial Times* and other similar newspapers covering particular topics can be a valuable source of industry information or data. When discussing the sources of information on an industry, it is worthwhile to mention Michael Porter's attitude on sources and information needed for industry analysis (Wheelen and Hunger, 1990).

He divided all the information resources into six basic groups, i.e. resources,[6] which are as follows:

1 Observers or overseers;
2 Suppliers or provisioners;
3 Sellers or distributors;
4 Buyers or users;
5 Competitors or adversaries;
6 Services or assistance.

Michael Porter particularly developed the resources from the first, fifth and sixth groups.

Michael Porter argues that the most important information resources in *group 1*, which consists of observers and overseers, include: (a) Networks, (b) unions, (c) publishers, (d) board, (e) associations, (f) agencies, (g) organisations and similar.

He argues that the most important information resources in *group 5*, which consists of competitors and adversaries, include: (a) Staff, (b) departments, (c) organisations, (d) employees, (e) agencies and similar.

He argues that the most important information resources in *group 6*, which consists of services and assistance, include: (a) Associations, (b) banks, (c) consultants, (d) supervisors, (e) auditors, (f) agencies and similar.

All the stated resource classifications (explained comprehensively and in detail) reinforce the hypothesis that there is a vast number of potential resources as well as the importance of their successful utilisation. A reaction is therefore needed based on the collected information on an industry.

When reacting to gathered information on an industry, it is necessary to *understand, interpret and correlate the information to reach relevant conclusions on the value of available information.* The information concerning the given industry is important since the industry has a direct impact on the company (Mašić, 2009).

According to Michael Porter (1983), the relative environment is considerably broad and it includes the respective social and economic factors and it is a key aspect of the environment of the industries (or an industry) which is the competing field of the organisation.

An analysis of the definition reveals that, in modern conditions, an industry does not have demarking lines. This means that each company can be both *a rival* and *a competitor,* simultaneously.

However, the partner relationship can be easily transformed into a competitive relationship. For example, if a buyer starts producing items which it formerly bought or if a supplier starts using products for his own business, rather than for sales. If we add potential competitors and the possibility of substitution to this scenario, it can be concluded that the competitive outreach, i.e. the range of contact with competitors, is much wider than the range indicated by the industry analysis.

However, the definition offered by Michael Porter is not accepted by contemporary theoreticians and practicians. Hence, he approached it from a broader aspect and expanded the competitive context beyond the industry (i.e. the competition among existing companies) to include suppliers, buyers, new competitors and substitute producers. He called it extended rivalry and he used it to set the boundaries of an industry. Considering his analysis of these five variables, there can be a so-called good and bad environment (Table 4.1; Bateman and Zeithaml, 1990).

Table 4.1 "Good" and "bad" environment

Factors	*Industry surrounding*	
	So-called "bad"	*So-called "good"*
Competitor rivalry	Numerous low industry growth	Few; high industry growth
Entry possibility	Numerous low industry growth	Few; high industry growth
Substitute possibility	Numerous	Few
Supplier strength	Few; strong negotiation power	Numerous; low negotiation power
Buyer strength	Few; strong negotiation power	Numerous; weak negotiation power

Source: Adapted from Bateman and Zeithaml (1990:228).

The level of profitability in an industry depends on the action of the competitive forces. The highest value is achieved in industries with a directed activity of competitive forces (oligopoly), whereas the lowest value is achieved in industries with extreme activities conducted by competitive forces (perfect competition on one side, and complete monopoly on the other side). Namely, when observing an industry environment from a company viewpoint, it is recognised as adverse if: *There are a lot of competitors, a lot of growth rate, a reduction of the entry barriers, lots of product substitutes, high negotiation strength and similar.* However, an industry surrounding is favourable if: *There is little competition, high growth rate, high entry barriers, few product substitutes, low negotiation strength and similar.*

However, the government needs to, directly or indirectly, manage the entry and exit terms, encourage the development of industries and substitutes, relativise the strength of suppliers and buyers and similar.

After almost 30 years, Michael Porter (2008) returned to his old magazine where he wrote about the five competitive forces. In his opinion, it is necessary to understand competition confrontation. Industry structure drives competition and profitability forward disregarding the character of the product or industry. When the industry structure is changed, new and promising strategic positions start emerging since the structural changes create new needs and new ways to meet the existing needs. Industry leaders have to predict such changes creating an opportunity for smaller companies to make profit. A careful definition of the relevant industry is suggested, one that is neither too narrow nor to broad, using two main dimensions of broadness of the industry in the process (Milisavljević, 2012): (1) Production broadness and (2) geographical broadness. The accent is on identifying the industry with good future opportunities.

In order to occupy an optimal strategic position in the environment as a form of strategic behaviour leading towards the creation of sustainable competitive advantage, Michael Porter (2008) recommended the concept of five competitive forces. The concept provides a way of conducting the *company analysis* versus *environment analysis* to form future business strategies in the *company-environment interaction.*

Namely, Michael Porter (1983) believes that the main goal of the analysis is to locate the strategic position in the industry where a company can have the best and most successful defense against the influence of other competitors in the industry and/or where it can have the best influence on them for their long-term benefit. The mutual power of the five competitive forces determines the basic potential of industry profitability and defines the inter-industry differences in the scenario of above the average profitability. The most powerful competitive forces prevalently determine the profitability of an industry.

On the one side, the profitability of an industry is *higher* if an industry has a stable competitive structure, a more favourable position in relation to suppliers, buyers and substitute industries and a lower degree of danger caused by the entrance of other companies. On the other side, the profitability of an industry is *lower* if it has a variable and undefined competitive structure, weaker position in relation to suppliers, buyers and substitute industries and if there is a high degree of danger caused by the entrance of other companies.

The concept introduced by Michael Porter (Kippenberg, 1998) requires conducting an exhaustive analysis of industry structure to reach a satisfying understanding of industry profitability and to locate the sources and incentives of each competitive force and to determine the possibility of a long-term influence on the profitability of the industry.

Understanding the industry structure alongside a conducted intern analysis of the company helps to gain a better insight into the real strengths and weaknesses of a company, develop the framework for positioning a company in an industry, identify the area where a strategic change is most beneficial and shed light on factors which offer the biggest chance for opportunities and threats according to industry trends.

The aim of conducting the analysis is directly linked with the process of shaping the business strategy. The strategic actions of a company in an industry (e.g. price policy, production manner, innovative capacity and similar) depend on the existing and future industry structure (e.g. competitive structure, production differentiation, industrial barriers and similar). Hence, the aim of the company during an industry analysis is clear: *Locate the industry position where a company can form the best defense against all of these forces and/or where it can have the best influence on its long-term benefit.*

Understanding the five competitive forces is the basis for evaluating the company position within the industry leading two fundamental goals (Barney, 1991):

1 *Maintaining the position* – if a company is content with its position (e.g. if it scores highest among its competitors);
2 *Repositioning* – if a company is not content with its position (e.g. if it wants to be distinguished among its competitors).

The constructs of the five competitive forces concept represent a somewhat threat to a company. Threats increase expenses, reduce income and reduce profit. The threats are identified as forces leading to an increase in the overall level of competitiveness in an industry, levelling the degree of created value with the national economy average. In other words, the competitive environment is determined by the following (Figure 4.3; Porter, 1985):

1 Rivalry among existing competitors;
2 Threat of new entrants;
3 Threat of substitution;
4 Bargain power of suppliers;
5 Bargain power of buyers.

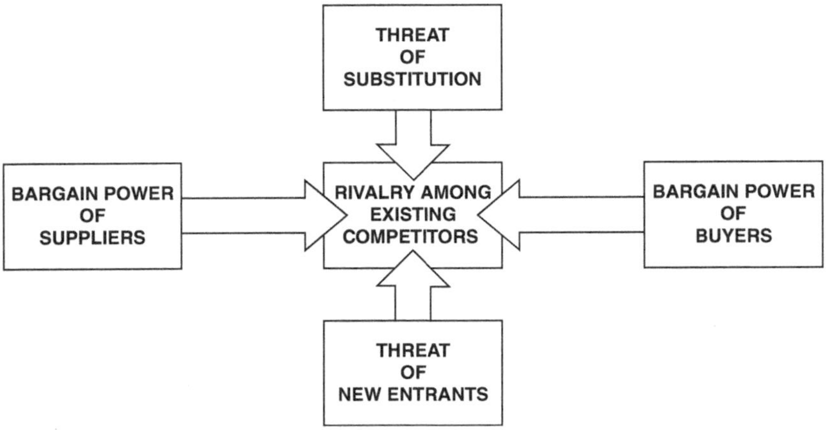

Figure 4.3 Porter's five competitive forces concept.

Source: Porter (1985:5).

Each construct in the five competitive forces concept has certain characteristics which are summed up in Figure 4.4.

> Looking at the image, it can be concluded that it is not in accordance with good economic intuition for all competitors to, more or less, follow their business strategies based on, more or less, the same resources of competitive advantage. Such an action limits the ***industrial organization*** approach which advocates that competition expresses itself through its prices. According to Joan Magretta (2012), this has led Michael Porter to oppose such attitudes in his works and suggest a new framework for analyzing the competitive game. Competition is not a war or a zero sum game where one player wins and the other loses. Competition is a win-win game.

Considering Michael Porter's contribution in that context, Joan Magreta (2012) states that there is a mindset change in rivalry among existing competitors which is shifting from the approach of beating competition to the approach of creating value. The comparison of the competitive rivalry mindset based on the industrial organisation approach and Michael Porter's approach can be seen Table 4.2.

Michael Porter's (Magretta, 2012) approach highlights the effect of the environment (industry) on the company (value chain). Namely, the profitability of the organisation is under the influence of the industry structure where the company is operating. The company must adapt to the conditions of the industry to survive and thrive. An industry with a favourable structure offers the best conditions for company profitability. A company can influence the industry structure with its innovative strategies rather than

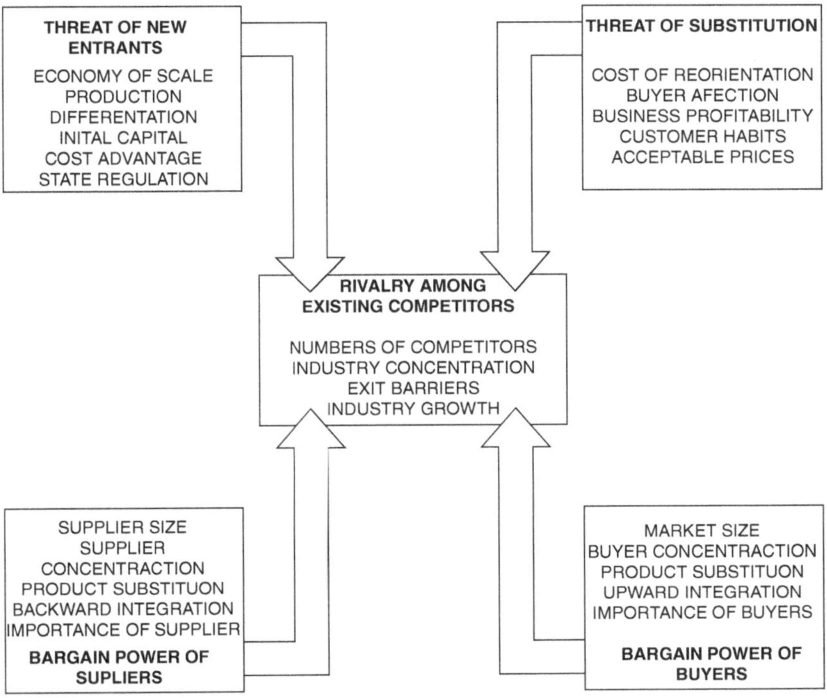

Figure 4.4 Elements of industry structure.

Source: Adapted from Porter (1985:6).

Table 4.2 Possible approaches to the analysis of the competitive game

The industrial organisation approach	*Michael Porter's approach*
Number one	Above the average profitability
Focus on market share	Focus on creating value
Serving the best buyer with the best product	Meeting the different needs for aimed buyers
Competing by imitating	Competing by innovation
Zero-sum game	Win-win game

Source: Adapted from Magretta (2012:32).

solely adapt to it. That is the reason why Michael Porter (Magretta, 2012) expands the rivalry of competitors to four additional factors widening the context of the market game: Buyer strength, supplier strength, substitute possibility and entry possibility.

This concept represents a sound analysis of flawed market structures. However, each competitive force has a different way of influencing the profit recognised as a difference between overall income (operative effectiveness) and overall expenses (operative efficiency), as shown in Figure 4.5.

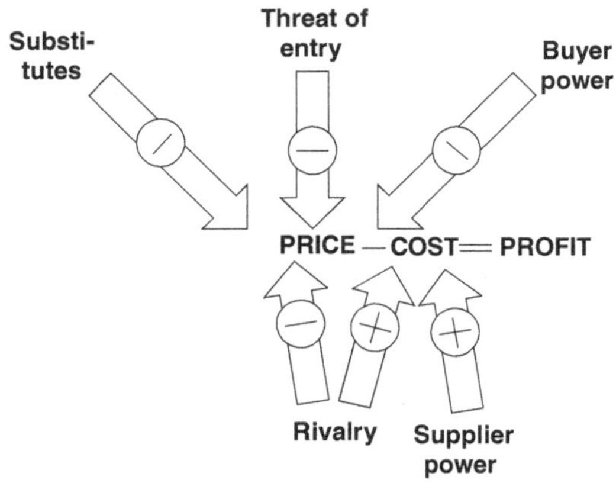

Figure 4.5 The influence of five competitive forces on profit.

Source: Magretta (2012:32).

Entry barriers – the danger of newcomers

The analysis of this force considers the entry barriers, i.e. the danger of newcomers. Newcomers are seen as potential competitors newly present in the industry or with an intention of entering the industry. Newcomers enter the industry guided by above the average profitability made by existing competitors in the industry. Michael Porter (1980) states that entry barriers are highlighted in the following cases:

1 When forcing potential competitors to start mass producing by applying the economy of scale with the risk of competitor reaction.
2 When there is a larger number of established market brands with loyal buyers in terms of reaching the sales level that minimises the cost per unit.
3 When there is a need for a big amount of initial capital of the company to attain an adequate level of competitive gravity.
4 When it is not possible for potential competitors to attain achieved cost advantage which has a highly set bar for potential competitors.
5 When there are institutional limitations imposed by the government through special permits needed to enter the industry (Table 4.3).

It is logical that an industry is more attractive when the danger of newcomers is lower, in the sense that there is more room for achieving a higher level of profitability for companies operating in the respective business. In other words, bigger market share for existing competitors means less opportunity for above the average profitability.

Table 4.3 Elements for assesing the influence of the danger of newcomer

Entry barriers	*Opportunity*	*Threat*
Considerable scales of economy		+
Marginal scale of economy	+	
Cost adversity from other aspects		+
Cost convenience from other aspects	+	
Strong product differentiation		+
Weak product differentiation	+	
Enormous needs for capital		+
Minor needs for capital	+	
Considerable costs of shifting		+
Minimal costs of shifting	+	
Controlled access to distribution channels		+
Opened access to distribution channels	+	
High government protection and limited entry		+
Low government protection without entry limitations	+	

Source: Adapted from Johnson and Scholes (2009:47).

The negotiation power of suppliers – the danger of suppliers

An analysis of this force looks into the negotiation power of the supplier, i.e. the danger of a supplier. Suppliers have a respectable negotiation power if the degree of concentration in their industry is higher than the concentration in the industry which buys their products. Suppliers can threaten with a price increase. According to Michael Porter (1980), the danger of suppliers is highlighted in the following cases:

1 When the number of potential suppliers is small, i.e. when a few suppliers dominate the industry which is more concentrated than the industry where they sell.
2 When suppliers sell unique products which significantly differ from others, or at least differentiated products.
3 When there is no danger that the product of the supplier can be substituted, i.e. replaced by a similar product.
4 When suppliers do not show interest for a step forward, i.e. for integrating the buyer (the corporation from the analysed industry) into its own value chain.
5 When corporations from the respective industry are not particularly important for suppliers, in the sense that more important buyers can be found at other industries.

It is logical that an industry is less attractive when the negotiation power of the supplier is higher, in the sense that there is less room for achieving a higher degree of profitability for corporations operating in the respective business. In other words, the negotiation power of suppliers to create

Table 4.4 Elements for assessing the influence of the negotiation power of suppliers

Negotiation power of supplier	*Opportunity*	*Threat*
The industry of suppliers has few companies and it is concentrated	+	
The industry of suppliers has many companies and it is fragmented		+
There are no substitute products for the supplier product	+	
There are substitute products for the supplier product		+
The industry is not an important client of the supplier industry	+	
The industry is an important client of the supplier industry		+
Supplier product is important for the industry	+	
Supplier product is not important for the industry		+
Supplier products are differentiated	+	
Supplier products are not differentiated		+
There are considerable costs of switching from the suppliers products	+	
There are no considerable costs of switching from the suppliers products		+
The supplier has the potential of a descending integration in the industry which purchases from it	+	
The supplier does not have the potential of a descending integration in the industry which purchases from it		+

Source: Adapted from Johnson and Scholes (2009:46).

higher product prices is more expressed resulting in higher product cost and less room for profitability (Table 4.4).

The negotiation power of buyers – the danger of buyers

An analysis of this force explains the negotiation power of buyers and the danger of buyers. Buyers have a respectable negotiation power if the degree of concentration in the buying industry is higher compared with the selling industry. Buyers can threaten with profit decrease. According to Michael Porter (1980), the danger of buyers is highlighted in the following cases:

1 When the number of potential buyers is small, i.e. when a few buyers dominate the industry which is more concentrated than the industry where they buy.
2 When buyers buy standardised and non-differentiated products which significantly differ from others, or at least non-differentiated products.
3 When there is a danger of standardising the supplier product, i.e. identifying it with a similar product.
4 When buyers show interest for a step back, i.e. for integrating the supplier (companies from the analysed industry) into their own value chain.

5 When companies from the respective industry are not particularly important suppliers for the buyers, in the sense that more important suppliers can be found in other industries.

It is logical that an industry is more attractive when the negotiation power of buyers is higher in the sense that there is less room for achieving a higher degree of profitability for companies operating in the respective business. In other words, the pressure from buyers for lower prices is higher resulting in lower sale prices and less room for profitability (Table 4.5).

Substitute pressure – the danger of substitutes

The analysis of this force considers the possibility of substitution, i.e. the danger of substitution. Substitution includes products coming from direct or indirect competitors with an equal function. Substitutes enter the industry guided by the notion of meeting the same needs which the current competitors in the industry are meeting. According to Michael Porter (1980), the possibilities of substitution are highlighted in the following cases:

1 When a buyer does not have to pay a high price for the transition to a substitute product directly jeopardising the products.
2 When buyers develop a tendency under equal price and performance, leading them to switch from products to substitutes.
3 When companies produce items that can substitute the respective product at a profit at their other markets.
4 When substitute consumption trends increase at the cost of the product, causing the substitute consumption increase to lead to a decrease in product consumption.
5 When there are many other products that can fulfil the same function as the product at hand but with acceptably low prices.

It is logical that an industry is less attractive when the danger of substitution is more expressed in the sense that there is more room to achieve a lower degree of profitability for companies operating in the respective business. In other words, a more attractive price-based positioning towards existing products leads to a lower possibility of above the average profitability (Table 4.6).

Competition intensity – the rivalry of competitors

The analysis of this force investigates the rivalry of companies in an industry as an important factor of industry profitability. The intensity of competition includes the mutual rivalry of companies within an industry to achieve the best possible technological and market position. More direct companies rivals within an industry lead to the assumption that the strength of industry

Table 4.5 Elements for assessing the influence of the negotiation power of buyers

The negotiating power of buyers	*Opportunity*	*Threat*
The buyer purchases big amounts from the company in the industry	+	
The buyer purchases small amounts from the company in the industry		+
Industry products present a considerable amount of the overall expenses of the buyer	+	
Industry products do not present a considerable amount of the overall expenses of the buyer		+
Industry products are standard and non-differentiated	+	
Industry products are differentiated and unique		+
The buyer is faced with minor switching costs	+	
The buyer is faced with major switching costs		+
The profit of the buyer is small	+	
The profit of the buyer is big		+
The buyer can produce the purchased products	+	
The buyer cannot produce the purchased products		+
Industry products are not important for the quality of buyer products	+	
Industry products are important for the quality of buyer products		+
Buyers have complete information on the industry and the product	+	
Buyers have limited information on the industry and the product		+

Source: Adapted from Johnson and Scholes (2009:47).

Table 4.6 Elements for assessing the influence of substitute pressure

The danger of substitution	*Opportunity*	*Threat*
There are very good substitution products, i.e. substitutes		+
There are several solid substitution products, i.e. substitutes	+	
There are very bad substitution products, i.e. substitutes		+

Source: Adapted from Johnson and Scholes (2009:48).

rivalry is higher. According to Michael Porter (1980), the intensity of competition is highlighted in the following cases:

1 When there is a big number of competitors in an industry similar in scale and power which influences their similar offer.
2 When there is a larger number of competitors of equal scale, there will be a higher intensity of rivalry among them, rather than the other way around.
3 When fixed costs are high or the product has a short-term nature creating evidently expressed efforts to reduce prices.

4 When there are high exit barriers preventing companies from exiting the industry despite the low return on investment.
5 When there is low industry growth among existing competitors since every competitor must work harder for its share.

It is logical that an industry is less attractive when the rivalry in it is more expressed in the sense that there is more room for achieving a lower degree of profitability for companies operating in the respective business. In other words, a higher degree of rivalry in relation to existing competitors leads to a lower possibility of above the average profitability (Table 4.7).

Strategic group analysis

The concept of strategic groups has a different approach to understanding an industry. According to Momčilo Milisavljević (2012), the following two problems can be found in an industry: (1) Two companies are not completely different and (2) two companies are completely the same. These problems indicate that it is harder to identify groups of companies which resemble each other than groups of companies that differ from each other. This is significant because the main competitiveness goes on among similar companies. Namely, strategic group analysis as the second step in the strategic analysis of the environment has a task of serving as a same kind of a bridge between

Table 4.7 Elements for evaluating the influence of competition intensity

Rivalry in an industry	*Opportunity*	*Threat*
An exceptionally large number of competitors in the industry	+	
An exceptionally low number of competitors in the industry		+
Competitors are balanced in terms of their power	+	
Competitors are not balanced in terms of their power		+
There is a differentiation or there are no switching costs	+	
There is not a differentiation or there are no switching costs		+
Fast sales growth in the industry	+	
Slow sales growth in the industry		+
High fixed costs	+	
Low fixed costs		+
Considerable differentiation or considerable switching costs	+	
Slight differentiation or slight switching costs		+
Industry capacity is increased in major leaps	+	
Industry capacity is increased in minor leaps		+
Different and diverse competitors	+	
Similar and generalised competitors		+
Major strategic interests of the company	+	
Minor strategic interests of the company		+
High exit barriers	+	
Low exit barriers		+

Source: Adapted from Johnson and Scholes (2009:48).

understanding the industry as a whole on one side and the focus on organisations within the respective industry on the other side (Šehić, 2002). A strategic group analysis is a useful tool when there are many participants in an industry without the possibility of an in-depth analysis of each individual participant. The idea of strategic groups was defined by Caves and Porter (1978). These two authors[7] defined a *strategic group as a group of organisations handling similar opportunities and threats which differ from similar opportunities and threats featured in the industry, while having the same business strategy*. This means that a strategic group is a group of competitive corporations following the same or similar strategy in all strategic dimensions, i.e. which (a) have similar choices (e.g. similar price policy), (b) have similar features (e.g. similar vertical integrity and similar) and (c) have similar means (e.g. similar technological basis) (Caves and Pugel, 1980).

However, the mentioned definition of strategic groups has not precisely clarified two things: (1) Industry boundaries and (2) the structure of opportunities and threats operating in the industry. Imprecision in defining the boundaries of the industry is less relevant when analysing organisation exposed to similar opportunities and threats. The definition of industry boundaries is less significant than the definition of the boundaries of the strategic group. If there are several strategic groups in a single industry, the difference in opportunity and threat structure must be included in the analysis of the industry.

An analytical tool used in the analysis of development and trends of an industry is *strategic group maps*. It presents a simple visualisation and graphical representation of the relation of the personal position and the position of competitors in the context of determining the mobility barriers, identifying marginal groups, labelling movement paths and similar (Ferguson et al., 2000). In any case, the organisation in different strategic groups have different competitive foundations and different competitive advantages. In order to draw out the map of strategic groups, the following steps must be followed:

1 Identifying the key features differentiating the organisation within an industry based on typical diverse variables;
2 Repositioning the organisation on a map defined by two variables using pairs with different features;
3 Labelling organisation that need to be repositioned in the same space which is the foundation for creating a strategic group;
4 Describing the area encircling each group and making sure it is proportional to the scale of group share in the overall profitability of the industry.

According to Hax and Majluf (1991), two dimensions (strategic dimension X and strategic dimension Y)[8] are crucial in the process of defining strategic groups (Figure 4.6). Possible strategic dimensions that can be considered

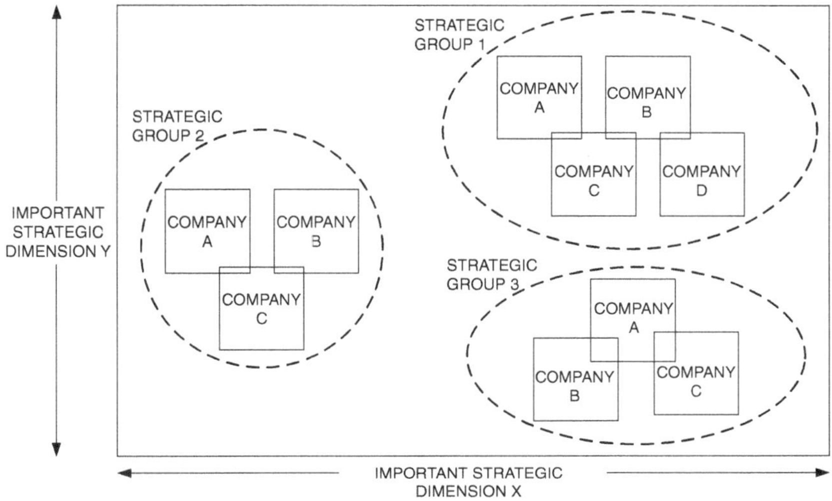

Figure 4.6 The map of strategic groups according to two key dimensions.

Source: Hax and Majluf (1991:36).

include the following: Quality (high, medium, low), area (local, regional, state, global), middlemen (one, some, all), services (without any, limited, full) and similar.

The alternative strategic positions of different competitors can be displayed based on either of the two mentioned dimensions. The main competitors of a company belong to its strategic group.[9]

They sell different products at similar prices to different buyers. The higher the similarity in the business strategies of companies in a strategic group, the bigger rivalry among them and vice versa; the more different business strategies in a strategic group, the weaker rivalry among them. There is direct competition in the first scenario, whereas there is indirect competition in the second one. It can be argued that the coordination of operating is more important than cooperation when forming strategic groups. It is due to the fact that strategic groups can be formed around mutual business strategies which can be a result of monitoring the business strategies of others.

According to Michael Porter (1979), strategic groups are not equivalents of strategic segments since they are defined on a broader platform of competition. They are an analytical tool in a strategic analysis. Different strategic groups have different mobility barriers giving some companies the edge over others. There is a certain link between entry barriers and mobility barriers. Although the entry barriers disable the entry of competitors into an industry, mobility barriers limit the movement of competitors between strategic groups within the same industry. Companies in a strategic group reach profitability which is higher than the profitability otherwise reached in the case of adapting to business strategy entering the strategic group or industry. That is the reason why companies try to compete with different business strategies despite the fact that all business strategies are not equally successful. If there were not any mobility barriers, it would be easy for some companies to imitate companies with successful business strategies influencing the profit equalisation.

According to Michael Porter (1979), the existence of strategic groups reduces the intensity of competition within an industry. It is a result of the cooperation and coordination of group members, which are the reason for the reduced intensity of the competition in the group, compared with competition among individual groups.

Such a situation is defined by three factors (Dess and Davis, 1984): (a) The number of groups and the distribution of their market shares; (b) the diversity of individual groups (the so-called strategic distance); and (c) the level of product buyer profile diversity.

Strategic groups have multiple advantages since they offer:

- Understanding and determination of the direct competitors of a company, which is the competitive foundation of rivalry within every strategic group;
- Identifying the similarities and differences of a company compared to existing competitors and competitors with an interest of entering the strategic group;
- The probability and possibility of a company to change a strategic group and overcome obstacles to enter a better strategic group;
- Recognising company opportunities and threats that need a timely identification since they occur at different intensity within strategic groups.

Competitors analysis from the environmental perspective

The competitor analysis has an aim of predicting the future decisions of competitors and their plausible reactions to the business strategy of a corporation as well as their initiatives and to determine the ways of influencing the competitors for the benefit of the company that initiated the analysis. Company competitors are those selling the same or similar products at same or similar prices to the same category of consumers. The existing business strategies of competitors, their assumptions on the industry and their potential should be monitored with special interest. All the stated participants are in a competitive game with companies from within the industry. Recognising them in such a way, the company can choose its competitors by classifying them into those which are important and those which are not, within the established industry boundaries. Determining the industry boundaries is important since it creates an opportunity for a corporation to identify direct and indirect competitors.

Direct competitors are a decisive factor since a lot of actions undertaken by companies are a result of an answer to the moves of the competition. Recognising and analysing the strategic group of the company located in an industry is a logical insight and a regular part of a detailed analysis of competitors.

Companies analyse the current, investigate the potential and predict the future competitors to position themselves in order to maximise the economic added value which differentiates the company from its competitors.

A constant collection of information on competitors is needed. The most common sources include the following: (1) *The competitors themselves* (e.g. reports, brochures, events, statements and similar), (2) *business partners* (e.g. suppliers, media, agencies and similar), (3) *internal sources* (e.g. analysts, acquisitionists, investigators and similar), (4) *competitor buyers* (e.g. interviews, surveys, groups and similar) and (8) *data bases* (e.g. the Internet, research, statistics and similar).

Intelligence on competition is a euphemism for economic espionage. Friedrich the Great used to say: You can be forgiven for being defeated, but you cannot be forgiven for being surprised.

Counter-intelligence consists of active actions to identify and neutralise the activity of data collection by competitors. The difference between intelligence and counter-intelligence is in the selection of posed questions.

If the following question is asked: *Why are competitors receiving benefits at the expense of our company?* You have a case of intelligence.

Counter-intelligence is featured by the following question: *What is it that our company does that provides it with the opportunity to make a profit at the expense of the competition?*

Michael Porter (1985) has established four diagnostic components (Figure 4.7) in an analysis of competitors:

1 Future goals;
2 Current strategies;
3 Assumptions;
4 Competences.

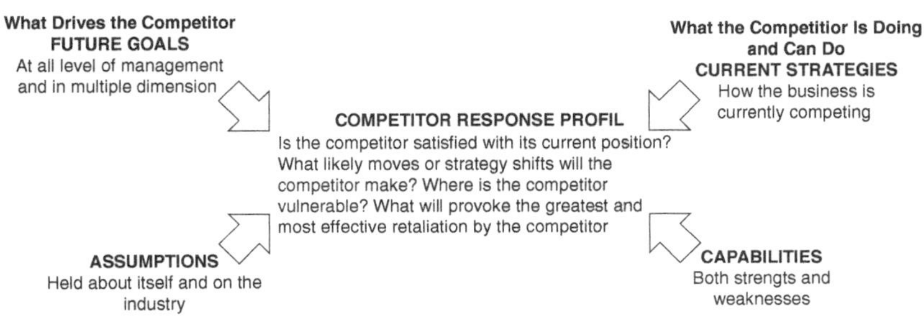

Figure 4.7 Porter's competitor analysis framework.

Source: Adapted from Porter (1985:49).

The first component of competitor analysis is future goals. Future goals enable the prediction of the level of satisfaction of competitors with their position, which offers information on the possible changes of their business strategy. The analysis needs to include the goals of the reaction of the strategic units of a company.

The second component of competitor analysis is current strategies. Forming attitudes on the current strategies reveals information on key operational policies of each individual business function and the type of connection between the business functions. The strategies can be explicit or implicit and always exist in one of these forms.

The third component of competitor analysis is assumptions. Identifying each competitor assumptions includes the assumptions of competitors on themselves and the assumptions of competitors on other competitors. Each company operates on a basis of a set of assumptions on their own situation as well as the industry and its competitors.

The fourth component of competitor analysis are capabilities. A realistic analysis of the competences of each competitor will affect the probability, definition, character and intensity of the reaction. Its strengths and weaknesses prompt its competence to either initiate or react to events taking place in the industry.

A company needs to analyse all noteworthy existing competitors which can have an active role in the market. The analysis should include current and potential competitors. The possibility for competitors to utilise their business strategies and goals greatly depends on their resources and capabilities. A company needs to gather information on each competitor. Generally speaking, a company needs to follow two variables during a competitor analysis:

1. Its share in buyer conscious – the percentage of buyers favouring a particular competitor when answering the following question: When you consider a particular industry, which company comes to your mind first?
2. Its share in buyer preferences – the percentage of buyers highlighting a competitor feature when answering the following question: Which product of a particular company does first come to your mind?

The general conclusion is that company with a big share in buyer conscious and preferences will reach a big market share and above the average profitability, too. However, companies enter and exit an industry. Although entry and exit barriers are conceptually different, there is often the possibility of their correlation. Figure 4.8 illustrates the exit barriers (which can be low or high) and entry barriers (which can be low or high).

Michael Porter (1980) argues that the most favourable position in terms of industry profitability is the one where the *entry barriers are high*, but the *exit barriers are low*. This makes entry difficult for potential competitors and creates an easier exit for existing unsuccessful competitors. There is capacity

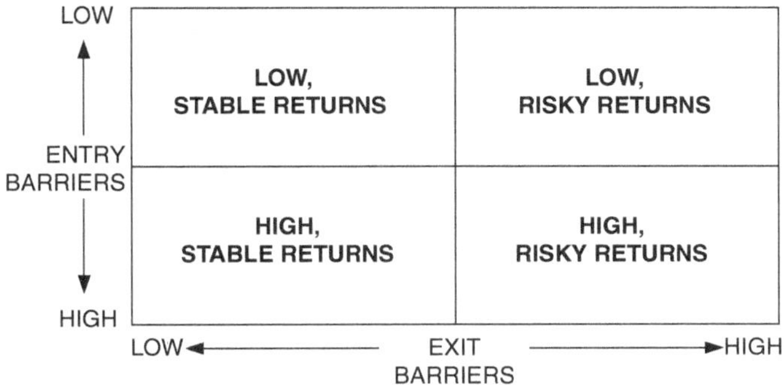

Figure 4.8 Industry barriers and profitability.

Source: Adapted from Porter (1980:22).

exploitation and high profitability in those industries. When both *entry and exit barriers are high,* the potential for profitability is high, but associated with high risk. This makes it difficult for existing unsuccessful competitors to exit. Weaker competitors do not leave and fight for a better spot in the existing industry. When both *entry and exit barriers are low,* the potential for profit is low, and associated with high risk. This makes it easier for unsuccessful competitors to exit. Weaker competitors leave the industry and fight for a better spot in a new industry. The least favourable position in terms of industry profitability is the one where *the entry barriers are low and the exit barriers are high.* This makes it easier for potential competitors to enter, and difficult for unsuccessful competitors to exit. There is unused capacity and low profitability in those industries.

Michael Porter (1995) points out some mistakes with companies trying to strategically react to the competition dynamics. *The first mistake concerns strategic thinking.* The biggest mistake is trying to apply universal business strategy. A good business strategy concerns dealing with structural characteristics of the industry economy and the unique position of a company in it. Industry leaders are the companies which do not optimise their performances, but rather redefine the industry. *The second mistake concerns the success in strategic adaptation.* A change alters the buyer's need. The continuity of business strategy and fast changes are not inconsistent. A differentiation needs to be made between business strategy and operative effectiveness in the process of operationalisation of the given position. Business strategy needs to be changed the very moment that the fundamental needs of the buyer are changed.

The development of new technology significantly influences the reshaping of industry structures. Given that context, industry participants significantly influence the creation of high barriers to reduce the newcomers, which leads to the reduction of industry competitiveness. Such a scenario creates artificial and highly unattractive industries for new participants. To what extent does such a relation favour the creation of investment-friendly attractive climate for investors to enhance the business environment which will lead to an increase in the national competitiveness of a country?

Analyse the strategic groups according to different variables established at the automotive industry example and include an explanation of reasons which had led the companies to start forming strategic groups within the industry.

Notes

1 Michael Porter and his researchers have conducted hundreds of interviews with top managers, leaders, consultants, researchers, bankers and others to research the role of a cluster in the growth of national competitiveness. In a cluster study conducted in San Diego, his group partly used the results obtained by a research based on the method of a profound psychological interview with over 160 top managers.

2 Jack Welch stated that the invention of Internet is the most significant event in American economy since the industrial revolution.

3 *Key success factors* can amount to 20% of factors conditioning 80% of company profitability or strategic business units.

4 There are a lot of different market structures placed between perfect competition and monopoly. The attempt of forging a unique theory uniting them in a microeconomic analysis has introduced the theory of games. The basic idea of Nash's balance from game theory is just a generalisation of Cournot's balance (Pascal, 1999).

5 Besides, the well-known book *Megatrends* by John Naisbitt, which has become a global bestseller, is the result of similar data collection.

6 Fahey, King and Narayanan compare the approaches of collecting information on an industry considering the following dimensions: means, scale, motif, time, dimension, range and holders. Following the listed items, the collection of information is conducted: irregularly (ad hoc updating, specific events, crisis at an initial phase, reactive level, retrospective data, short deadline, different agencies and similar), occasionally (periodic updating, selected events, ongoing crisis, proactive level, current data, medium deadline, particular agencies and similar) and continuously (structured updating, broad events, deep crisis, overactive level, prospect data, long deadlines and similar).

7 There is a theory and belief that strategic groups were initially introduced by Hunt in 1972 and further developed by Newman in 1978.

8 The level of vertical integration and the broadness of the production line are two key dimensions leading towards the separation of the company with completely covered production lines which in turn enables complete superiority in relation to other narrowly focused companies. In addition to these key dimensions, the authors argue that the following ones can be considered: Price/quality (high, medium, low), area (local, regional, state, global), middlemen (one, some, all), services (without any, limited, full) and similar.

9 Strategic groups in the automotive industry are, for example, positioned according to key dimensions: price (low and high) and product (many and few). The strategic group characterised by high price and a small programme includes: Ferrari, Lamborghini and Porsche. The strategic group characterised by low price and a small programme includes: Hyundai and Kia. The strategic group characterised by high price and high programme includes: Mercedes and BMW. The strategic group characterised by large programmes and low price includes: Toyota, Ford, Chrysler, Honda and Nissan.

References

Abell, D. (1993): *Managing with Dual Strategies: Mastering the Present, Preempting the Future*, New York: The Free Press.

Barney, B. (1991): *Gaining and Sustaining Competitive Advantage*, Boston: Addison-Wesley Publishing.

Bateman, S., Zeithaml, P. (1990): *Management*, Boston: Irwin.

Caves, R. E., Porter, M. (1978): "Market Structure, Oligopoly and Stability of Market Shares." *Journal of Industrial Economics*, vol. 26, no. 4, 289–313.

Caves, R., Pugel, T. (1980): *Intraindustry Differences in Conduct and Performance: Viable Strategies in US Manufacturing Industries*, New York: New York University.

Certo, C., Peter, J. (1991): *Strategic Management Concepts and Application*, Boston: McGraw-Hill.

Dess, G., Davis, P. (1984): "Porter's (1980) Generic Strategies as Determinants of Strategic Group Membership and Organizational Performance." *Academy of Management Journal*, vol. 27, 467–488.

Dess, G., Miller, A., Eisner, F. (2007): *Strategijski menadžment*, Beograd: Data Status.

Dragičević, M. (2012): *Konkurentnost: Projekt za Hrvatsku*, Zagreb: Školska knjiga.

Đuričin, D., Janošević, S., Kaličanin, Đ. (2011): *Menadžment i strategija*, Beograd: Ekonomski fakultet.

Ferguson, T., Deephouse, D., Ferguson, W. (2000): "Do Strategic Groups Differ in Reputation." *Strategic Management Journal*, vol. 21, no. 12, 1195–1214.

Harrigan, K. R., Porter, M. (1983): "End-Game Strategies for Declining Industries," *Harvard Business Review*, vol. 61, no. 4, 111–120.

Hax, A., Majluf, N. (1991): *The Strategy Concept and Process: A Pragmatic Approach*, New Jersey: Prentice-Hall.

Hill, C., Jones, R. (1998): *Strategic Management: An Integrated Approach*, Boston: Houghton Mifflin Company.

Jarillo, J. (2003): *Strategic Logic*, New York: Palgrave.

Johnson, G., Scholes, K., Whittinghton, R. (2007): *Exploring Corporate Strategy*, Harlow: Prentice Hall Financial Times.

Kippenberg, T. (1998): Strategy according to Michael Porter, Antidote, vol. 3, no. 6, 24–25.

Lancolla, G., Suarez, F. (2012): Closing the Technology Adoption–Use Divide: The Role of Contiguous User Bandwagon, *Journal of Management*, vol. 38, no. 3.

Magretta, J. (2012): *Understanding Michael Porter: The Essential Guide to Competition and Strategy*, Boston: Harvard Business Review Press.

Mašić, B. (2009): *Strategijski menadžment*, Beograd: Univerzitet Singidunum.

Milisavljević, M. (2012): *Strategijski menadžment: analiza, izbor, promena*, Beograd: Ekonomski fakultet.

Porter, M. (1979): *The Structure within Industries and Companies Performance*, Review of Economics and Strategy, vol. 61, no. 2, 214–227.

Porter, M. (1980): *Competitive Strategy: Techniques for Analyzing Industries and Competitors*, New York: The Free Press.

Porter, M. (1983): *Note on Structural Analysis of Industries*, Harvard Business Review, Background Note 376-054.

Porter, M. (1985): *Competitive Advantage: Creating and Sustaining Superior Performance*, New York: The Free Press.

Porter, M. (1990): *The Competitive Advantage of Nations*, London: The MacMillan.

Porter, M. (1991): *Green Competitiveness*, New York Times.

Porter, M. (1998a): *Clusters and the New Economics of Competition*, Harvard Business Review, vol. 76, no. 6, 77–90.

Porter, M. (1998b): *On Competition*, Boston: Harvard Business Review Book.

Porter, M. (2001): *Strategy and Internet*, Harvard Business Review.

Porter, M. (2008): *The Five Competitive Forces That Shapes Strategy*, Harvard Business Review, vol. 86, no. 1, 79–93.

Porter, M., van der Linde, C. (September-October 1995a): *Green and Competitive: Ending the Stalemate*, Harvard Business Review, vol. 73, no. 5, 120–134.

Porter, M., van der Linde, C. (1995b): "Toward a New Conception of the Environmental-Competitiveness Relationship." *Journal of Economic Perspectives.*

Šehić, D. (2002): *Strateški menadžment*, Mostar: Slovo.

"The Role of Continuous User Bandwagon." *Journal of Management.*

Vizjak, A. (2007): *Pobednici tržišnih niša: perspektive slovenačkih preduzećau borbi protiv globalne konkurencije*, Beograd: Fakultet za ekonomiju, finansije i administraciju.

Wheelen, T., Hunger, D. (1990): *Strategic Management and Business Policy*, New York: Addison Wesley.

5 Company Analysis: *Porter's Value Chain Concept*

Strategic company analysis

A company is a socioeconomic phenomenon focused on shaping the value system in the relationship with suppliers, distributors and customers.[1] There are two approaches to determine the paradigm of company success. These approaches model the company profile (its internal foundations and its created effects). The two approaches are as follows: (a) The conventional approach and (b) the contemporary approach. The *conventional approach* starts with the basic goal – the profit. The purpose of this approach is to strive towards an optimal combination of limited resources (maximal yield with reduced costs). According to Michael Porter, one of two sources of competitive advantage – low cost – can be found at the basis of this approach. In this approach, the underlying criteria for following a business strategy is the so-called *comparative advantage*. The effect should surpass the investment through the possibility of low prices or higher profit at identical prices in relation to competitors. The *contemporary approach* starts from the basic goal – economic added value. The purpose of this approach is to strive towards an optimal combination of limited resources (maximal yield with reduced costs). According to Michael Porter, the basic criteria for following business strategy is one of the two sources of competitive advantage – differentiation. This approach recognises the so-called *competitive advantage* as the main criteria for following a business strategy. The effect should surpass the investment through the possibility of higher prices or higher economic added value at increased prices in relation to competitors.

The new concept of organisation is composed of strategic business units – SBUs, which represent the infrastructure for achieving goals. In up-to-date practice, the companies have optimised their business operations following the logics of SBUs (Mašić, 2014), whereas companies will optimise their business operations following the essential core competences in its future practical work. The two concepts of organisational structure change are shown in Table 5.1.

According to Michael Porter (1980), the direction of strategic business unit operations can be offensive and defensive, i.e. oriented towards positioning starting from a given schedule of factors which define the industry

DOI: 10.4324/9781003359173-5

Table 5.1 Two concepts: strategic business unit or essential core competences

Characteristics	*Strategic business unit*	*Essential core competences*
Competition framework	Competitiveness among companies to establish a position	Companies competing to build core competences
Organisational structure	Portfolio of associated jobs in terms of the product-market relation	Portfolio of core competence in terms of the product-job relation
Unit status	Autonomy is sacred; SBU is the source of all resources	Alliance is sacred; SBU is the reservoir of all resources
Resource allocation	Particular businesses are analysis units; individual capital allocation	Core competences are analysis units; collective capital allocation
Added value	Optimising the yield on invested capital through capital allocation and business balance	Creating the architecture strategy by building core competence and securing the future

Source: Adapted from Prahalad and Hamel (1990).

structure, occupying such a position to successfully amortise the effect of unfavourable circumstances and focusing its activities at areas where the effect of the given factors is the weakest.

This influences the balance of given factors by actively influencing the constellation of the previously mentioned industry structure factors by means of different innovations or integrations, securing a perspective of business development in an industry. The result of such actions can be the utilisation of expected changes by relying on a timely application of new opportunities which will arise in an anticipated evolution of industry business conditions. A strategic business unit is *the smallest organisational part of a company for which there is a possibility of forming a business strategy* (Todorović et al., 2000).

After a company defines its mission,[2] vision[3] and goals,[4] it positions its own business in a company value chain. Following the logic of a systematic approach in the context of input-output relations, the company takes over the supplier value as its input to transform the respective value into a new value which is transferred to customers via distributors. This means that the company value chain describes the way of observing the business process as a chain of activities transforming inputs into buyer outputs. It also adds value to the final product in the process (Šunje, 2002).

The concept of added value analysis was introduced by Michael Porter (1985) who based his research on accounting practices of calculating added value through individual stages in the production process. This has led Michael Porter to transfer the idea to a company as a whole, proving that there is a necessity for a separate research of each individual activity in order to determine the sources of competitive advantage (Tipurić et al., 2010). Such an approach creates the possibility of treating the value chain as a separate unity, but keeping in mind that the company value chain is just a part of industry chain forming the following: (a) Upstream value, (b) channel value and (c) downstream value. Sustaining competitive advantage depends on the manner in which the company manages its own value chain. This leads to the creation of the *value system*. The basis of business operations is the business model which is most accurately described by the configuration of activities. Today, it is possible to measure and quantify the contribution of each individual activity due to modern development. Michael Porter defines the activity configuration as a value chain. Value chain, in its formation phase, copied the value chain rationale called the *thread* (French *filirere*), which describes the physical flow of the input, operations and output reflecting the relations in a particular period of time. Value chain[5] is a *concept that facilitates the disaggregation of a business into strategically relevant activities*. The process offers an easier way of considering the value chain and identifying the activities where there is a key competence which can be exploited through business strategy. Focusing on the activities within the value chain provides an insight into activities which can be utilised to create competitive advantage. Value chain generates a value which represents the amount a buyer is willing to pay for the product. Buyer value is calculated using three core groups of activities:

1 Activities differentiating a product from other same products;
2 Activities creating low cost of a product compared with other same products;
3 Activities that offer the possibility of quickly meeting the buyer's demands.

Such defined value is characterised by *total revenue*. A company generates *profit* if *the value* surpasses *the expenses*. Consequently, the analysis of creating and sustaining competitive advantage focuses on *value* rather than *cost*. This is the purpose of a business strategy, particularly to differentiate between business strategy and operational effectiveness. The company value chain portraits the total value, i.e. it consists of activities and profit (Todorović et al., 2000).

A company has to analyse the three aforementioned activities, irrespective of whether it conducts them or not since it is the sole condition for creating a value system to be used as a platform for building competitive advantage. The following needs to be defined in the process (Đuričin et al., 2015):

a The most critical activities in a value chain which either reduce costs or increase value;
b Key expenses or leading activities in a value chain which either reduce costs or increase value;
c The most important relations in a value chain which either reduce costs or increase value.

Activities include physical steps to be taken to create a product, whereas the profit is the difference between total income and total cost. Activities are identified solely at companies whereas profit is identified at companies and at suppliers and distributors too, since it is a part of total cost covered by the buyer. Correlating is important since the supplier, the distributor and the buyer all influence the value in a value system. Only a handful of companies cover each and every activity in a value chain. Ford Motor Company can serve as an example since it has been completely vertically integrated[6] from producing steel to selling cars. However, it had a negative effect on the employees who were being exploited. Charlie Chaplin pointed out their status in the company as well as the general exploitation of workers in his popular parody *Modern Times.*[7] There are no two identical company value chains. Although some companies try to copy value chains, Michael Porter warns against such attempts since the differences existing among company value chains of competitors present the key sources of competitive advantage.

In order to identify the differences, Michael Porter (1985) states that the following three steps need to be taken:

1 Analyse activities following the product lines to identify weak and strong sides;
2 Identify connections between value chains of different product lines to determine the effect of cost and value of one value chain on the cost and value of another value chain;
3 Identify the synergy between the value chain and different product lines.

Companies most often unite different businesses, each representing an autonomous unit which demands a business strategy to be shaped. Most corporations are involved in hundreds and even thousands of activities in the process of input to output conversion. The company cannot increase value or reduce costs by considering the activities as a whole. Creating and sustaining competitive advantage comes from various separate activities conducted by a company On Competition. The basic features of a strategic business unit are as follows:

1 That it has its own business operations;
2 That it has its own competitors;
3 That it has its own manager.

Some strategic business units can be merged either due to their scale or connection in terms of identical suppliers, identical distributor or identical customers. Michael Porter highlights the correlation of strategic business units. Such correlation is established by iterating several mutually connected steps:

First, *to identify the basic correlations within the company* which are really or potentially present between strategic units of a newly founded company since all the specific activities need to be identified to represent the foundation

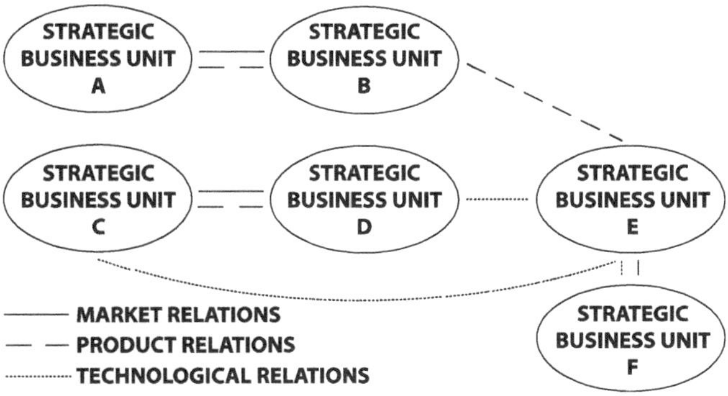

Figure 5.1 The correlation of strategic business units in a company.

Source: Adapted from Porter (1985:369).

for future repositioning and organisation of strategic business units. This means that it is necessary to evaluate which of the activities can be common for particular strategic business units. Figure 5.1 illustrates a correlation matrix in a company with a smaller number of strategic business units.

It offers the opportunity of grouping strategic business units with particularly strong correlations and it can facilitate their visualisation as a cornerstone for certain business functions. Disregarding the manner of their presentation, potential correlations must be clearly set apart from those which are actually realised in practice. Different strategic business groups are often correlated in different ways. One strategic business unit can be associated with the market, whereas another one can be associated with production. Figure 5.2 illustrates the correlation matrix of a company with a larger number of business units.

	STRATEGIC BUSINESS UNIT A	STRATEGIC BUSINESS UNIT B	STRATEGIC BUSINESS UNIT C
STRATEGIC BUSINESS UNIT B	COMMON BUYER		
STRATEGIC BUSINESS UNIT C	COMMON BUYER COMMON RAW MATERIAL COMMON COMPONENT	COMMON BUYER	
STRATEGIC BUSINESS UNIT D	COMMON RAW MATERIAL COMMON COMPONENT		COMMON RAW MATERIAL COMMON COMPONENT

Figure 5.2 The correlations among strategic business units in a company (correlation matrix).

Source: Adapted from Porter (1985:369).

In order to identify the correlations in an easier way, each company can be divided into such strategic business unit groups which have different correlations but their quantity is relatively small compared with the possible number and correlation type of strategic business units of other groups.

Second, *to determine the basic correlations outside the organisation*, i.e. to identify the relation between the existing strategic business units and other businesses which are currently not a part of the company portfolio.

A company needs to be careful in selecting those activities which are essential in a value chain for an opportunity to locate related businesses to share their activities with in the future. It is highly advisable to use the same formula to identify completely new relations never used before by a single competitor and which can be fitted into the company.

Third, *to identify possible side correlations*. This step follows the identification of basic correlations. It includes considering activities individually in a value chain where a company has valuable innovations that can be used in other strategic business units. In addition, this process includes the identification of new businesses which can be an asset to existing strategic business units of a company. Possible side correlations manifest themselves as a similarity in the configuration of activities in a value chain.

Fourth, *to identify the correlations with the competitors*. This means that a company needs to determine the multiple competitors which are an actual or potential adversary in more than one business. The existence of multiple competitors indicates the existence of correlations and it can aid in their identification. After a company determines the existence of such competition, it must record each type of correlation within each competitor portfolio. However, they are often different and involve different type of work making it difficult to identify with them.

Fifth, *the importance of correlation for competitive advantage*. Despite a host of overall relations, there is only a handful of those that strategically matter. The competitive advantage resulting from basic correlations from within a company serves as a benefit for sharing activities, sharing costs and difficulties with correlation integration. Common activities must be measured against respective competitor activities in all the mentioned dimensions. The side relations lead to competitive advantage if the benefit of the know-how transfer surpasses its costs.

Sixth, *developing a horizontal integration to enhance the most important correlations* which can be achieved in the following ways:

1 Distributing appropriate activities in the value chain for an easier coordination of the stated activities for everyone;
2 Coordinating the strategic positioning of particular strategic business units;
3 Separately observing the aims of individual strategic business units by equally including all participants in the discussion;

4 Coordinating offensive and defensive business strategies towards multiple competitors and competitors with different correlations;
5 Diversifying in order to reinforce the important correlations which will result in the creation of completely new unknown relations;
6 Using relevant basic relations of formal programmes of personal innovation transferal exchange;
7 Selling strategic business units which do not have significant common ground with others, making their relations notably difficult.

If there are several models of correlations within a company, including different groups of strategic business units, the implementation of the tactics mentioned earlier can lead to activity overlapping. When this happens, it is necessary to stimulate those relations which have the biggest influence on competitive advantage even if that subsequently results in higher costs. Organisational mechanisms are established to complete this task and they enable a simultaneous progression of correlation of different strategic business units.

Seventh, *the movement of horizontal organisational mechanisms* with the aim of successful strategy implementation is an important step for the entire process of shaping the business strategy since companies cannot successfully utilise correlations without horizontal structure which offers coordination and the transfer of competencies using connections among strategic business units. That is why the processes of defining strategic business units including classifications in appropriate groups to achieve maximum mutual coordination are vital. Creating and sustaining competitive advantage of a company does not solely depend on its value chain, it depends on its value system, too. Value chain is formed at the industry level. Michael Porter (1985) differentiates two important elements within the concept of a value chain:

1 Different activities conducted in particular chain connections;
2 The concept of a value chain with more connections called a value system.

If a company has a single product (or if it is non-diversified), the value chain is formed at the company level and it consists of its activities. If a company has multiple products (or if it is diversified), the value chain is formed at the strategic business unit level and consists of strategic business unit activities (Figure 5.3).

Such a relation requires an agreement on the company – *strategic business units* relation[8] concerning:

1 The planned changes in the strategic business unit portfolio (changes planned by the company and changes to be planned by the strategic business unit), i.e. demands the decisions on issues such as which

strategic business units will grow, which will consolidate, which will be liquidated and which will be renewed. Such decision-making requires distribution of needed resources to reach the portfolio development of strategic business units in a company.

2 The business area where the strategic business unit will operate (which business area will be covered by the company and which business it will assign to the strategic business unit), i.e. demands a decision on the connection between strategic business units which should lead to certain synergic effects.

3 The operational limitations in relation to other strategic business units (which operations are allowed by the companies and which operations it will pass on to the strategic business unit for it to decide on the permission), i.e. it demands a decision on balancing the relations between the sales scale and income to be achieved by the strategic business unit. Such decision-making requires an assessment of the acceptable level of strategic business unit profit oscillation within a company, too.

4 The needed capital for investing in the development of strategic business units (which investments does the company need and which investments it believes the strategic unit business will need), i.e. it demands a decision on the question of balancing money flows in strategic business units. In addition, such decision-making requires an estimate for increasing long-term and permanent capital of strategic business units in a company.

5 The expected results to be reached by a strategic business unit (the results of the company and the expected results of the strategic business unit), i.e. it demands a decision on the results to be reached by each individual strategic business unit. In addition, such decision-making requires a common definition of clear and scalable goals of strategic business units in a company.

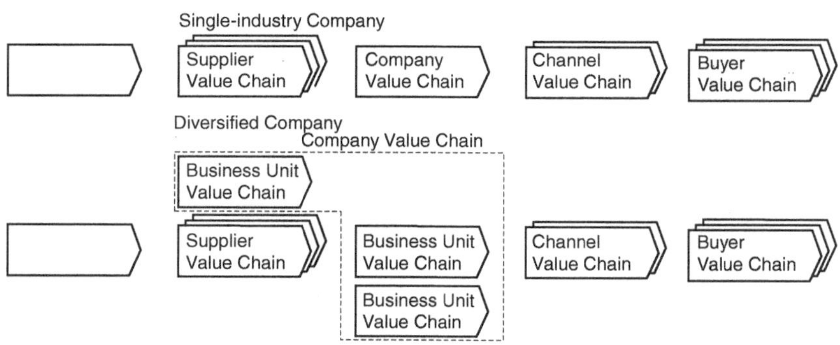

Figure 5.3 Value system.

Source: Adapted from Porter (1985:35).

The company-strategic business unit agreement can be reached to include both the lower and higher levels (top managers and strategic business unit managers) in the process of setting aims. Therefore, it is advisable for these levels to work together when setting aims to facilitate their implementation. In order to properly set the strategic aims, it is possible to use the management by objectives – MBO to promote the idea on the need of cooperation during the process of forming strategic goals which have been agreed upon (based on mutually agreement) by senior managers (top managers) and junior managers (strategic business unit managers). Management by objectives has gained high popularity in the 1960s and 1970s and it was used by many companies not only in its origin country of the USA but also the whole world. Management by objectives is focused on reaching aims that have been mutually defined and revised by top managers and strategic business unit managers. It should be noted that the process of management by objectives must start from top managers by transforming the company aims into specific aims of strategic business units. However, the process must follow the bottom-up procedure by including the strategic business unit managers into the process of setting the strategic aims of the company. Hence, the following needs to be closely considered (Hicks and Gullet, 1972):

1 *The type, significance and mutual coordination of goals*– respecting the fact that there are classifications of strategic goals according to different aspects which are used to facilitate the application of this concept, the role and significance of goals on the level of a company as an entity and strategic business units as its components is highlighted.
2 *Mechanisms, benefits and the degree of setting goals* – abandoning the autocratic approach which is replaced by the democratic one, highlighting the benefits of participation which should result in an agreement-based strategic goal definition as the most efficient mechanism at the level of a company as an entity and strategic business units as its components.
3 *Executives, monitoring and the analysis of goal realisation* – controlling the realisation of goals by all included in the defining process, regularly holding meetings and highlighting the role and significance of self-control on the level of a company as an entity and strategic business units as its components.

Michael Porter (1991) identifies the criteria applied in the practice of diversified companies during the conceptualisation of the mix of strategic business units. Namely, he differentiates the four following approaches:

1 Concept of portfolio management;
2 Reducing cost by restructuring;
3 Transfer of core competences;
4 Sharing of activities.

The portfolio management concept is mostly associated with successful, overrated and developed strategic business units. Michael Porter (1987) argues that the concept of portfolio management offers a type of optimisation or a schedule of activities. Top management appears in a role of an auditor conducting a regular business audit.

Reducing cost by restructuring is mostly associated with unsuccessful, underrated and undeveloped strategic business units. Top management appears in the role of a restructurer conducting special business restructuring. Michael Porter (1987) believes that restructuring offers a type of cost reduction.

The other two concepts (*key competencies transfer* and *mutual utilisation of activities*) are based on studying the strategic business units to achieve competitive advantage. Namely, the optimisation of the mix of strategic business units has the aim of creating premises for creating synergy based on a better distribution of cost and assets throughout the activities in a value chain of a company. Considering the fact that each strategic business unit is a value chain per se, there is a tendency to consider the capitalisation of the relations among strategic business units. Such relations are considered from the following aspects (Todorović et al., 2000):

1 Transfer of core competences from one strategic business unit to some of the activities in a value chain of another strategic business unit;
2 The possibility of a mutual utilisation of some of the activities in a value chain by multiple strategic business units.

The realisation of the aforementioned concepts depends on several premises. The most important ones are the following (Montgomery and Porter, 1991):

1 The existence of similarity, i.e. coherency among activities in a value chain of strategic business units;
2 The possibility to achieve sufficient competitive advantage by a transfer of core competences and mutual utilisation of activities in a value chain.

It is evident that each approach has its benefits and limitations and it is up to the top management to determine their attractiveness and the possibility of combining. Such an action requires a detailed analysis including an interactive procedure.

Constructs of strategic company analysis

A strategic organisational analysis includes the following:

1 Value chain analysis;
2 Strategic activities analysis;
3 The analysis of competitors from the company perspective.

Value chain analysis

Michael Porter (1985) suggest a procedure for analysing the value chain by disaggregating it into activities. Chain value activities of a company represent only a part of activities called the value system. Each product line has its value chain; hence, a company can be seen as a group of different value chains. The value chain is formulated at the level of a strategic business unit in diversified company (Đuričin et al., 2015). Recognised as a set of relative activities, a value chain is united by the internal and external company relations. The relations are links between (a) the way a particular value activity is conducted and (b) the cost of conducting another value activity. The sum of internal and external links of an activity forms the *configuration of value chain activities in a* company. Their importance is recognised in the possibility of creating and sustaining competitive advantage in two ways: (a) Forming an optimal configuration and (b) mutually coordinating activities. There are a host (Porter, 2007) of relations used in a value chain: The same function can be completed in different ways, the cost of conducting direct activities can be reduced through enhancements, the need for long-term product service, quality assurance functions can be reduced and completed in a different way and similar.

Identifying the relations is a process of finding ways in which each company locates the path of influence of each activity which creates costs and higher value compared with another activity. However, establishing quality relations is possible if a company has quality information at its disposal. The lack of information or incorrect information such as imprecise data can result in cost increase and value decrease. This phenomenon is known as the *bullwhip effect* (Russel and Taylor, 2009). This effect occurs when all value chains in a value system make decisions from the aspect of their own interest or lack precise information on the demand of an adjacent value chain in a value system. This can result in, for example, an increased level of safety stock.

Value chain activities surpass the company and the configuration, i.e. the relations of activities are spread on the value chain of the company, the distributors value chain and the buyer value chain. Establishing the complete configuration provides the company with the opportunity for profit from both founding and managing the relations among value chain activities of a company and from founding and managing relations among value chain activities of the supplier, value chain activities of distributors and value chain activities of the buyer. The configuration of relations covering both the supplier value chain and the distributor value chain is known as the *vertical relation* in literature, whereas the configuration of relations covering the buyer value chain is known as the *horizontal relation* in literature. The aim of establishing a complete activity configuration is to establish a certain order in a company. Establishing an order requires the coordination between value chain activities.

Tasks scheduled to be completed by the company must be mutually coordinated by unification and management to fulfil the previously set aims. The background of failure in fulfilling aims can be found in bad coordination of activities in a value chain of a company. An important notion of a value chain analysis is to break down the chain into activities starting from initial raw material to end customers and strategically relevant segments to understand the cost drivers and the differentiation drivers (Shank and Govindarajan, 1992). Value chain analysis explains the way in which the business process creates buyer value. It is evident that it can be done through two sources of competitive advantage (overall low cost and differentiation). Consequently, the value chain analysis disaggregates the business process into activities occurring within the process, starting from business process input to business process output.

Value chain of a company is being recognised as a utility diagnostic tool to identify the profitability of each phase in the business process. The analysis attempts to determine the costs of these activities to reveal whether a company has got the low cost advantage in relation to competitors. This forms the foundation of Michael Porter's attitude of company inaptness as a unit to locate the sources of competitive advantage. Namely, he argues that each individual activity must be considered independently and separately from others to identify its influence. That is the reason why activity features are examined to determine the way in which each activity participating in the value chain can lead to company product differentiation. Independent of the value chain area in which the given corporation operates, there is always the zone of primary expertise. Namely, this is the value chain gravity centre, the zone of the highest expertise and the possibility which presents the source of competitive advantage. The gravity centre is usually associated with activities conducted by the corporation to start off with its business operations. It is a question of *core business* (Đuričin et al., 2015). Nowadays, it is becoming an increasing trend for company to seek personal solutions in fundamental changes of their position in an industry where they operate. Company are increasingly following the technological trends, i.e. making notable changes in their core business through technological strategy.

According to Michael Porter (1980), the technological strategy determines the ways in which a company can create and use technology. Since technological changes affect the industry structure, the technological strategy is an important element of the overall strategy of a company (Figure 5.4).

Michael Porter believes that the technological strategy is a powerful tool for following the sources of competitive advantage. In his opinion, it is often wrongly assumed that a change in the process should cover its cost and that product change should yield differentiation. That is the reason why the revision of technologies at the disposal of the company needs to indicate areas in which a company should favour the option of cost reduction and

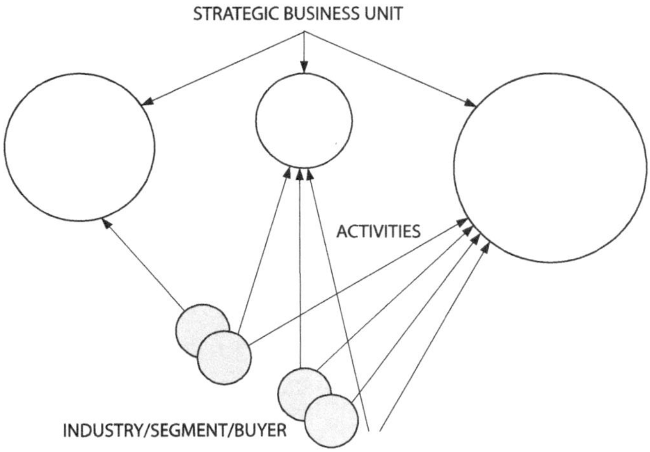

Figure 5.4 Activity identification.
Source: Đuričin et al. (2015:399).

areas where it should favour the option of differentiation as a source of competitive advantage.

The selection of a specific technology in a value chain to be focused on is important due to the relations between technological change and competitive advantage. A company should divert its attention to the technologies that have the biggest direct or indirect influence on low cost or differentiation. The premise is to always balance the cost of technology enhancements with its following benefits on the strategic positioning of a company in its environment. It should be noted that low cost orientation does not consequently rule out differentiation. Each activity in a value chain is different both in terms of strategy and technology. The activities are separable sequences of a business process which consume either time or resources where value or cost drivers operate. A strategic business unit corresponds with the market, segment or buyer through activities (Đuričin et al., 2015).

Michael Porter has significantly improved the analysis of business process disaggregation into activities considering the specific relations within the activities themselves in the process. Consequently, the business process is perceived as an activity chain rather than a series of business functions. The value chain idea is actually founded on a process-based perspective of a company. It presents a way of overviewing the company production as a system comprised of subsystems with individual inputs, transformation procedures and individual outputs. Activity identification involves the disaggregation of the business process and its classification into two basic groups (Porter, 1980): (1) Primary activities and (2) support activities (Figure 5.5).

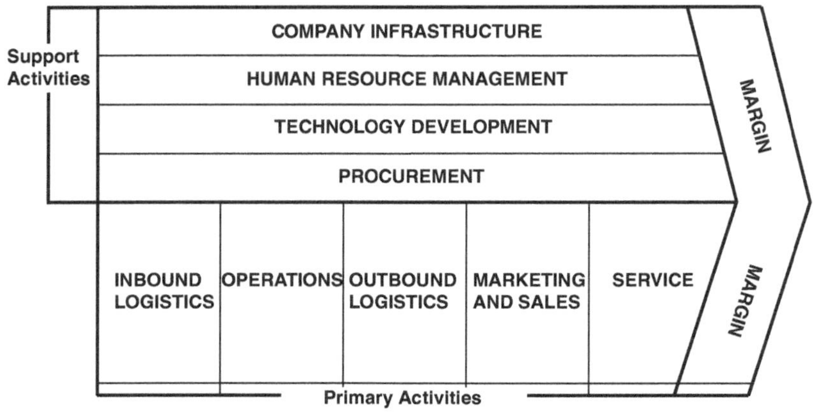

Figure 5.5 Porter's value chain concept.

Source: Porter (1985:37).

Primary activities include all the procedures involved in the final product production and its delivery to customers. These activities include the following: Inbound logistics, operations, outbound logistics, marketing and product sales (Pearce and Robinson, 2000).

- *Inbound logistics*: Activities, costs and assets related to the supply of fuel, energy, raw material, materials, parts, merchandise, and consumables provided by suppliers including reception, storage, input issuing, the handling of material in warehouses, workplace delivery, supply management and return to suppliers.
- *Operations*: Activities, costs and assets related to the transfer of input into outputs concerning the productions, assembling, testing, packing, equipment and installation maintenance, quality assurance and environmental protection.
- *Outbound logistic*: Activities, costs and assets related to the physical product distribution to customers concerning the storage of final products, warehouse manipulation, order processing, selection, packing, delivery and distribution operations.
- *Marketing and sales*: Activities, costs and assets related to the efforts of sales forces, marketing and promotions, market research and distributor planning and support.
- *Service*: Activities, costs and assets related to ensuring customer assistance such as assembling, spare part delivery, maintenance and fixing, technical assistance, buyer information and complaints.

Support activities include the company infrastructure which supports the normal conduction of primary activities including the company infrastructure, human resource management, technology development and supply (Pearce and Robinson, 2000).

- *Firm infrastructure*: Activities, costs and asset related to top management, finance, accounting, legal issues, safety and security, information systems for managers and other overhead functions.
- *Human resource management*: Activities, costs and assets related to recruiting, hiring, training, development, compensating and work relations of all types of employees.
- *Technology development*: Activities, costs and assets related to product research and development, process research and development, enhancing the design process, tool and equipment formations, computer software development, telecommunication systems, computer-integrated designing and engineering, new data base development, the development of computerised support systems.
- *Procurement:* Activities, costs and assets related to the supply of raw material and materials, services, machinery and other input necessities needed to back up company activities by supporting all value chain activities.

The type of work conducted by the company determines whether the value chain analysis will be focused on all support activities or only some of them, and which activities will receive the highest amount of attention.

The value chain also includes the profit which is the difference between the cost of the activity and the sales price, a price which is the result of the process of buyer value creation in a value chain.

In order to generate profit, the company has notably altered the business paradigm from production orientation to market orientation, as shown in Figure 5.6. This has shifted the focus in the value chain from the activities of inbound logistics, operations and outbound logistics to the activities of marketing, sales and service. The level of generated profit is still one of the fundamental benchmarks of company success. Activities involved in every individual situation must be kept in mind in a value chain analysis considering that a single activity, which is a support activity in one activity, can be a primary activity in another one.

According to Michael Porter (1985), the sources of competitive advantage include the following:

1 Low cost;
2 Differentiation.

Low cost

Low cost can be achieved if a company has a low cost cumulate when conducting activities compared with competitors (Todorović et al., 2000).

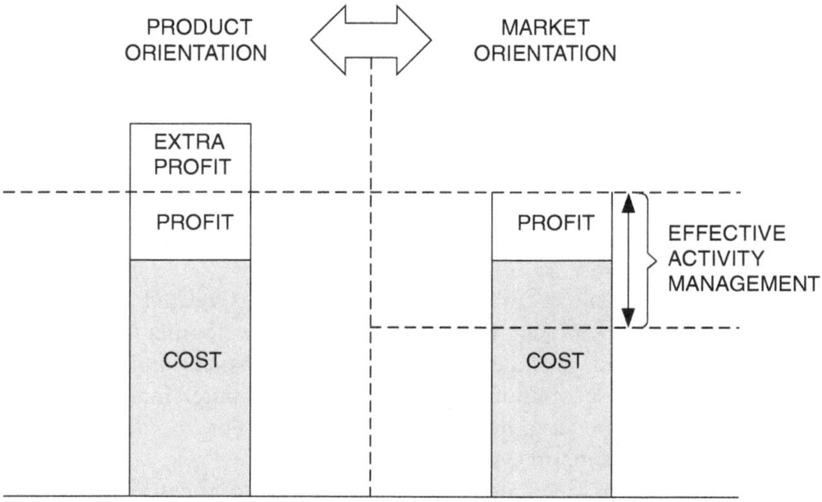

Figure 5.6 The change of the company business paradigm.

Source: Pearce and Robinson (2000:207).

This means that a company can achieve competitive advantage if it creates and sustains considerably low cost than its industry competitors. Low cost offer a favourable position for a company in terms of lower price formation, reaching market share, extra sales profit and similar.

Costs have an indirect impact on the second source of competitive advantage as well. Specifically, as long as the price growth does not surpass the differentiation cost, a company cannot achieve competitive advantage. Consequently, a differentiated competitor cannot endlessly increase the costs of differentiation. Cost analysis is based on the existing accounting system which categorises the costs of a single value chain activity of a company into direct, indirect and general costs (Porter, 1985).

However, the data provided by such an analysis are insufficient for a strategic cost analysis. In each and every company, costs are a consequence of its activities in a value chain. This fact leads to different costs in every company so this analysis is becoming simplified and factitious (Todorović et al., 2000). Each position in a value chain of a company where costs are aggregated is different in terms of activities and behaviour. Having low costs than competitors must be an obsessive focal point of each company.

According to Michael Porter (1985), company orientation towards low cost in all business segments must include the utilisation of the following: economy of scale (using the capacities which ensure the economy of scale), curve of experience (using the potential provided by the curve of experience), positional annuity (using distributors which provide cheaper supplies) and technological change (using technology which will ensure cost reduction). However, to maintain low cost than competitors, a company must constantly monitor the cost drivers in its value chain activities, which is not an easy task by all means. Several cost drivers influence the cost of a single activity. Cost drivers reflect the relations among the activity within a company on one side and the relation of a corporation and its surrounding, on the other side. Special attention must be focused on the relations of particular activities to establish or sustain a relation among activities within the value chain and within the value system. The only way to monitor cost behaviour is through the activity conduction cost analysis and the analysis of necessary assets. It includes the cost structure determinants of a particular activity variably controlled by the company (Đuričin et al., 2015).

The aim is to reach low cost in every activity considering the best ways to conduct the activity and showing ingenuity in reducing and eliminating certain activities in a company value chain. Cost drivers can either support each other or have a contrasting effect on each other. According to Michael Porter (1985), there are ten cost drivers:

- *Economy of scale*: It can exist in any activity segment in a value chain. It is created in production by narrowing down the production programme and increasing the production range on several types of products.
- *The curve of learning*: It can exist as a consequence of production enhancement through process redesign. It is created by correlating the costs with the cumulated production units in a value chain.
- *Capacity exploitation*: It can exist as a consequence of cost digression per product unit. The efficiency of fixed company assets is increased through a sound distribution throughout the activities in a value chain.
- *Correlating all that matters*: It can exist when all that matters is correlated with other value chain activities which leads to cost reduction through the enhancement of activity coordination and common optimisation.
- *Mutual correlation*: It can exist as a consequence of mutually strong bonds among certain value chain activities which is reflected on the simplification of the conduction of certain value chain activities.
- *Vertical integration*: It can operate forward or backward. It is achieved through the transfer of experience between strategic business units which leads to a decreased pressure on the company from powerful customers or suppliers.
- *Capacity optimisation*: It can exist if a company has information from the market and it is achieved by utilising the advantages or reducing the disadvantages of the notion to introduce a pioneer product to customers.
- *Discretion policies*: It can exist when a company makes tactical decisions. They are created by their influence on company costs such as expansion or reduction of the production programme, customer service and similar.
- *Company location*: It can exist when a company utilises the positive location effects. It is created by a direct influence on cost reduction, transport, construction and tax on all activities in a value chain and similar.

- *Institutional factors*: It can exist when a company is up to date with the surrounding changes and it is achieved by acknowledging government policy and regulations which can have an effect on cost increase as a major cost driver.

The concept of cost drivers is one way of understanding cost behaviour in every value chain activity. A company needs to identify its value chain and diagnose its cost drivers. Michael Porter (1985) suggests the following phases for a company to create the foundations for a low cost environment:

1 Identify the needed value chain and distribute the costs and assets throughout its activities.
2 Identify cost drivers for each value chain activity and observe their interaction.
3 Identify the competitor value chain and establish relevant competitor costs and the source of cost difference.
4 Shape the business strategy to reduce the relative cost position by controlling cost drivers or by reconfiguring the value chain.
5 Ensure that the cost reduction does not decrease differentiation or to purposely make a decision which leads to such a scenario.
6 Test the cost leadership strategy to determine its long-term sustainability so that the company can rely on it.

A strategic cost analysis should include a definition of value chain activities, an asset distribution (both fixed assets and working capital) and a cost distribution (business and non-business costs) for each company value chain activity (both primary and support activities).

Each value chain activity is associated with assets and costs through working capital and capital investments (Đuričin et al., 2015). The input entry into the value chain has an influence on each value chain activity through the costs of business operations (raw material supply) and fixed assets (capital investment). The need for asset distribution throughout the value chain can be traced back to the fact that a certain asset percentage needed for conducting a particular activity in a value chain has a significant influence on costs. The strategic cost analysis embodies (Todorović et al., 2000): (a) Activities with a significant and/or growing share in total costs or defined asset and (b) activities with different factors which are cost drivers. This places an individual activity as the subject of a cost analysis.

The disintegration of total costs of value chain activities leads to the identification of components with the highest share. Cost drivers of those components are identified, analysed and monitored. If more than one cost driver influences an activity, it is necessary to continue with the disaggregation until reaching a "one cost driver per one activity" scenario. Next, it is necessary to distribute costs and asset throughout the value chain activities. Costs are distributed to the activities which create them, whereas the asset is distributed to the activities that use it. Asset distribution can be done in two ways: Following the asset value or following the replacement value. There is an alternative to these two ways which relies on the methodology of transferring asset or replacement value into costs through amortisation (Porter, 1985).

The distribution of costs and assets leads to the creation of a value chain which showcases the way in which costs and assets are distributed in the process of profit generation. To make a high-quality analysis, the costs must be distributed into (a) raw material and materials costs, and (b) workforce costs. The assets must be distributed into the following: (a) current assets and (b) fixed assets.

Figures 5.7 and 5.8 illustrate the zones where it is possible to reduce costs.

For example, raw material costs are usually at the highest level of production needs due to safety stock. In addition to the substitutability among cost drivers, there is also an interaction expressed in the two following forms (Stern and Stalk, 1998): (1) The increase of influence and (2) the cancellation of influence.

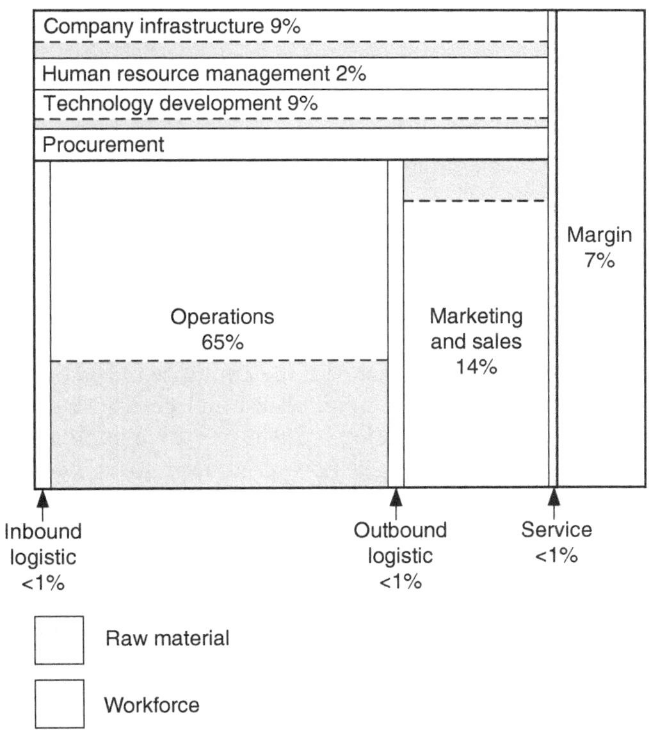

Figure 5.7 Value chain activity cost distribution.

Source: Porter (1985:68).

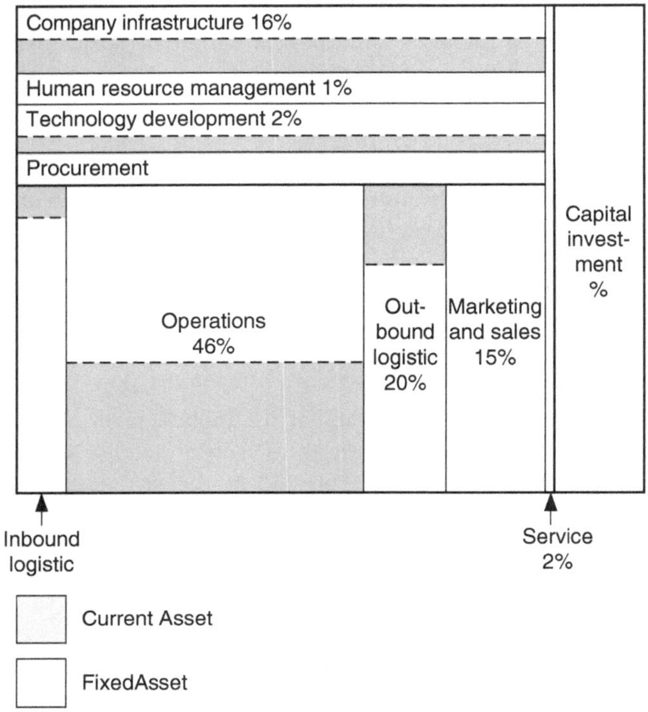

Figure 5.8 Assets distribution in value chain activities.

Source: Porter (1985:69).

Hence, the relation of the production programme and the economy of scale is an example of the increase of influence, whereas the relation between vertical integration and capacity exploitation is an example of influence cancelation. Low costs can be reached if the cumulate of all costs in a company value chain is lower than the cumulate of all costs in a competitor value chain. Orientation towards low costs is worthwhile only if it creates sustainable competitive advantage. Low costs lead to above the average profitability only if an appropriate value is provided to customers so that competitive advantage based on low costs is not cancelled out by the need to offer lower product prices conditioned by cost leadership among competitors.

Competitors can have a similar or different value chain configuration. The similarity or difference can have a stronger (if they are different) or weaker (if they are similar) influence on company position concerning low costs.

Companies sometimes make an effort to imitate competitor value chains which is not a good idea due to different cost drivers which arise in their activities. A company can achieve competitive advantage based on low costs in the following two ways (Porter, 1985):

1 Cost driver control;
2 Value chain reconfiguration.

Cost driver control is exercised on the cost drivers which have a significant influence on total costs. Value chain reconfiguration is exercised on those activities which have a significant influence on the company business operations.

Former ways of achieving low costs are not mutually exclusive. The sustainability of low cost-based competitive advantage is affected by the permanent control of cost drivers and constant value chain regulation. Even competitors with different value chains have some common activities whose relative low cost position can significantly influence the cost cumulate.

Low costs as a source of competitive advantage are associated with the so-called differentiation proximity (Porter, 1980), i.e. when a low cost-based competitive advantage of a company is higher than the price difference between the company and other competitors. Hence, the nature of necessary price compromises does not prevent a company from creating higher value than competitors nor from sustaining it above the average profitability. Michael Porter (1985) believes that low cost orientation can, but it does not have to, result in sustainable competitive advantage.

Choosing low costs as a basis for achieving competitive advantage means following the cost leadership strategy, too. The strategic orientation is to be the industry leader and not just another company in the race for that position. The strategic rivalry of multiple industry participants for the position of industry leader in fragmented industries is very dangerous. As long as a company does not achieve competitive advantage based on low costs and does not convince its competitors to abandon their current business strategies, the consequences of generating profitability in an industry can be fatal. Considering this danger, Besanko et al. (1996) state that the following conditions are needed to create low cost-based competitive advantage:

a If an industry is characterised by the economy of scale and the economy of experience, but they are not exploited by a single company on the market.
b It the possibilities for improvement of the observed benefit of the industry product are limited by the nature of the product.
c If the customers are relatively price-sensitive and unwilling to pay premium prices for additional increases in quality, form and image of the product.
d If the industry product has product features whose objective quality attributes can be assessed by customers at the moment of purchase.

Differentiation

Differentiation occurs if a company is unique in relation to its competitors in terms of something that has buyer value with lower price. Differentiation opens up the possibility for a company to offer products at lower prices than competitors, higher sales at existing prices or continuous sales in periods of seasonal demand (Todorović et al., 2000). Differentiation based competitive advantage can lead to above the average profitability if the price difference is higher than differentiation costs.

Although a company can be different from its competitors, that does not automatically imply that it is using differentiation as a basis for its competitive advantage, if the difference does not have buyer value. This means that a company should use its unique position in an industry having in mind differentiation costs and position duration.

Differentiation as a source of competitive advantage includes the shaping or adapting of the business process which will be the foundation for setting the company apart from its competitors. This means that differentiation is a tool used to offer customers something unique that other competitors cannot offer. Differentiation can be easily placed within value chain activities, where each continuous activity represents a source of differentiation.

Value chain activities, which make up a small percentage of total costs, can have a big impact on the degree of differentiation. A value chain adapted to strategic cost analysis does not have the potential to identify the activities which can be used a source of differentiation (Todorović et al., 2000). However, a value chain adapted to the analysis of differentiation requires a, perhaps, more delicate classification of particular activities and the aggregation of other activities estimated not to have a major effect on the degree of differentiation.

According to Michael Porter (1985), a company orienting towards low costs in all segments of business operations needs to utilise the distributor advantage (the difference in the achieved level of raw material supplies), the technological development (the difference in the achieved level of technological development), the production activities (the difference in the achieved level of production activities), the distribution system (the difference in the achieved level of the distribution systems) and sales activities (the difference in the achieved level of sales activities).

Differentiation sources can be looked for in every value chain activity conducted by its company. The difference among company is a consequence of special activities conducted by the company in creating value and the way it influences the customers. A company can be differentiated against competitors and against the competitive range. The competitive range is influenced by the possibility of the company to meet different buyer needs at different locations. In addition, the differentiation basis can be found in suppliers and distributors.

According to Michael Porter (1985), there are ten drivers of uniqueness:

- *Activity definition* – activities which can have a significant contribution to the company value chain configuration which will be capable of creating the basis for differentiation which will result in the future establishment of correlations.
- *Activity selection* – it includes the decision on selecting the activities that need to be done in the value chain to generate value which will result in created value after covering all the costs.
- *Activity bonding* – it includes the establishment of relations between activities in a company value chain or the relation with the value chain of the supplier or value chain of the distributor to form strong relationships.
- *The employment of timing* – determining when to conduct an activity in a company value chain to achieve notable cost reductions of activity conduction in a value chain.
- *The use of location* – which influences the configuration and reconfiguration of a value chain whose favourable utilisation can notably enhance the value chain activity configuration to benefit from the future prosperous effects.
- *Possible liaisons* – the existence of possible liaisons in the parent company which opens up the possibility of mutual activity conduction in a value chain forming a basis for value creations.
- *The learning effect* – the possibility of conducting activities in a far better way than before creating significant savings which were not considered before and which created a cost increase.
- *Vertical integration* – which represents a combination of different activities in a value chain with a company orientation towards using intern rather than extern transactions to generate above the average profitability.
- *Operation scale* – the scale of operations acting exclusively as a differentiating factor which can create value without generating any low cost features for the customers.
- *Institutional factors* – which particularly concern the development of good relations with the union and other important groups of interest which have a notable influence on the company and *vice versa*.

Independent of the existing or potential differentiation factors of a corporation, the buyer perception that something special is being offered is the foundation of a successful differentiation. Differentiation will lead to above the average profitability if the value created by the buyer surpasses the differentiation costs.

Michael Porter (1985) suggests the following phases needed for a corporation to create the differentiation foundation:

1 Identify the real customers and analyse the way customers rank shopping criteria.

2 Identify the buyer value chain and direct or indirect effects of the company on it.
3 Assess the cost of existing and potential sources of uniqueness in a company value chain.
4 Select a value chain activity configuration which forms the most valuable buyer differentiation with a relative ratio to differentiation costs.
5 Create the background for cost reduction in activities which do not affect the chosen differentiation forms.
6 Test the differentiation strategy to determine its sustainability from the aspect of sustainable competitive advantage.

The goal is to create a bigger difference between created buyer value and costs of creating the uniqueness of a value chain. Differentiation creates costs since uniqueness requires a better conduction of company value chain activities in relation to its competitors. However, it should be highlighted that different forms of differentiation created different costs. Generally, differentiation costs reflect the factors which account for activity cost of the activities which provide uniqueness. There are two types of relations between factors (Stern and Stalk, 1998): (1) Factors driving the uniqueness and (2) factors driving costs. For example, the factors that initiate uniqueness influence the factors that initiate costs and factors that initiate costs influence the factors that initiate uniqueness.

The basis of understanding the things that a buyer has is buyer value. A company can easily visualise the value chain of a buyer based on information on the influence of its product on its cost reduction. Differentiation is the factor that reduces buyer costs in many ways. A company creates added value for customers through premium price or a preference at the same level in two ways:

1 Reducing buyer costs;
2 Increasing buyer value.

If a company is capable of reducing costs for its buyer or to increase his value, the buyer is proportionally willing to accept the higher price of a product. Differentiation is possible in all types of industries, particularly in industries with various differences of products which are particularly valued by customers.

The sustainability of differentiation is at stake if the differentiation initiators are at risk since it eliminates the possibility of introducing premium prices. Differentiation as a source of competitive advantage can be sustainable in the long term if it is based on a complex set of differences which are hard to imitate by competitors, because the imitation of uniqueness leads to the loss of differentiation. According to Besanko et al. (1996), such a scenario requires the following conditions to create differentiation-based competitive advantage:

a If a typical buyer is willing to pay a notable premium price for product features that enhance the received benefit.
b If a company contains a notable number of economies of scale and experiences which are already vastly exploited by existing participants.
c If the product quality features in an industry can be evaluated based solely on the experience of using the product by the buyer.

Strategic activities analysis

Considering the fact that competitive advantage can be achieved in two ways (overall low costs and differentiation), a company identifies the so-called cost drivers and so-called value drivers. Cost drivers are associated with support activities (company infrastructure, human resource managements, technology development and supply), whereas value drivers are associated with primary activities (inbound logistics, production, outbound logistics, marketing, sales and services).

The essence of business strategy is to maximally utilise the value drivers and maximally reduce the cost drivers by an adequate value chain configuration or reconfiguration. Each value chain activity creates costs (raw material and materials) and spends assets (fixed and current). Activity-based costing(ABC) method can be used to distribute costs and assets throughout the value chain activities. The traditional accounting technique used earlier does not fit the bill for this type of analysis because it traces costs according to types, places and cost holders. In the process it, according to Marin Buble (2005), distributes direct costs on the holders and general costs are distributed following a pattern.

The application of a traditional accounting technique does not offer the possibility of tracking costs by activities. That is why activity based costing is applied. Each value chain activities creates cost so a value chain analysis seeks to determine the cost of each activity. A detailed analysis provides a cost comparison with key competitors or the industry average which can be used as a starting point to realise whether we are in front, behind or equal with competitors on one side and whether we are better, worse or equal with the industry average, on the other side. Consequently, it can be discussed whether certain cost entries are increasing or reducing.

A value chain is suitable for the company competitive advantage resource diagnosis and differences existing among competitors. Each basic and following activity need to be divided into less separate activities. The activities with the best demonstration of the real and potential competitive advantage of a company should be highlighted.

Each separated activity (irrespective of its aggregation degree) must have its own economy, a powerful real and potential influence on differentiation and significantly contribute to total costs. After the documentation of the value chain, activities which are the key for customer satisfaction and market success need to be identified. Such activities must be placed in the spotlight during the analysis research. Three reasons play an essential role in this phase of value chain analysis (Pearce and Robinson, 2000).

First, the fundamental mission of a company should influence the selection of activities to be researched in detail. Hence, top management needs to focus all of its attention to achieving low costs. Second, the value chain nature and the relative importance of its activities are variable in some industries. Hence, top management needs to focus all of its attention to activities important for the company. Third, the relative importance of activity value can vary considering the company position in a broader value system. Consequently, top management must see the bigger picture of a value chain.

However, it is not enough just to identify activities, a step further needs to be taken to identify the activity within each of the two groups. Looking at the inner structure of the categories of primary activities and support activities, we can find three types of activities with different roles in creating competitive advantage. These activities include the following:

1. *Direct activities* – which directly create buyer value (e.g. assembling, promotion and similar).
2. *Indirect activities* – which indirectly offer the conduction of primary activities (e.g. administration, maintenance and similar).
3. *Quality insurance activities* – which ensure the quality of other activities (e.g. control, supervision and similar).

Each company has each of these three activities which can be found in primary and support activities. The essence of activity analysis is to identify the four groups of activities. *First, the activities that do not exist, but they are important for business strategy.* The aim is to introduce these activities. *Second, to identify activities which do not follow the mission.* The aim is to eliminate these activities. *Third, to analyse activities vital for business processes.* The aim is to keep these activities. *Fourth, to analyse activities which add value.* The aim is to enhance these activities. The essence of activity analysis is shown in Figure 5.10.

The value chain concept previously explained in detail is an ideal type of form associated with the condition in a company. A company often does not have all the stated and explained activities, so it has to create its own value chain. The necessity which is the starting point for creating a favourable company value chain is the analysis of the current state. Hence, it is necessary to revise whether there are sound reasons for conducting particular activities in a company – sourcing, or should particular activities be given to third parties – outsourcing. Most companies focus on their core competences outsourcing everything else following the motto: *Do what you*

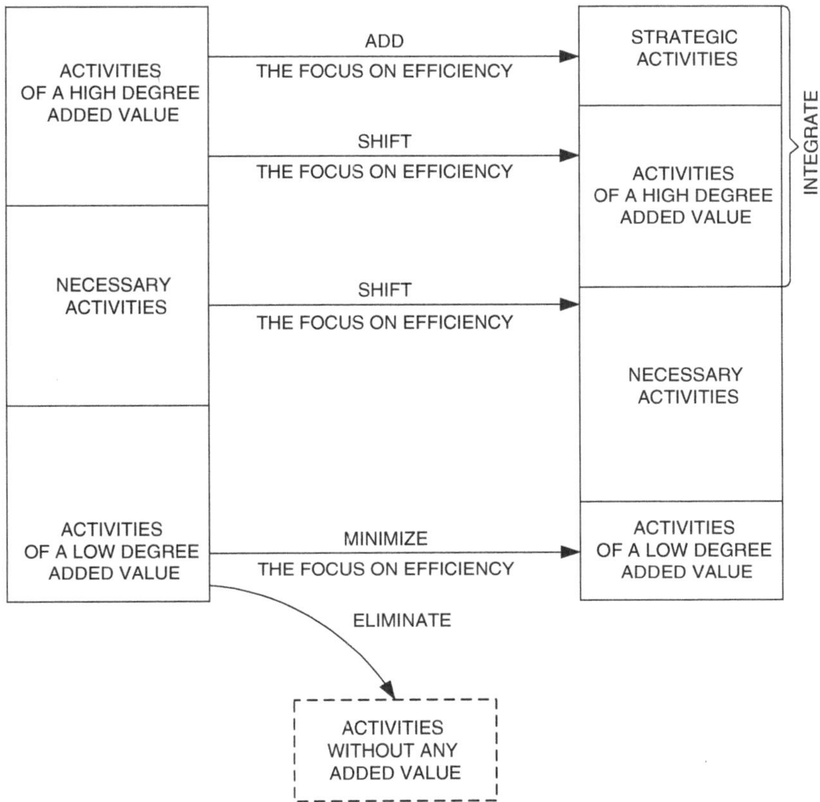

Figure 5.9 Activity analysis.

Source: Adapted from Johnson and Scholes (1999:36).

do best – outsource the rest. To get results, a cost benefit analysis needs to be carried out (Figure 5.9).

The comparison between the company costs and the cost of external suppliers should be the criteria for selection (Voss and Chalupsky, 1996). That is the essence and the aim of value chain activities analysis. A decision made on that basis offers the opportunity for a company to focus its attention on conducting strategically important activities.

Competitors analysis from the company perspective

A quality value chain activity analysis requires the comparison of a corporation value chain with the value chain of its competitors. This comparison can be done at different levels of value chain disaggregation, but the best one in practice is the one carried out at the core business level (Figure 5.10). The best way to evaluate the internal factors and value

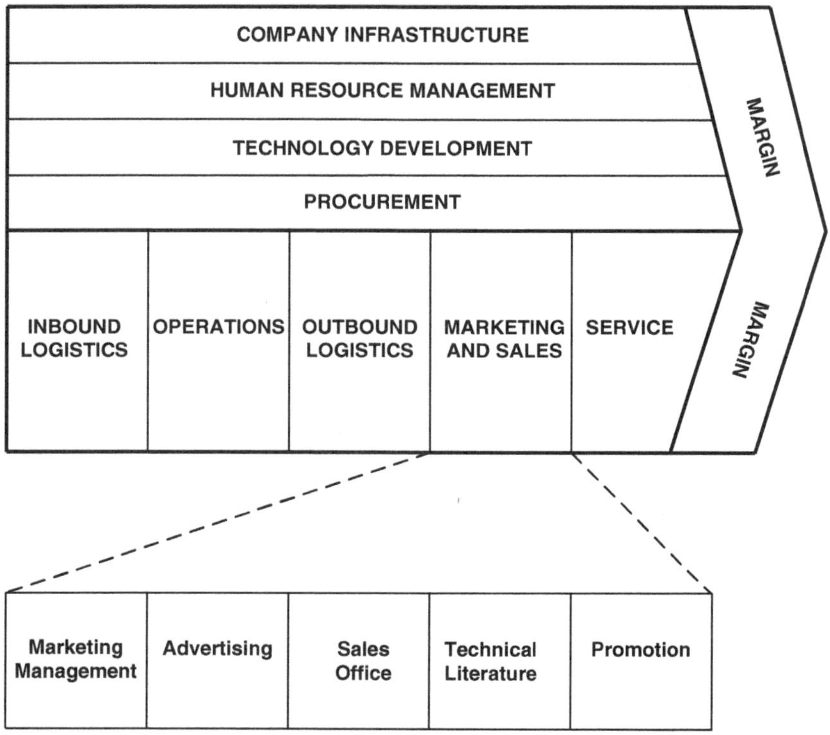

Figure 5.10 Disaggregation of value chain activities.

Source: Adapted from Porter (1985:46).

activities during that process is by using competitive benchmarking which represents a comparison with the best practice. In the end, it should be noted that the benefit of a value chain analysis is the identification of the activities in the total business process which have their share of influence on the level of costs, quality, image and similar features in the final product. Such identification is the foundation for following at least one of the business strategies (sometimes even following both simultaneously) – the strategy of cost leadership or the strategy of differentiation.

Competitive benchmarking is a word used in the sense of comparison. It is actually a buzzword. The root of the word is benchmark, meaning a standard or a reference point. According to the definition of the *American Productivity and Quality Center* – APQC, *competitive benchmarking is a systematic and continuous process of measuring profitability and comparing the followers with the leader, irrespective of his position, to receive information on profitability increasement.* Actually, it is a series of successive observations and reflections which should lead to the identification and application of the so called best practice (Đuričin et al., 2015).

According to Michael Porter (1999), each industry has both leaders and followers. The companies which are the first to enter the market are called pioneers. Companies which are the first to develop a new technology are called technological pioneers. Companies which are the first to discover new markets are called market pioneers. Both types of corporations are called first movers. Competitive advantage achieved on the basis of the new entrance is called first mover advantage. Companies that enter the market after the pioneers are called followers. Companies that enter the market earlier are called early followers. Companies that enter the market later are called late entrants. Both types of companies are called late movers. Competitive advantage achieved based on later market entrance is called later-mover disadvantages.

The selection of follower or leader strategy must be a part of consistent decision making: Planning component (decision making) and action component (decision implementation). Followers can attack the leader, but first they have to evaluate whom to attach and how. In this sense, depending on personal capabilities and the positioning of competitors, it is possible to attack the market leader led by the idea of a better way to serve the market. Such an action requires a comparison with the competitor to evaluate personal possibilities and the positioning of the competitor.

Competitive benchmarking is possible if there is a high degree of comparability between the leader and followers in an industry. Competitive benchmarking can be beneficial both for the leader and the follower due to its impartial positioning. Competitive benchmarking advantage of direct competitors is conditioned by the possibility of establishing different forms of communication among them.

However, competitive benchmarking disadvantage is conditioned by the possibility of penetration in the same market among them. In the first variant, it is a case of a mild intern discussion due to the perception that the company is *playing with a friend*, whereas in the second variant, it is a case of a heated intern discussion due to the perception that the company is *playing with an enemy*.

Competitive benchmarking is conducted one step at a time until the key success factors relevant for the follower when comparing to the leader are reached. That way, a thorough analysis has been carried out following the principle that the devil lays in the details. Figure 5.11 illustrates the cost analysis of an activity for three competitors.

Company B has notably lower costs than the other two companies owing to the advantage of low cost activity conduction. It is a signal to annul the personal costs of the activity. Devastating technologies vastly undermine the company value chain making it more flexible and unstable which is reflected in the value system in terms of a significant decrease of profitability. The externalisation of the business process leads to the decrease of internalisation which in turn reconfigures the existing value chain which receives a completely new form.

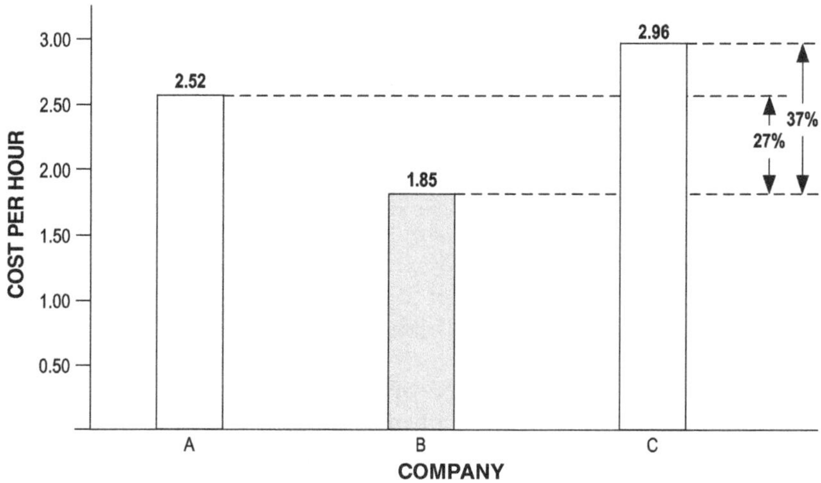

Figure 5.11 Cost comparison of one activity.

Source: Adapted from Karlof and Ostblom (1995:61).

What is the degree of influence of Internet technology on value chain activities in terms of cost drivers and uniqueness, in a way that the profit is increased or decreased which is reflected on the erosion of competitive advantage?

Analyse a company value chain based on business operation data by classifying activities into primary and supporting ones and assign each activity with cost drivers and differentiation drivers which serve as tools for competitive advantage.

Notes

1 Being a socioeconomic phenomenon, a company is oriented towards stakeholders. Depending on the character of the correlation, stakeholders are classified into (1) insiders – all the people, individuals or groups inside the company who can be influenced by the corporation and the company can adapt their behaviour to its benefit. Insiders include owners, managers and employees; (2) outsiders – all the organisations, individuals or groups outside the company who cannot be influenced by the company, and the company adapts its behaviour to them. Outsiders include customers, suppliers, government, unions and the community.

2 In its shortest form, the mission can be defined as the reason for the existence of the company. It answers the following question: Where are we now?

3 In its shortest form, the vision is defined as an attitude on the desired future of the company. It answers the question: Where do we want to be?

4 In its shortest form, the goals are defined as the results which a company wants to reach. They answer the following question: How will we get there?

5 The older approach was developed by the famous consulting agency McKinsey&Co. This relatively simple model suggests the inclusion of the following six distinctive and mutually conditioned activities in creating companyvalues: (1) Technological development, (2) production design, (3) production, (4) marketing, (5) distribution

and (6) services. The new approach was developed by Krüger and Homp and it is often called the Krüger – Homp value chain. It offers a precise analysis of the significance and the role of each activity by analysing their key competences. Krüger and Homp differentiate two categories of key competences in acompany value chain: (a) Basic competences, which refer to an efficient and effective control of existing operations and (b) developing (meta) competences, which refer to their growth.

6 According to Michael Porter, quasi integration represents a relationship of vertically connected companies placed between a long-term contract and full ownership. This includes the following forms: (1) Asset share, (2) loan or loan guarantee, (3) exclusive business contracts, (4) specialised logistics devices and (5) cooperative research and development. Quasi integration should be observed as an alternative to full integration. It is vital to recognise whether the common interest reached through quasi integration is sufficient enough to achieve cost (and risk) reduction compared with full integration.

7 Dealing with inhumane modern work conditions and the negative side of technological advancement, Charlie Chaplin used the *Modern Times* to scene out the immortal satire of a man and his position in the modern society which is both funny and tragic at the same time. A worker in a modern company does not get around well working among machines. He is unable to catch up with the conveyor belt he is assigned to and suffers a mental breakdown and ends up in a hospital. After leaving the hospital, the doctors advise him to live a stress-free life, but he immediately stumbles upon a strike and ends up in prison, being convicted as a communist leader. Charlie Chaplin created the silent movie *Modern Times* in a period when movies with sound were replacing silent movies and he used audio only on several occasion throughout the movie (the speech of the factory director, prison radio, Chaplin's singing).

8 Newman et al. (1989).

References

Besanko, D., Dranove, D., Shanley, M. (1996): *Economics of Strategy*, London: Wiley.

Buble, M. et al. (1997): *Strategijski Management*, Split: Ekonomski fakultet.

Buble, M. (Ed.) (2005): *Strateški menadžment*, Zagreb: Sinergija.

Đuričin, D., Janošević, S., Kaličanin, Đ. (2015): *Menadžment i strategija*, Beograd: Ekonomski fakultet.

Henderson, D. (1981): *The Concept of Strategy*, Boston: The Boston Consulting Group.

Hicks, G., Gullet, R. (1972): *The Management of Organization*, New York: Mc Graw-Hill.

Johnson, G., & Scholes, K. (1999). *Exploring Corporate Strategy*, London: Prentice Hall.

Karloff, B., Ostblom, S. (1993): *Benchmarking: A Singpost to Excellence in Quality and Productivity*, Chichester: Wiley.

Mašić, B. (Ed.) (2014): *Menadžment: principi, koncepti i procesi*, Beograd: Singidunum.

Mašić, B., Džunić, M., Nešić, S. (2014): *Savremena teorija menadžmenta: škole i novi pristupi*, Beograd: Data Status.

Montgomery, C. A., Porter, M. E. (Eds) (1991): *Strategy: Seeking and Securing Competitive Advantage*, Boston: Harvard Business Press.

Newman, H., Logan, P., Hegary, H. (1989): *Strategy, a Multi-level, Integrative Approach*, Cincinnati: South-Western Publishing Co.

Pearce, A., Robinson, B. (2000): *Formulation, Implementation and Control of Competitive Strategy*, Boston: Irwin McGraw-Hill.

Porter, M. (1980): *Competitive Strategy: Technique for Analyzing Industries and Competitors*, New York: The Free Press.
Porter, M. (1985): *Competitive Advantage: Creating and Sustaining Superior Performance*, New York: The Free Press.
Porter, M. (1987): *The Stage of Strategic Thinking*, The Economist, May 23, 21.
Porter, M. (1998). Clusters and The New Economics of Competition, *Harvard Business Review*, vol. 76, no. 6, 77–90.
Porter, M. (1998). *On Competition*, Boston: Harvard Business Review Press.
Porter, M. (2007): *Konkurentska prednost*, Zagreb: Masmedia.
Prahalad, C. K., Hamel, G. (1990): *The Core Competence of the Corporation*, Harvard Business Review, vol. 68, no. 3, 79–91.
Russel, S., Taylor, B. (2009): *Operation Management: Along the Supply Chain*, New Delhi: Jonh Wiley & Sons.
Shank, K., Govindarajan, V. (1992): *Strategic Cost Management: The Value Chain Perspective*, Management Accounting Research.
Shank, J.K., & Govindarajan, V. (1993). *Strategic Cost Management: The New Tool for Competitive Advantage*, New York: Free Press.
Stern, C., Stalk, G. (1998): *Perspective on Strategy from the Boston Consulting Group*, New York: Wiley & Sons.
Šunje, A. (2002): *Top-menadžer: vizionar i strateg*, Sarajevo: Tirada.
Tipurić, D. (Ed.) (2010): *Korporativno upravljanje*, Zagreb: Sinergija.
Todorović, J., Đuričin, D., Janošević, S. (2000): *Strategijski menadžment*, Beograd: Institut za tržišna istraživanja.
Voss, P., Chalupsky, J. (1996): *Outsourcing im Personalwesen: Weiterbildun- gsabteilung als Cost-Profit-Investment Center*, Personalfuehrung.

6 The Company and Environmental Interaction: *Porter's Concept of Generic Strategies*

The company and environment interaction

The company is interlocked with the environment. Due to an increasing association of a company with the happenings in its surrounding, the co-ordination of its value chain configuration with its surrounding needs emerges as an important component.

A company deals with the environmental influences due to the following reasons:

a To convert inputs into outputs aimed at meeting the needs of the environment.
b To conduct managerial activities in each life cycle phase in order to justify its social legitimacy.

A company relates its operating mode with the demands of its environment. A company must have the support of the environment. A bad corporation value chain configuration, which leads to a decrease in operational efficiency and operational effectiveness, prompts sanctions imposed by the environment.

Business strategy is in charge of coordinating, i.e. balancing that relationship. Hence, a business strategy is a binding agent creating an interaction between the company and its environment. It is clear that the success of a company depends on its relation with its environment. A company uses the environment as its information resource needed for the orientation in its business activities. There are different viewpoints on the coordination between the company and the environment. According to one viewpoint, company *are not capable of adopting to the environment*, whereas another viewpoint advocates the idea that *companies are capable of adopting to its environment*. Both viewpoints are incomplete because they consider both approaches in an alternating manner. Consequently, the two approaches have been integrated into the so-called *strategic perspective*, which goes a step further. This dominant approach is based on the hypothesis that *companies not only adapt to the environment, but they can shape it, too.*

DOI: 10.4324/9781003359173-6

The core message of these two approaches is that business definition must be based on: (1) environmental influences and (2) company capabilities. Consequently, a company is not founded only on existing production possibilities, it also considers the conditions of the environment. As a consequence, the *adaption to the known* (ex-post analysis) is insufficient, and the *recognition of the unknown* (ex-ante analysis) is needed. This shifts the focus from the intern organisation (the company) to the extern orientation (the environment).

In addition to its adaptation and influence, a company has a host of other options when interacting with its environment. A company must provide a strategic consonance with the environment by a trade-off approach between *everything that the environment wants and everything that the company can offer* on one side and *everything that a company needs and everything that the environment can offer,* on the other. Creating a sustainable competitive advantage depends on the interaction between the company and the environment.

According to Michael Porter (Kiechel, 2010), a scenario is an *internally consistent view (in a company) of all possible future changes (in an environment).* He based his claims on a set of convincing assumptions on important uncertainties from the environment which can influence a company which has an effect on creating sustainable competitive advantage. The scenario of an environment presents one possible future structure of the environment. A set of environmental scenarios has been carefully selected to point out to the frame of possible (and sound) future aspects of the environment, with significant implications for the company. The environmental scenario time period should reflect the time horizon of the most important decisions (Milisavljević, 2005).

Michael Porter (Kiechel, 2010) suggests the following process of creating environmental scenarios:

1 Identify the uncertainties which could influence the environment
2 Determine the causative factors which initiate them
3 Create a frame of reliable assumptions on each causative factor
4 Combine the assumptions on individual factors into an internally consistent scenario
5 Environmental analysis which will be dominant in each scenario
6 Determine the sources of competitive advantage in each scenario
7 Predict the behaviour of competitors in each scenario.

A company systematically includes the possible consequences of environmental uncertainty into its formation of business strategy by constructing several scenarios. An analysis of each industry scenario should specify the resulting implications on the value chain. The purpose of creating one or more scenarios is for the company to understand the way to change the industry structure and competitive conditions. That is, when a scenario becomes an important part of the strategic arsenal. Forming a business strategy with a goal of ensuing success in a single scenario is risky, whereas forming a business strategy with a goal of ensuring success in all scenarios is expensive. Hence, a scenario alone is insufficient to form a business strategy. It only offers an initiative conceptual frame for its formation.

Business strategy – the manner of interaction between the company and the environment

The interaction between the company and its environment is conducted with the help of business strategy. The essence of business strategy is to maximise the benefit of value drivers and minimise the benefit of cost drivers. This can be completed by combining the influence of five competitive forces (environmental analysis) with value chain activities (company analysis) (Đuričin et al., 2015). This leads to the identification of business strategy elements, which enables the achievement of competitive advantage (Table 6.1).

An important fact should not be put aside; there is no appropriate interaction between the company and the environment without a clear perception of the company position in a competitive environment. In order to understand business strategy in the right way, the key dimensions of business strategy need to be identified. A provocative work titled *Strategy as a practice* (Whitinghton, 1996) offers the following four viewpoints on business strategy:

The first viewpoint was established in the 1960s with the focus on the portfolio techniques. Business strategy relies heavily on methods and techniques.

The second viewpoint was established in the 1970s with the focus on alternative options. Business strategy relies heavily on internationalisation and diversification.

The third viewpoint was established in the 1980s with the focus on strategic changes. Business strategy relies heavily on innovation and development.

The fourth viewpoint was established in the 1990s with the focus on practical competence. Business strategy relies heavily on knowledge and expertise.

The key dimensions are located in a strategic triangle which Kenchi Ohmae (1982) called the *3C business model.*

Table 6.1 Business strategy elements

Activity	*Five competitive forces*	*Value chain*
Focus	Industry value drivers	Activity differences
Result	Industry average prices and costs	Industry relative prices and costs

Source: Adapted from Đuričin et al., 2015, *86*.

Michael Porter raises the following question: *What comes first: business strategy or the business model?* A business model should include a discussion on business strategy, whereas a business strategy should have a model for generating profitability. The author highlights three key factors for success in the development of business strategy. The factors represent a cornerstone of each business which is aimed at profitability. Namely, when developing a business strategy, three main players must be considered (Ohmae, 1982):

1 Company
2 Customer
3 Competition

Only after integrating the 3C in the so-called strategic triangle, it is possible to create sustainable competitive advantage (Figure 6.1). As seen from the model, the three key players include the *company* which defines its own business strategy, *customers* who satisfy their needs and *competitors* who satisfy the needs of customers. Considering the context of these three main players, business strategy is perceived as a way of company differentiation in relation to its competitors using its own advantages to better meet the needs of customers (Ohmae, 1982).

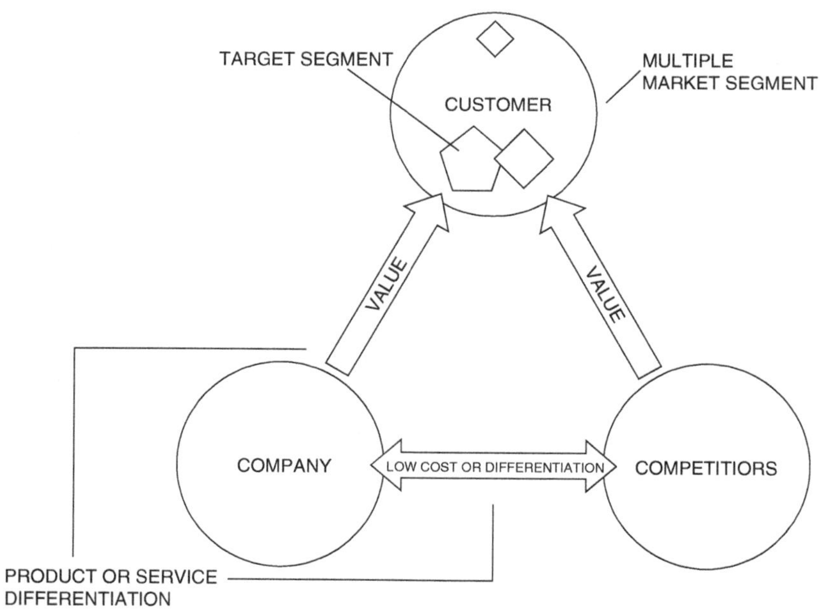

Figure 6.1 The strategic triangle.

Source: Adapted form Ohmae, 1982, 92.

Porter's generic strategies

Considering the context of three key players, the defined business strategy includes a clear definition of the company towards customers on one side and a definition towards competitors, on the other. Having in mind the previous conclusion, the following must be considered (Thompson and Strickland, 1998):

1 Strategic contemplation in terms of the environment.
2 Strategic contemplation in terms of the company.

The process of defining the condition of the company and the dynamics of the environment requires an assessment and evaluation of the value chain activities (the company) and the identification of the industry structure (the environment) using an analytic procedure based on strategic contemplation in order to identify strategic alternatives. A meticulous diagnosis of the condition of the company and the dynamics of the environment is a necessary prerequisite in the process of long-term decision-making concerning the company course in relation to its environment.

According to Arthur Thompson and John Strickland (1998), a company which does not understand its environment will form its business strategy that does not offer the interaction between the company and the environment and cannot provide the generation of sustainable competitive advantage as such.

A strategy defined in that way features all the relevant aspects of strategic architecture and Michael Porter (1980) labelled it as *generic strategy*. These business strategies are called generic strategic because all companies (value chain) can use them in their environment (industry) whether they work with production or services, or if they are profitable, non-profitable, big or small.

This was Michael Porter's contribution to the contemporary view of business strategy with a highlight on the significance of achieving competitive advantage. The starting point of generic strategies is the curve of experience which is the result of empirical research conducted by the *Boston Consulting Group* – BCG.[1] The concept of the curve of experience was introduced in the late 1960s based on research which relied on hypotheses on the relation of movements of costs and prices in a large number of companies in the USA.

Based on the results of the conducted research, the following theory has been created: *total costs per unit generally have a realistic decrease of 20–30% every time the accumulated experience is doubled*. The theory is presented in Figure 6.2 (Henderson, 1981).

The 80% curve of experience means that every time the experience is doubled, the costs per unit are decreased by 80% of their initial level (costs per unit are decreased by 20%). That is the rate of learning. The curve of experience is the change rate in cost movement in relation to the accumulated

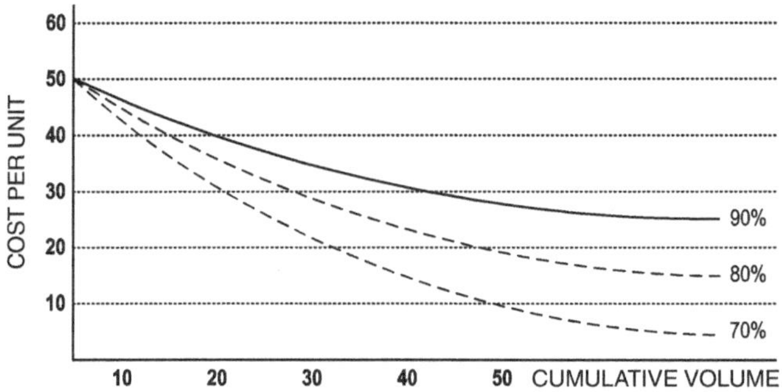

Figure 6.2 The curve of experience.

Source: Henderson, 1981, *116*.

product units. After its introduction, the curve of experience had a wide practical application. Empirical research has revealed that the curve of experience can have different forms. According to Momčilo Milisavljević, the curve of experience is a formal model illustrating the relation between production costs per product unit and the experience gained in the production process. Following the popularisation of the curve of experience in the 1970s, Michael Porter (1980) based his generic strategy of cost leadership on the curve of experience and expanded this concept by the strategies of differentiation and focusing as alternative strategies to creating competitive advantage.

To put it simply, prior to the identification of the generic strategy type followed by the company, it is necessary to design the two following dimensions to foster a better understanding (Porter, 1980):

1 Competitive advantage
2 Competitive volume.

Competitive advantage

The way of playing the strategic game is the formula for company success in the environment. The selection of the way of playing the strategic game depends on the possibility of creating superior value for customers, which enables the generation of above-the-average profitability for the corporation. This represents the principal element of competitive advantage which is used by a company to create a set of assumptions to deliver superior value to its customers generating above-the-average profitability.

According to Michael Porter (1985) there are two main sources of competitive advantage:

1 Low cost
2 Differentiation

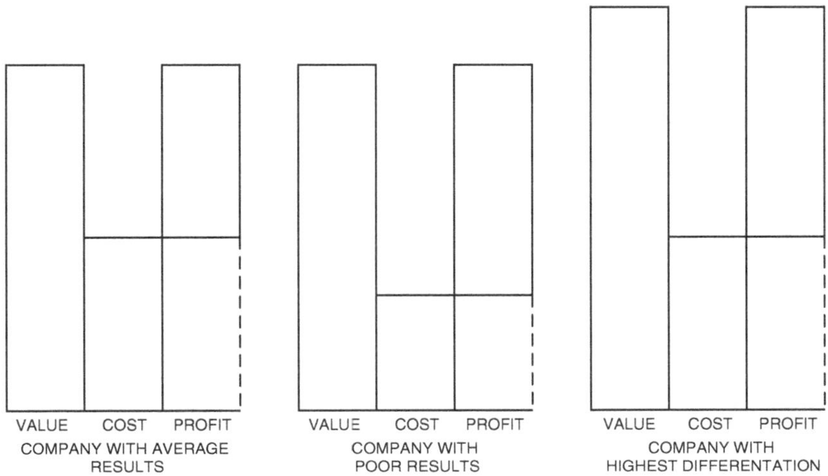

Figure 6.3 Low cost vs. differentiation.

Source: Đuričin et al., 2015, *435*.

This means that competitive advantage is created by either delivering equal value to customers with lower cost compared to competitors (low cost advantage) or by delivering higher value to customers with average industry cost (differentiation). If a company wants to create competitive advantage, it is necessary to choose which the type of competitive advantage it wants to achieve and the market volume it wants to cover.

Both generic strategies provide above-the-average profitability, i.e. higher profits which represent the difference between total revenue (operative effectiveness) and total cost (operative efficiency), i.e. more value at lower cost compared to competitors (Đuričin et al., 2015). That is the foundation of sustainable competitive advantage and the ultimate goal of generic strategy (Figure 6.3).

Simultaneous creation of competitive advantage based on both low cost and differentiation is scarce and it exists only in special cases. There is a limited number of cases where it is possible to apply both sources of competitive advantage. It can hardly have a long-lasting character; it is sooner or later surpassed or neutralised by the competition. However, that does not imply that a company cannot simultaneously focus both on low cost and differentiation in some situations. As long as the company is not at the level of above-the-average profitability of the industry, the steps taken towards low cost and differentiation are compatible.

A company transfers from one source (low cost) to another source (differentiation) based on four generic blocks (Hill and Jones, 1998): (1) superior efficiency, (2) superior quality, (3) superior innovation and (4) superior responsiveness (Figure 6.4).

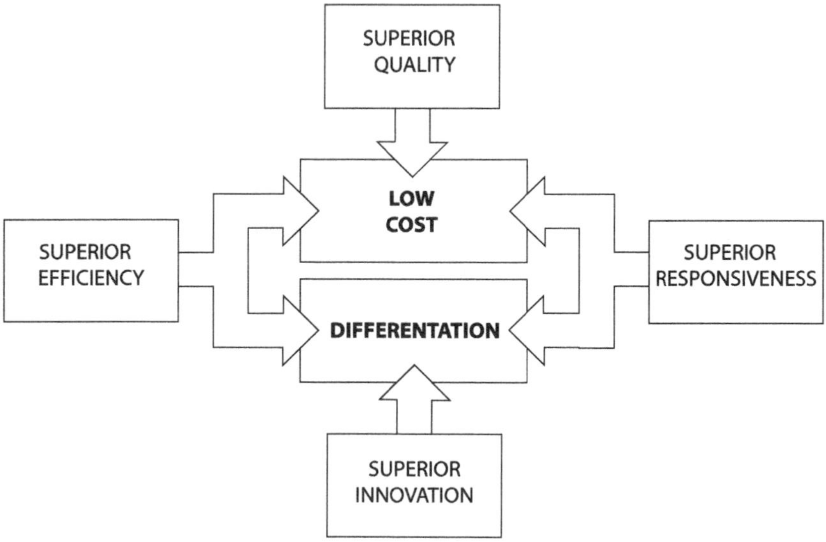

Figure 6.4 The transfer from low cost to differentiation.

Source: Adapted from Hill, Jones, 1999, *113*.

Superior efficiency results in increased company productivity and reduction in production costs. The focus of this generic block of competitiveness is to reduce the company cost.

Superior quality results in decreased company cost or a superior product quality. The focus of this generic block of competitiveness is to reduce the company cost.

Superior innovation results in the reduction of production cost or a more superior way of satisfying needs. The focus of this generic block of competitiveness is to increase the product price.

Superior responsiveness results in an increase of the perceived value and product price increase. The focus of this generic block of competiveness is to increase the product price.

Although generic blocks are perceived separately in the sense of a simultaneous change, there is undoubtedly a vast network of connections among these four generic blocks (e.g. quality can reflect on efficiency, whereas innovativeness can reflect on readability) (Šunje, 2002).

Competitive volume

The second dimension of generic strategies, competitive volume, is important because the company determines the degree of market coverage. An industry is not homogenous because it consists of more or less segments, making it discrepant. Industry segmentation is a broader term than market segmentation.

Market segmentation represents the identification of differences in customer behaviour to form adequate marketing strategies, whereas industry segmentation presents the identification of differences in customer behaviour to form generic strategies (Todorović et al., 2000).

That is why market segmentation is oriented towards marketing activities within a set of activities conducted by the company, whereas industry segmentation is oriented towards all the activities conducted by the company.

The segments forming an industry have the same structure as the industry, with a difference in the influence of competitive forces which varies from one segment to another. In addition, each segment has different suppliers, middlemen (if there are any) and customers. Each segment has an attractive nature which creates opportunities for the generation of competitive advantage (Figure 6.5).

This forms the basis for identifying the following two key variables of industry segmentation (Porter, 1985):

1 Products
2 Customers.

It is important to have an insight into the desired customer category on one side and their needs, on the other, for a company to fulfil their needs at the expected level. This means that all the focus is placed on the customer, his needs and the way of their fulfilment.

The reason for industry segmentation lies in the fact that products and/or customers within each industry have mutual differences implying that there are differences in creating competitive advantage. Hence, industry segments are formed as a consequence of differences in customer behaviour and the difference in the ways of fulfilling their needs. This means that the company focuses on the needs it wants to fulfil, the customer category it wants to contact and the way in which it wants to fulfil their needs. The differences in products or customers influence the formation of industry segments since they inevitably lead to changes in one or more competitive forces.

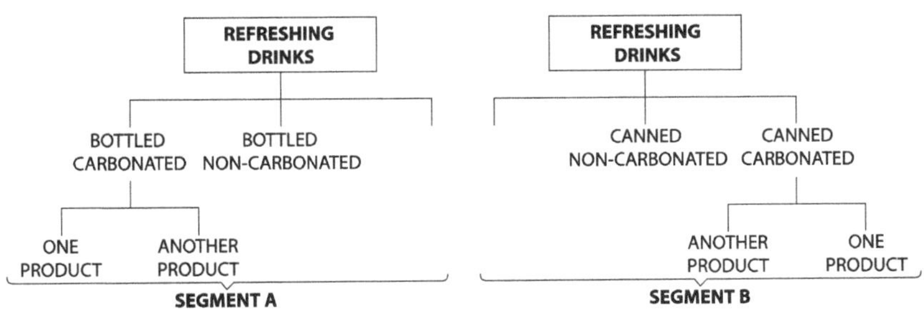

Figure 6.5 Different market segments.

Source: Kotler, 1998, *56*.

Considering these facts, two key issues are raised: (1) Which industry segment to focus on considering the possibility of the presence of a series of different segments? (2) Which segment does have a permanent focus considering the possibility of creating barriers among segments?

The process of determining the industry segment to focus on requires a full-scale industry analysis from the aspect of demand in the terms of understanding the real customer needs to be satisfied which are present at the aimed industry segment (Šunje, 2002).

A company can focus on larger number of segments (more coverage) or on a lower number of segments (less coverage), with an understanding of the industry structure offering more or less space for a subtler market positioning. Following the identification of aimed customers, the preconditions for product profiling have been created based on orientation towards one of the two sources of competitive advantage (low cost or differentiation) with an extension of the highest possible degree of aimed customer satisfaction fulfilment with quality product features (Figure 6.6).

According to Philip Kotler and Kevin Keller (2009), a company will be successful if the value is delivered and if the satisfaction of the aimed customers has been fulfilled. Customers choose between different offers based on their evaluation which represents the highest delivered value.

According to their opinion, value is estimated based on the consideration of tangible and intangible customer benefits and costs. It is actually a combination of quality, service and price which is known as the *customer value triad*.

The value is increased by quality enhancement and it is lowered by price decrease, although some other factors can play a significant role in customer perception, too. An identification of industry segments is needed, which will be used as a foundation for offering the formed product with a goal of satisfying the aimed customers in that segment.

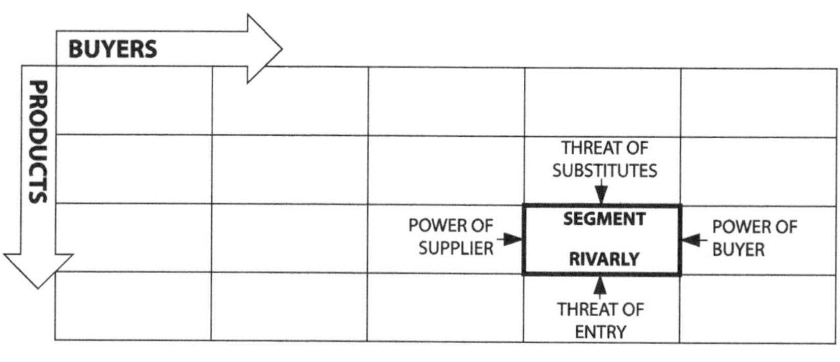

Figure 6.6 Competitive strengths in an industry segment.

Source: Porter, 1985, *235*.

Competitive strategies

Since Michael Porter classifies the generic strategies in the context of the market game, the full name used for business strategy is actually *competitive strategy.* Porter (1980) defines business strategy as a *selection of a different set of activities to deliver a unique mix of values.* It is described as a way of taking offensive or defensive action with an aim of creating a position in an industry which is possible to defend. This means that, when using generic strategies to generate competitive advantage (as a single variable), they turn into *competitive strategies.*

Each generic strategy is a result of a consistent selection between competitive advantage on one side and the competitive volume, on the other. Both of these concepts mutually support competitive advantage. The basis of the generic strategy concept is that competitive advantage is the heart of business strategy and the creation of competitive advantage requires a selection on behalf of the company concerning the type of competitive advantage it plans to create and the range of competitive volume where it wants to create it. The generic strategy concept is founded on the premise that there is a host of ways for a company to create competitive advantage depending on the environment.

According to Michael Porter (1980), competitive strategies include the location of a favourable competitive position in an industry seen as an arena where competitive activity is taking place.

The goal of competitive strategies is to generate above-the-average profitability acknowledging the strengths which determine the industry competition.

If we were to compare two companies following generic strategies, each one would select a different basis for its competitive advantage. According Michael Porter (1980), there are three, i.e. four generic strategies used by a company in relation to its customers and competitors (Figure 6.7).

According to Michael Porter (1980), the combination of competitive advantage with competitive volume leads to the creation of three, i.e. four competitive strategies: (1) cost leadership, (2) differentiation, (3) focus based on (a) cost leadership and (b) differentiation.

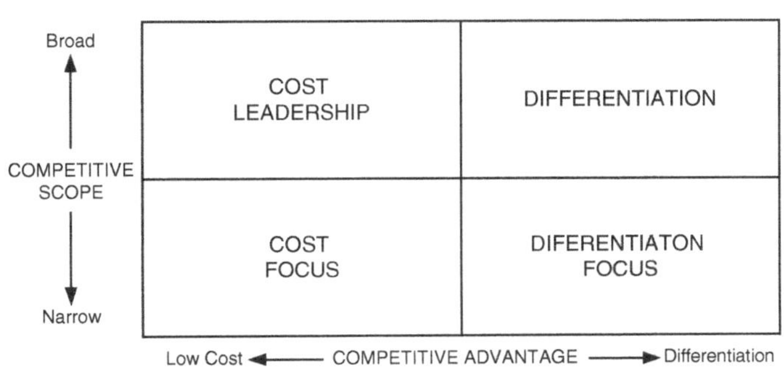

Figure 6.7 Generic strategies types.

Source: Porter, 1980, *39.*

According to Michael Porter (1985), when low cost or differentiation is used as sources of competitive advantage in an industry recognised as a part of competitive volume, the respective competitive strategies are known as overall cost leadership and differentiation. When low cost or differentiation is used as a source of competitive advantage in a segment recognised as a part of competitive volume, then the respective competitive strategies are known as focus based on cost leadership and focus based on differentiation.

Each of the three generic strategies requires fundamentally different paths to competitive advantage combining the type of desired competitive advantage with the range of competitive volume where the company wants to create competitive advantage.

Strategists

Competitive strategies in contemporary conditions are recognised as fundamental decisions prepared and conducted by strategists (Smith, 2003). Due to their highly important rule, strategists cannot afford to prepare bad decisions and implement them well or *vice versa*, to prepare good decisions and implement them poorly. Michael Porter (2004) points out the significance of strategies highlighting that they believe in changes and consider all options and use the reports as a foundation for creating ways of changing the competition. They energise the company while facing competitive challenges.

In addition to planning, strategists act, too, according to Đuričin et al. (2015). If correctly established, the association between planning and acting can result in company prosperity. However, if it is established in a wrong way, it can result in company failure, too. The concept of competitive strategy has two parts:

1 The planning component (preparing decisions)
2 The action component (implementing decisions).

The planning components

The planning component includes preparing decisions which are a starting point for the process of forming the business strategy as the key decision. The interaction between the company and the environment via competitive strategy is the *conditio sine qua non* of decision preparation (Figure 6.8).

When discussing the planning component, Michael (1999) believes that there are two levels of shaping competitive strategies:

a Company strategy (or organisational strategy)
b Strategic business unit strategy (or competitive strategy).

Figure 6.8 Competitive strategy: the manner of company and environmental interaction.

Source: The authors.

The company strategy or company strategy is a business strategy associated with a corporation as a single unit. Considering the company strategy includes the general orientation of the entire company. It could be argued that its essence is to define the portfolio of the strategic business units which will be used to generate competitive advantage. It concerns the manner of defining the market position for strategic business units by the company as a whole. Strategic business unit strategy or business strategy is a strategy of doing business with a particular strategic business unit. Observed within the frame of a strategic business unit, it concerns the general orientation of each strategic business unit. It could be argued that its essence is to determine the path to company competitive advantage through each individual strategic unit. It concerns the way in which strategic business units enhance the market positions.

The company strategy (or corporate strategy) is oriented towards the following question: *How to choose the strategic business units which will be the spotlight of a corporation to a certain degree?* The strategy of the strategic business unit is oriented towards the following question: *How to create competitive advantage in each business where a company competes at the market?*

The strategy of the company (organisational strategy) is present exclusively at the level of the company as a whole, only if the company has a certain degree of diversification with a tendency of diversification continuation. It is used as a foundation for developing the strategies of strategic business units (competitive strategies).

Generally speaking, this implies that company strategies must develop diversified (multi-product) company, whereas competitive strategies must develop non-diversified (single-product) company.

The selection of the appropriate competitive strategy is one of the competitive business strategies developed by Michael Porter (1998) to upgrade the aspect of the company arsenal of strategies. According to Michael Porter (2008), two questions stand out when choosing competitive strategies.

The first question concerns the attractiveness of the industry for above-the-average profitability including the determining factors. The second one concerns the determination of the competitive position of the relative competitive advantage in an industry. Using the given dimensions, competitive strategy can easily be classified in one of the three following types of competitive strategies (Hill and Jones, 1998): (1) overall cost leadership, (2) differentiation and (3) focusing based on (a) overall cost leadership and (b) differentiation.

Overall cost leadership is a competitive strategy type based on low costs as a source of competitive advantage with a tendency of establishing communication with a higher number of market segments at the aimed market. This competitive strategy leads towards the generation of overall cost leadership through the curve of experience, economy of scale, cost control and similar. Overall cost leadership includes the creation of lower costs in relation to the costs of competitors. In an ideal scenario, overall cost leadership is achieved throughout several cost dimensions. The fundamental mindset behind this competitive strategy is that cost reduction in relation to competitors will lead to the creation of higher value which is recognised as a fundamental guideline for generating long-term above-the-average profitability. Overall cost leadership is achieved by those that manage to develop standardised products which the customers want. It is founded on creating quantitative differences in their own products in relation to its competitors with an aim of creating a lower price. The fundamental idea of this competitive strategy is to become the real market leader of overall costs, rather than just one of several similar ones (Figure 6.9).

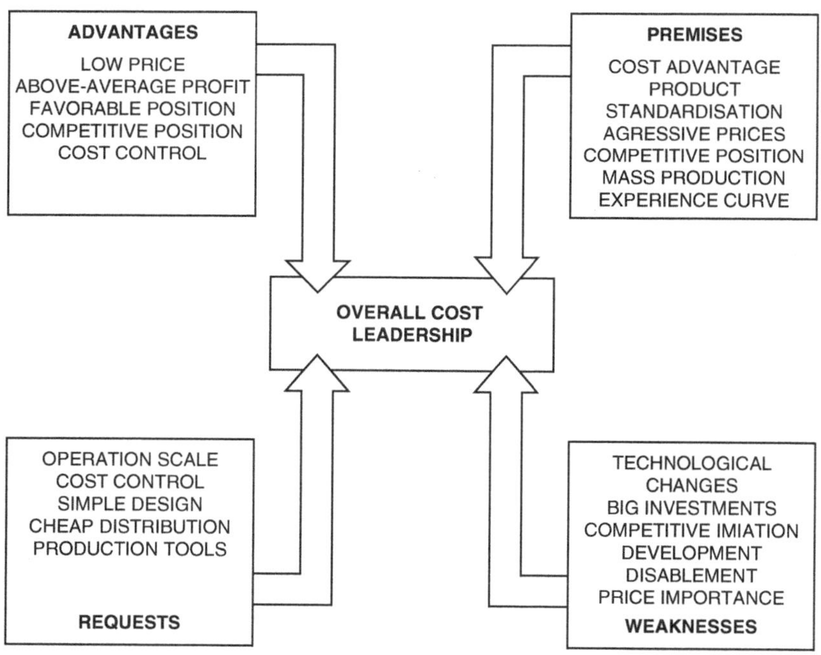

Figure 6.9 Overall cost leadership features.

Source: Adapted from McGee et al., 2005, *210*.

Differentiation is a competitive strategy type based on differentiation as a source of competitive advantage with a tendency of establishing communication with a higher number of market segments. This competitive strategy leads towards the creation of differentiation through brand image, distribution channel, services and similar. Differentiation includes the generation of profitability which is higher than the average profitability of the industry. In an ideal scenario, differentiation is achieved throughout several dimensions of differentiation. The fundamental mindset behind this competitive strategy is that differentiation will lead to a higher product valuation by the customers which is recognised as a fundamental guideline for generating above-the-average profitability. Differentiation is achieved by those who manage to develop non-standardised products which the customers want. It is based on creating qualitative differences in their own products in relation to competitors, with an aim of being different. The fundamental request of this competitive strategy is to be the real market leader in uniqueness, rather than one of several similar ones (Figure 6.10).

Focus is a type of competitive strategy derived from two basic competitive strategies (overall cost leadership and differentiation). The basic feature of focus is to be carried out at the focused market segment. This competitive strategy is used to directly meet the needs of a limited group of customers. i.e.

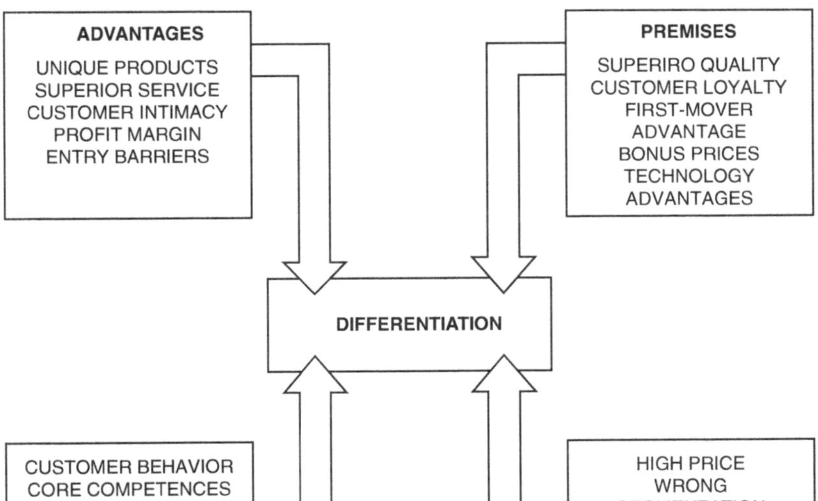

Figure 6.10 Differentiation features.

Source: Adapted to McGee et al., 2005, *210*.

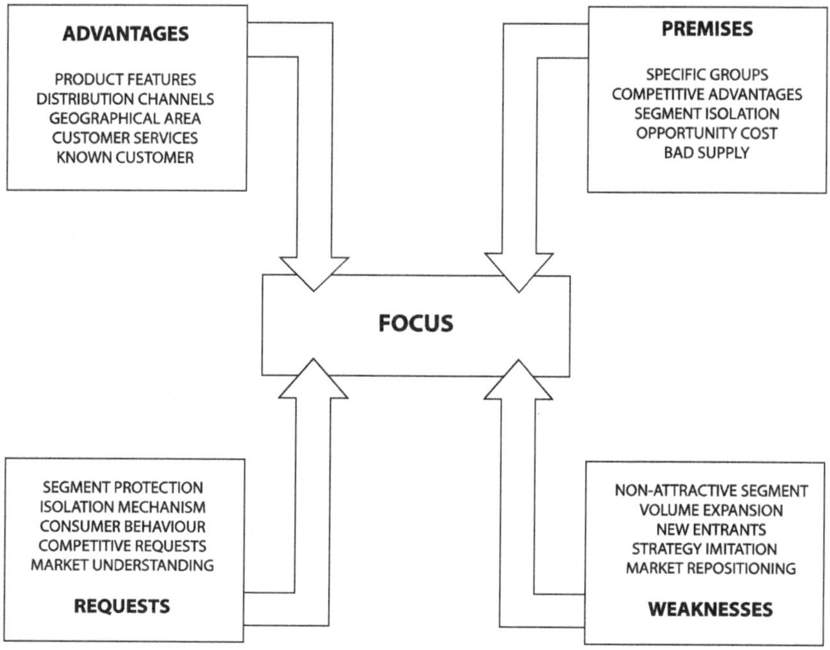

Figure 6.11 Focus features.

Source: Adapted from McGee et al., 2005, *211*.

market segment. Since focus is a competitive strategy derived from two previous competitive strategies (overall cost leadership and differentiation), two subtypes of focus should be differentiated: (1) low-cost focus with a primary focus (orientation) on low-cost products aimed at a market segment and (2) differentiation focus with a primary focus (orientation) on differentiated products aimed at a market segment (Figure 6.11).

The action component

The action component includes the implementation of decisions which initiate the process of conducting a competitive strategy as a key decision. The interaction between the competitive strategy and the organisational structure is the *conditio sine qua non* for the application of the decision (Figure 6.12).

According to Tom Burns and George Stalker (Burns and Stalker, 1971), the action component consists of two groups which shape the organisational structures of business:

1 Bureaucratic (or mechanical) structure which can be applied to traditional, i.e. classic structures,

2 Organic (or adaptive) structure which can be applied to contemporary, i.e. modern structures. The features of bureaucratic and organic structures appear as extremes suitable for different strategic business units (Figure 6.13).

The relation between competitive strategy and organisational structure has changed over time depending on the environment and the company. Alfred Chandler (1962) conducted the most extensive research concerning the

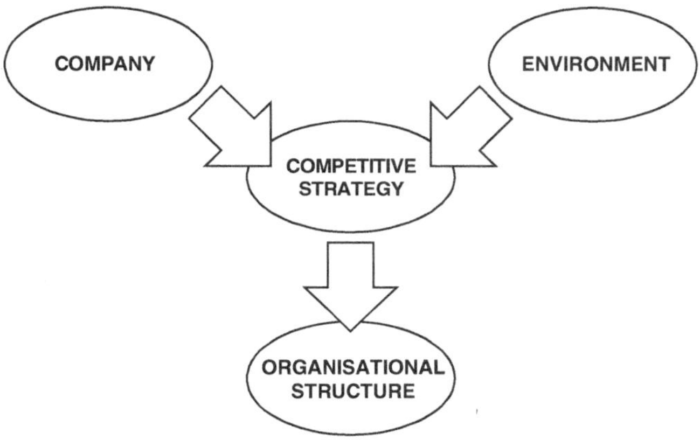

Figure 6.12 The synchronisation between competitive strategy and organisational structure.

Source: The authors.

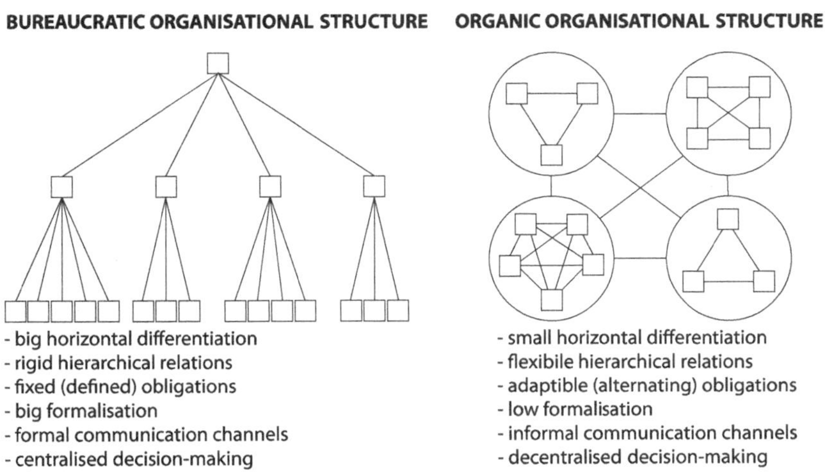

Figure 6.13 Bureaucratic versus organic organisational structure.

Source: Adapted from Burns and Stalker, 1971, *54*.

relation between competitive strategy and organisational structure. He based his work titled *Strategy and structure – chapters form the history of the American industrial company* on an intensive study of the history of company such as DuPont, General Motors, Standard Oil of New Jersey and Sears, Roebuck and Co., and he proved the hypothesis that competitive strategies of a company determine the organisational structure of a company and that its common name is the use of company resources (tangible and intangible) to meet the market demands. Organisational structure is a tool for an integrated application of the existing resources of a company in the process, whereas competitive strategy is a plan for resource allocation (relevant distribution) for future market demands.

Based on that notion, Alfred Chandler formulated his famous *structure follows strategy* statement. There has been an ongoing discussion on the nature and the character of that relation ever since from the 1960s. According to this statement, environmental changes and the opportunities and the danger it produces inform the company about the manner of adapting competitive strategies to fit the changed circumstances (geographical expansion, vertical integration, i.e. product diversification).

Alongside to following these competitive strategies, a change of the organisational structure becomes a necessity after a certain period of time.

Alfred Chandler studied the big American companies in detail and reached some satisfactory generalisations. Observed from the aspect of time, many of those companies have been in the process of initial resource accumulation in the period between 1880 and World War I. They established their top management in the period of the first two decades of the 20th century. Some of them initiated the process of further expansion mostly through diversification in the third decade, whereas most saw this expansion after the 1930 crisis. The outset of the new organisational structure formation dates back to the third decade. However, a vast number of organisational unit reorganisations took place in the fifth and sixth decade.

The operation and achievement of those companies have shown that a desire for self-regeneration and growth within the market economy frame was the driving force which knew how to efficiently utilise the existing resources. American companies gave no visible signal of comprehending the association between organisational structure and competitive strategy up until the 1920s.

Considering everything said, the organisational structure of companies following overall cost leadership and differentiation will be different from the organisational structure of companies following the strategy of focus (Petković et al., 2002) (Table 6.2).

Generally speaking, overall cost leadership requires a bureaucratic organisational structure, whereas differentiation requires an organic organisational structure.

The decision to follow a certain competitive strategy requires a strict application of completely different models of organisational structure since

Table 6.2 Common requests from competitive strategies to organisational structure

Competitive strategy	*Common requests for organisational structure*
Overall cost leadership	• Strong cost control • Detailed control reports • Organisational responsibility of employees • Achieving quantitative goals
Differentiation	• Coordination between functions • Subjective goal measurement • Highly skilled workers
Focus	• The combination of the above stated features (focus on a particular segment)

Source: Adapted from Daft, 2002, *112*.

the three competitive strategies include completely different demands. Overall cost leadership requires high productivity and low costs from a company. Differentiation requires company competence to achieve a certain degree of flexibility and advanced innovations. Focus requires company competence to achieve a combination of the two previous strategies. Here, company success requires an adequate organisational structure. Different organisational structure features displayed in Table 6.3 compete for the two competitive strategies too. Previously mentioned attitudes on the relation between competitive strategies and organisational structures are displayed in Figure 6.14.

The organisational structure needs to follow the competitive strategy, whereas the business functions within the organisational structure have a task of securing the sources of competitive advantage (low cost and differentiation) to optimise the organisational structure to follow one of the selected competitive strategies (overall cost leadership, differentiation and focus), as shown in Table 6.4.

Table 6.3 The features of an organisational structure in three competitive strategies

Organisational structure features	*Overall cost leadership*	*Differentiation*	*Focus*
Specialisation	High	Low	Combination
Decentralisation	Low	High	Combination
Degrees	High	Low	Combination
Range	Narrow	Wide	Combination
Grouping	Functional	Market	Combination
Relations	Low	High	Combination
Integration	Low	High	Combination
Formalisation	High	Low	Combination
Coordination	Process standardisation	Team communication	Combination
Overall	Mechanical	Organic	Combination

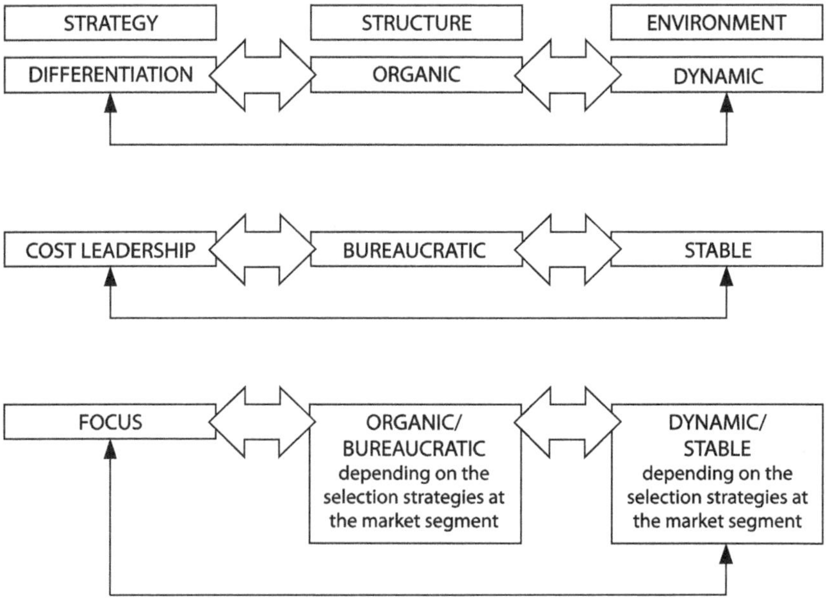

Figure 6.14 The relationship between strategy, structure and environment.
Source: Adapted from Daft, 2013, *71*,Šehić, Delić, 2012, *405*.

Table 6.4 Competitive advantage resources in business functions

Business function	*Overall low costs*	*Differentiation*
Production	Productivity enhancement	Flexible production
Human resource management	Decrease and elimination of the absence and fluctuation	Attracting and educating experts and workers
Marketing and sales	Increase in demand and the scale of sales	Targeting customers and brand creation
Technology development	Enhancing the efficiency of production technology	Enhancing the quality of existing products
Logistics	Reducing logistics costs through the just-in-time system	Ensuring the most quality logistics through long-term cooperation

Source: Jones, 2001, *236*.

Each competitive strategy type requires employees with different roles of behaviour (DeNisi and Griffin, 2008). The role of behaviour (Nankervis et al., 2002) implies the behaviour which an employee needs to have functioning as a job holder in a company. These behaviour roles vary across different dimensions. In addition, different behaviour roles concern different competitive strategies. Company following the overall cost leadership (Kulović, 2012) demand that their employees take care of quantity, have a short-term approach, be comfortable with stability and be prone to risk. These employees are expected to foster a behaviour type which is repetitive and conducted independently or automatically. Hence, companies following overall cost leadership, due to the focus on production efficiency, have a tendency to narrowly define the desired competencies and to invest in the development of desired competencies. Such companies develop consistent payment systems with a huge difference in income between supervisors and subordinates.

Companies following differentiation (Kulović, 2012) demand that their employees are creative and cooperative, to have low interest in quantity, a long-term approach, to tolerate insecurity and to accept risk. Employees in such companies are expected to practice behaviour type which includes the willingness to cooperate with others, to accept risk, to develop new ideas and to have a balanced approach on the work-results relation. Hence, companies following differentiation will encourage creativity through widely defined jobs. Such companies hire more people from the outside with a limited socialisation of newcomers and with a provision of broader career paths. Activities related to the development of competencies are focused on cooperation. The compensation system is characterised by movement towards external equality since external influences manage the recruitment needs.

Such companies develop a performance system based on results and company success evaluation to encourage top managers to accept risk[2]. The selection of competitive strategies influences the choice of respective policies and practices concerning the employees, as seen in Table 6.5 (Storey and Sisson, 1990).

Control indicates the degree of success to which companies follow the selected competitive strategy. However, the type of control to be selected depends on the competitive strategy followed by the companies,

Table 6.5 The influence of competitive strategies on employee policies and practices

Overall cost leadership	*Differentiation*	*Focus*
Low rate of employee involvement in decision making	High rate of employee involvement in decision making	High rate of employee involvement in decision making
Internal recruiting only	Internal recruiting only	Partial internal and external recruiting
Small share of variable incomes in total profit	High share of variable incomes in total profit	Medium share of variable incomes in total profit
Small investments in training	Big investments in training	Big investments in training
Classic relation between employer and employees	Employer-employee cooperation	Employer-employee cooperation

Source: Adapted from Storey and Sisson, 1990.

Table 6.6 Competitive strategies and control types

Control type	*Overall cost leadership*	*Differentiation*	*Focus*
Output control	High application (e.g. cost control)	Somewhat application (e.g. aim control)	Somewhat application (e.g. quality control)
Bureaucratic control	Somewhat application (e.g. budget control)	High application (e.g. rule control)	Somewhat application (e.g. budget control)
Group control	Low application (e.g. quality control	High application (e.g. culture control)	High application (e.g. norm control)

Source: Buble et al., 1997, *404*.

i.e. whether it is following overall cost leadership or differentiation if it is focused on a particular market segment. Based on this notion, the following three types of control have emerged:

1 Output control,
2 Bureaucratic control
3 Group control.

Unlike bureaucratic control which presents a mechanism outside the group, group control is a mechanism created by the group itself. The system of norms and values in a bureaucratic control is established by the company, whereas the system of norms and values in group control is established by the group. An individual feels he is *forced* to work *the best he can* in bureaucratic control, whereas an individual feels *responsibility* to work *the way he needs to work* in group control. Accordingly, bureaucratic control employees are controlled by an external system imposed upon them, whereas group control employees are controlled by an internal system which they have established themselves.

Following overall cost leadership (Mintzberg et al., 1995) is achieved by creating an economic factory, a permanent cost control, minimising the costs of services and similar. Hence, a complete output control and lower bureaucratic control and group control are applied here (Table 6.6).

Following differentiation (Mintzberg et al., 1995) is achieved by innovating existing products, a developed customer service, product quality control and similar. Hence, bureaucratic and group control is used here to its full extent, whereas output control is used to a lesser degree.

The interaction between the planning and the action component

The association between the planning and the action component is completed through the adoption of the strategic plan. During the process of strategic plan adoption, it is important to understand the management apparatus. In the literature, the role of management apparatus in the process of strategic plan adoption is identified as the main factor of the competitive position of a company.

The aim is to provide the correlation between the purposes of the company with the interests of the owner. A number of recent studies suggest that the management apparatus plays a key role in the process. However, that role is insufficiently realised in practice. Either way, it can be exclusively realised in the partnership between the board (supervising or managing) and the top management of the company.

However, they often hold one or two functions simultaneously: the first being managing (owner's), whereas the second one is executive (top managerial) (Drucker, 1955).

Although the two functions can be observed individually, they are intertwined in practice. Since it is hard to determine the difference between governance and management, terminological ambiguity often emerges when trying to understand these terms. Hence, Anglo-Saxon literature includes the following terms related to governance: *direction*, *governing*, *administration*, *control* and the following terms related to management: *guidance*, *management*, *generalship*, *leadership*. The first author to deal with this issue was Chester Barnard.

The association between the governance (owner's) and executive (top management) function is defined by a set of combinations (Mašić, 2008): (a) The owners can do all the top-managerial tasks themselves, (b) they can hire professional top managers and simultaneously do some top managerial work and (c) they can leave all the top-managerial work to professional top managers.

In addition, this association is defined by a set of contract relations which are known as managerial contracts in the literature. The following two theories explaining the set of contract relations more closely were formed based on these associations.

- Agency theory
- Stewardship theory

The premise of the agency theory (Nyberg et al., 2010) is the economic man who has a rational desire to maximise his own benefit, whereas the premise of the stewardship theory (Davies et al., 1997) is the self-proclaimed man who wants to raise his personal bar in his desire to maximise collective benefit. An individual places personal interests as the goal, whereas the collective interest is highlighted in stewardship theory.

In the agency theory, there is a relationship between the capital owner (the so-called principal) and the professional top-manager (the so-called agent) in which they sign a contract which states that the principal is paid to work in the interest of the owner. In stewardship theory, there is a relationship where the capital owner and the professional top-manager (known as the governor) close a deal which indicates that the governor is motivated to work in the interest of the owner. In other words, when discussing agency theory, if an agent has to choose between the maximisation of personal benefit or principal benefit, he will opt for the maximisation of personal benefit at the expense of principal interest (there is an emergence of the so-called agency cost for the principal), whereas in stewardship theory, if a governor chooses between maximisation of personal benefit or principal benefit, he will opt for the maximisation of principal benefit at the expense of personal interest (there is an emergence of the so-called opportunity cost for the governor).

According to Branislav Mašić et al. (2008), the 20th and 21st centuries are characterised by a tendency to leave the majority of top-managerial work to professionals. It does make sense since there are numerous factors justifying this phenomenon. There has been a revelation that professionals are individuals whose competencies (knowledge, skills and abilities) guarantee that they will do a better job completing top-managerial tasks compared to the owner. The previously stated facts indicate that every owner does not have to be (both) a top manager too to successfully manage his capital, i.e. to generate an income to its invested capital, which is the ultimate goal of each capital investment. However, top managers can participate in the ownership structure of a company where they conduct their top-managerial tasks, which does not influence their position, status, role and behaviour as holders of top-managerial work. The association between the managerial (owner's) and the executive (top-managerial) function observed as an example of private companies (partnership companies) is different compared with the example of corporations (shareholders company).

There are only a few owners in partnership companies whereas there are many owners in shareholder's companies. Owners complete top-managerial tasks in partnership companies too (there is no separation between ownership and top-managerial function), whereas owners leave top-managerial tasks to professionals in shareholders' companies (there is a separation between the ownership and top-managerial function) (Erić, 2000). People can be simultaneously involved in the managerial (ownership) and the executive (top-managerial) level. Our legislation does not allow that since members of the board of directors cannot be members of the board of supervisors at the same time.

Although the separation of the governing (ownership) and executive (top-managerial) function is advocated in the recent literature, companies where both these functions are united in a single person still dominate in practice. Namely, the same person is both the owner and top manager in most companies (Higgins, 1994). Those who oppose the separation and favour the current state of affairs argue that the separation into two functions (owner and top manager) would jeopardise company leadership.

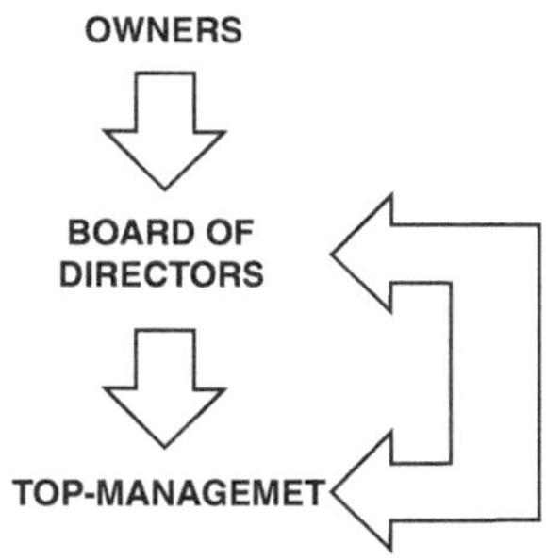

Figure 6.15 The relationship between the governing and the top-managerial position.
Source: Adapted from Manus and Minow, 1995, *104*.

Those who favour the separation and oppose the current state of affairs highlight that the unification of the two functions (owner and top manager) in a single person would make it harder to make changes in a company (Figure 6.15) (Milisavljević, 1999).

To understand their role requires a comprehension of the models (Manus and Minow, 1995) which are a framework of the functionality of different levels in an organisational structure of a company.

The first model is the unitary or the single-stage model: This model includes only the board of directors. The essence of this model is the unification of the governing (ownership) and the executive (top-managerial) level which is comprised of the internal and external members of the board of directors. This model is applied by the USA and Great Britain. Since the chief executive office is a member of the board of directors, and quite often the chairman of the board of directors at the same time, it is necessary to evaluate his work from time to time, particularly by external members of the board of directors.

It is necessary that everyone, external participants in particular, should have the information needed for discussion to make sure it does not end up being dull.

It can be argued that external members of the board of directors are free and independent and have a much more favourable position to evaluate the company business in a more serious way compared to the so-called internal members. External members, in contrast with internal ones, are given priority due to the following (Payne et al., 2009): (a) they use financial performances as central parameters when evaluating the company success, (b) they have a tendency to dismiss the CEO due to bad performance, (c) they have a tendency to carefully scrutinise the work of the CEO to protect their own reputation and (d) they are more objective when evaluating the company business operations since they use financial performances. However, according to Jay Lorsh, giving advice is the one thing a CEO expects most from the external members of the board of directors. In order to maintain the unification of the functions of the president of the board and the CEO in a single person and to increase the system of top-management control, there have been recent suggestion of introducing the so-called leading director, i.e. to assign this role to one of the members of the board of directors. Hence, the role of the board of directors in modern company needs to be strengthened through authorisation. Jay Lorsh states several reasons for authorisation: (a) the owners indirectly pressure the board of directors to influence the top management to work in their interest, (b) increase of public interest through the specification of institutional frameworks for enhancing the work of top managers, (c) it is believed that top managers are overpaid considering their achieved results. According to Momčilo Milisavljević (1999), the degree of authorisation needs to be adapted to the company needs. Hence, authorisation does not mean that the board of directors should take over the role of the top management of the company and govern it directly through its business activities. It is recommendable to have a small-numbered board of directors to constantly monitor the work of top management. The members of the board of directors need to have experience to successfully monitor the work of top management. Jay Lorsh (1995) argues that there are no indicators that a board of directors, in companies where it has the authority to monitor the work of top management, has lost its power to lead the company.

The second model is the dual or the two-stage model:This model recognises the existence of the supervisory board and the management. The essence of this model is to separate the governing (ownership) level from the executive (top managerial) level. This model is applied by the EU and Japan. The role of the board of supervisors is limited to the selection of top managers, monitoring their work and their dismissal if the company performances are not satisfactory. The role of shareholders is to dismiss the board of supervisors if the company has not operated successfully. This means that top managers depend on the board of supervisors and the board of supervisors depends on the shareholders. This model has not been successful since many companies applying it has operated unsuccessfully. It has been discussed that a companies failure is not associated with power distribution, but rather with bad decision-making. The disadvantages can be found in decision making, with the cause being the way in which the board of supervisors and top management make decision and monitor the company development. Accordingly, power reform is not the key for correcting the problem, but it does not undermine its importance. It is common for top managers to have certain power since power is a permanent follower of capital management. The power possessed by top managers today is vast. Branislav Mašić et al. (2005) argue that, here, it needs to be highlighted that the power of top managers has a tendency of permanent growth due to the process of globalisation.

Company capital management autonomy (particularly in big companies since they have huge capital at their disposal) includes the possession of vast power on the behalf of top managers. The possession of power raises the issue of its abuse. This has led to the inauguration of the problem of top-management control, i.e. the problem of controlling the behaviour of top managers to protect stakeholders and owners. The basics of top-manager control can be found in each company. Hence, each company includes the forms and the dynamic of top-manager control in its statute. This includes the need to control the behaviour displayed by the top manager on one side and controlling the results achieved by the top manager on the other. Accordingly, special place and role are assigned to (Manus and Minow, 1995): (a) direct control conducted by the apparatus in relation to the shareholder assembly, board of supervisors and certified auditors and (b) indirect control conducted according to indicators in relation to the growth level, market position and price dynamics. Well-organised companies ensure a timely protection from irresponsible behaviour in terms of the disposition of their capital. However, practically, the existing control system of top-manager behaviour in the area of capital management does not have all the performances needed to successfully control the behaviours of managers. It has been often proven that even top managers, who are often associated with financial and legal consultants, are prone to falsify and tamper business reports and audit companies sometimes give more advice than exercise control which altogether harms the shareholders[3].

Based on model comprehension, we can apply the following two terms (Buble et al. 2007):

1 Governing (ownership),
2 Executive (managerial) level.

The governing (ownership) level consists of company owners and/or their representatives appointed by the assembly to be a part of the board. In the Anglo-American model, the board consists of members of *the board of directors headed by the chairman of the board of directors.* In the European-continental model, *the board consists of members of the board of supervisors headed by the chairman of a board of supervisors.*

The *executives* or those with a share in the ownership structure of the company (major or minor shareholders) are known as *insiders*, whereas *non-executives* or those without a share in the ownership structure of the company (major or minor) are known as *outsiders*. Outsiders are nominated into the governing board or board of supervisors on a temporary basis with a goal of solving financial, legal, investment and other questions. In order for the governing or board of supervisors to function properly, it is recommendable to hold 6 to 12 regular annual meetings with additional meetings depending on the circumstances. The revision of the company business strategy needs to be done at least once a year.

The executive (top managerial) level consists of a manager and/or their substitutes appointed by the board into the top management[4]. In the Anglo-American model, *the top management consists of executive officers headed by the*

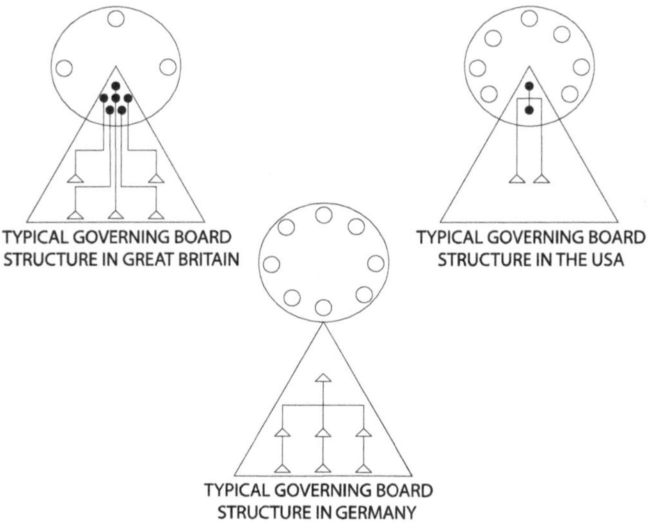

Figure 6.16 Typical board structure (either governing or supervisory) in some companies.
Source: Buble et al., 1997, *32*.

chief executive officers. In the European-continental model, the *top management consists of board members (executive officers) and the board chairman (managing director)*. Top management is responsible for the functioning of the company as a whole. The term top management does not imply a formalised management based on the group system, but rather a constellation of 3 to 10 managers at the top of the organisational structure of a company[5].

Figure 6.16 illustrates a typical board structure (either governing or supervisory) in some companies. As seen in the figure, the outsider chairmen are a minority in companies in Great Britain. It is common for a governing board to have more than one outsider member, but certainly less than half of the total number of members. In sharp contrast, most members of the governing board are outsiders in companies in the USA. Unlike the USA and Great Britain, Germany has completely separated membership in the governing board and top management. Anyway, the governing board consists of an odd number of members, at least three, whereas the main assembly of the company nominates them for a period of 3 years, with the possibility of a reelection.

Priorities must be defined to focus on. According to Momčilo Milisavljević (1999), there are the following three points of view of the increased role of the board (governing or supervisory) in the process of strategic management:

1 First, who is responsible for the minimisation of the management board (governing and supervisory) in the strategic management process and who considers it to be the jurisdiction of the top management of the company

2 Second, who assigned the board (governing or supervisory) with the role of providing an insight and monitoring of the realisation of the strategic management process
3 Third, who is responsible for favouring the partnership between the board (governing or supervisory) and top management in the process of strategic management.

Members of the board (governing or supervisory) are legally obliged to give their vote on some company decisions such as merging other companies, merging with other companies, the division of the company into other companies and similar. The board (board of directors or board of supervisors) can directly influence the strategic planning process by incorporating its members into respective sub-boards (sub-board for strategy, for instance), by indirect suggestions concerning the top-management tasks and by direct supervision over the decisions of the top management.

The board (board of directors or board of supervisors) can directly influence the strategic planning process by reducing the corporation dependency on the resources and the influence of the environment by providing the top management of the company with relevant information.

The role of the board (board of directors or board of supervisors) is narrowed down to the *authorisation of the strategic plan* of the company which is adopted by the *executive officers* headed by the *chief executive officer* in the Anglo-American model or *the members of the board of directors* (executive officers) headed by the *chairman of the board of directors* (managing director) in the European-continental model.

It is recommendable and even necessary to have this document to establish the needed communication between the board (board of directors or board of supervisors) and top management in the strategic planning process, since competitive strategy is put to paper by its application. Disregarding the methodological framework[6] of the strategic plan, the document should be short, a few pages only. It is believed that the best practice is for the initiative to start from the top-managerial level with the participation of all levels of strategic business units with their suggestion and initiatives. The board (board of directors or board of supervisors) which has, in the past, only passively authorised the strategic plan of the company recommended by top-managerial team is now more active in its creation. In addition, strategic business unit managers receive a more important role in the creation of the strategic plan, whereas the role of professional planners is beginning to fade (Babić et al. 2008).

Each manager has clearly delimited authorisation and responsibilities in relation to their function in the company. It is important to clarify the positions of individual top-managers involved in the task to ensure work efficiency. Strategic business unit managers have a narrower area of jurisdiction and responsibility compared with the CEO or the managing director. However, they perform the same activities as them. The difference is that the CEO or the managing directors of the company perform activities referring to the entire

Table 6.7 The role of the board (board of directors or board of supervisors) and the top management in the strategic plan

	Formulates	*Authorises*	*Implementation*	*Monitors*
Board (board of directors or board of supervisors)		x		x
Top management	x		x	

Source: Milisavljević, 1999, *36*.

company, whereas the strategic business unit managers do the same activities for its segments. A number of board members (board of directors or board of supervisors) do not feel comfortable to discuss the company strategic plan together with the members of the top management (Babić et al., 2008). The board (board of directors or board of supervisors) members feeling competent and free to take part in the discussion represent a real challenge for the top management, particularly if there is a request for an alteration or a change of the suggested strategic plan. A timely intervention by the board members (board of directors or board of supervisors) is required in many cases when there are changes in the strategic plan.

Hence, brainstorming[7] is the best option to reach quality solutions and avoid conflicts. Many companies organised the so-called days of strategic planning (Pozen, 2011), where board members (board of directors or board of supervisors) and top-management members discuss the strategic plan using the *brainstorming* technique. Brainstorming is coin formed by two words: brain and storm[8]. The method was developed in the 1950s when empirical research revealed that meetings held to solve the burning business problems attended by highly paid experts were not yielding results. The development and application of brainstorming has solved the problem. The evaluation of the strategic plan cannot be completed through the aspect of current and past results, but rather through the comparison of the invested capital income generated by the existing competitive strategy and invested capital income which could be generated using other competitive strategies (Milisavljević, 2012) (Table 6.7).

As seen in the table, the top management formulates a strategic plan and submits it to the board (board of directors or board of supervisors) for adoption. The top management applies the strategy plan and the board (board of directors or board of supervisors) monitors its application.

The sustainability of generic strategies

Michael Porter (1998) states that a generic strategy will not lead to above-the-average profitability if it is not sustainable in comparison with its competitors, disregarding the fact that activities enhancing the industry can increase the profitability of the entire industry, even when imitated.

Table 6.8 Distinctive features of generic strategies

Accent	*Generic strategies*		
	Overall cost leadership	*Differentiation*	*Focus*
Production	Nobody can produce cheaper	Nobody can produce better	We make products only for you
Marketing	We have a better price than them	Our product is better than their product	We exist because of you

Source: Adapted from Hill, Jones, 1989, *136*.

The sustainability of generic strategies requires the competitive advantage of the company to resist the erosion caused by the behaviours of competitors or industry development.

Each generic strategy represents a potential and considerable danger for another generic strategy, e.g. companies following the strategy of focus must pay attention to competitors which fulfil the needs of multiple segments and *vice versa*. It should be noted that a company must keep in mind that generic strategies (overall cost leadership, differentiation and focus) cannot be applied simultaneously (Table 6.8).

Namely, overall cost leadership does not provide simultaneous differentiation since it leads to cost increase just as differentiation does not provide simultaneous overall cost leadership since it leads to cost increase. Hence, attention should be paid to avoid getting stuck in the middle, i.e. based on the average level, what are the things that can result in the lack of possibility to reinforce the competitive position in an industry (Hill and Jones, 1989).

However, generic strategies can coexist profitably in many industries as long as companies follow different generic strategies or select a different basis for overall cost leadership, differentiation or focus. If, e.g. two or more companies follow a strategy based on the same principle, an exceptionally painstaking, long and unprofitable battle can be expected. Each generic strategy necessarily includes different competences and demands for request, as shown in Table 6.8.

Overall cost leadership usually requires a firmer control system, general cost minimisation, using the economy of scale and the specialisation of employee skills which can have a counter-effect on the company trying to differentiate itself through orientation towards new products (Table 6.9).

The former or present understanding of generic strategies by competitors influences the choice offered to the company and the costs needed to change its position. The concept of generic strategies is based on the premise that there is more than one way to generate competitive advantage, depending on the industry. If all companies within a single industry were to follow the principles of generic strategies, each one would have to select a different basis for creating competitive advantage. Although not all

Table 6.9 General features of the three generic strategies

Generic strategy	*General requirements for the company*
Overall cost leadership	• Considerable capital investment • The development of technical-technological competence • Intensive employee supervision • Product facilitation through design • Low-cost distribution
Differentiation	• Big marketing abilities • Production engineering • The existence of meaningful creativity • High reputation of the company • Long tradition of the industry • Help from distribution channels
Focus	• Combination of the above-mentioned items (focus on a particular segment)

Source: Adapted from Daft, 1995, 71.

companies would succeed, the generic strategies would provide alternative paths for generating above-the-average profitability.

The sustainability of overall cost leadership

Overall cost leadership sustainability depends on many factors. The following three are the most important:

1 Sustainability concerning the interrelation among strategic business units – factors needed to force the competitor to diversify in order to achieve the same cost advantage.
2 Sustainability concerning the presence of entry barriers to related industries – factors needed to create entry barriers for related industries which significantly increases costs, hindering the potential newcomers.
3 Sustainability concerning the value chain configuration – it is almost inevitable for competitors to face considerably high costs in each attempt to counteract the reconfigured value chain.

The sustainability of differentiation

Differentiation sustainability depends on many factors. The following three are the most important:

1 Sustainability concerning the uniqueness sources of the company created by lifting barriers – advantages gained through early market entry are more sustainable uniqueness drivers.
2 Sustainability concerning the cost advantage created as a consequence of the differentiation effect – sustainable competitive advantage used

when conducting activities leading to differentiation will generate sustainability.

3 Sustainability concerning the differentiation as a consequence of high costs – fixed costs covered by the customers due to the reorientation on another supplier enable premium prices.

The sustainability of focus

Focus sustainability depends on many factors. The following three are the most important:

1 Sustainability concerning competitors oriented towards multiple segments – the scale and sustainability of competitive advantage generated through focus in relation to company operating in multiple segments.
2 Sustainability concerning the imitators creating barriers against mobility which prevent the focus strategy from being imitated or prevents competitors, who have narrower goals, to increase their focus.
3 Sustainability concerning the substitution of products which attract customers – the existence of intentional or unintentional risk that segments which are not covered by the company could attract customers.

Upgrading Porter's generic strategies concept

Raymond Miles and Charles Snow (1978) have upgraded Michael Porter's concept of generic strategies. The authors believe that company develop adaptive strategies based on the perception of the environment by the company (i.e. the company sees what it wants to see in its environment). Since company have different perceptions of their environment, it is safe to say that they develop different *adaptive strategies*. Different business strategies enable some companies to be more adaptive or sensible to its environment in relation to the adaptability or sensibility of other companies. The authors particularly single out the development of *strategic configurations* with the goal of creating compatibility between the company and the environment. Such compatibility is referred to as the *adaptive cycle*.

The cycle should consist of three problems than need to be solved during the interaction between the company and the environment. The authors call these problems *the problems of the complex and dynamic process of strategic selection* and they usually occur simultaneously. The three problems are as follows (Miles and Snow, 1978):

1 Entrepreneurial problems concerning the way of developing markets and products
2 Engineering problems concerning the way of acquiring and using technology

3 Administrative problems concerning the way of organising and controlling the business operations.

Raymond Miles and Charles Snow (1978) have offered the following four configurations of strategic behaviour which can solve the problem of the adaptive cycle:

1 Explorer – He generates competitive advantage by achieving success in new markets using new products with the highest possible risk compared to other configurations. He is fast to accept new technologies. The corporation retains its external focus on a broadly defined production-market domain with possible losses due to adaptability to changes.
2 Prospector – He generates competitive advantage by achieving success on the existing markets using the existing products with the lowest possible risk compared to other configurations. He is slow to accept new technologies. The company retains its external focus on a broadly defined production-market domain with possible losses due to operative efficiency.
3 Analyst- He generates competitive advantage by combining the previous two configurations
4 Reactor - He does not generate competitive advantage.

The business strategy typology employed by Raymond Miles and Charles Snow (1978) is similar to the typology used by Michael Porter.

Whereas Michael Porter's typology presents the method of competition (the way a company generates value for its customers), the typology employed by Raymond Miles and Charles Snow presents the approach of the competition (the way in which the company applies the method of competition). If we were to compare the two typologies, we could conclude that the resemblance is undisputed (Figure 6.17).

It should be noted that Michael Porter's typology is based on the principles of *economic logic*, whereas the typology of Raymond Miles and Charles Snow is based on the principles of a *philosophical approach* to business. Both typologies contain an equal number of configurations (four), with three successful ones. The successful configuration patterns consist of the following (Miles and Snow, 1978):

1 Two existing, pure types positioned at the opposite ends of the strategic continuum (Porter's *overall cost leadership and* differentiation and Miles' and Snow's *explorer and prospector*)
2 One idiosyncratic combination of pure types which is closer to the middle of the strategy continuum (Porter's *focus* and Miles' and Snow's *analyst*).

Michael Porter (1998) labelled the unsuccessful and unsustainable types as *stuck in the middle*, whereas Raymond Miles and Charles Snow (1978) refer to them as *reactors*.

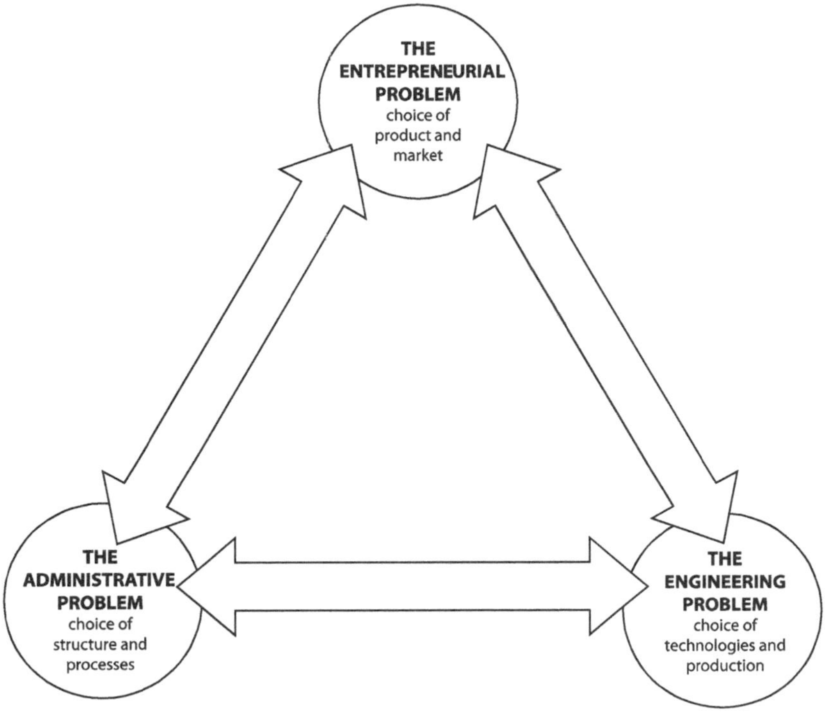

Figure 6.17 Miles' and Snow's adaptive cycle.

Source: Miles and Snow, 1978, *24*.

Their common feature is their inconsistency to follow a single configuration at the strategic continuum representing a somewhat combination of the three successful types in that way (Figure 6.18).

Looking back at the previous facts, we could argue that there is not a real contrast between the two typologies (Porter's and Miles' and Snow's) which indicates the possibility of their combination. Disregarding the sole classification into the respective typology, the question of balance between different typologies emerges as a more relevant issue. When discussing balance, it is important to understand the matrix displaying the combined typologies (Figure 6.19).

Hence, *the explorer* and the *reactor* are homogenous categories. *Low-cost analyst* and *high-cost prospector* use overall cost leadership as a basis for reinforcing the competitive advantage, whereas *differentiation analyst* and *differentiation prospector* use differentiation as a basis for reinforcing the competitive advantage. An explorer is successful in defining the competitive volume. A reactor does not have success in defining the competitive volume. Low-cost analyst does not have success in defining the competitive volume. Differentiation analyst and differentiation prospector are successful in defining the competitive volume (Boyd and Walker, 1999).

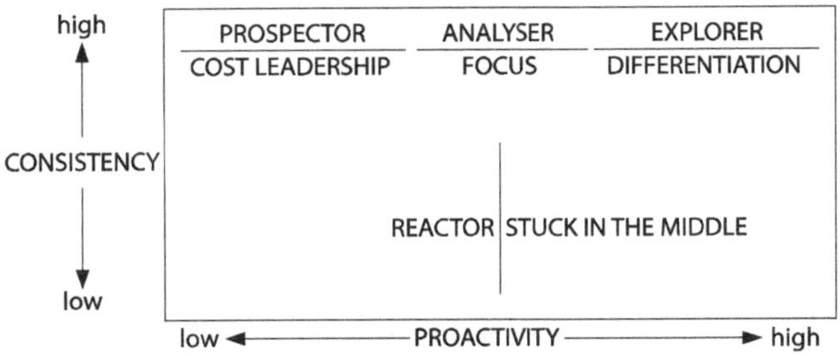

Figure 6.18 The combination of Porter's and Miles' and Snow's typology.

Source: Miles, Snow, 1978, *24*.

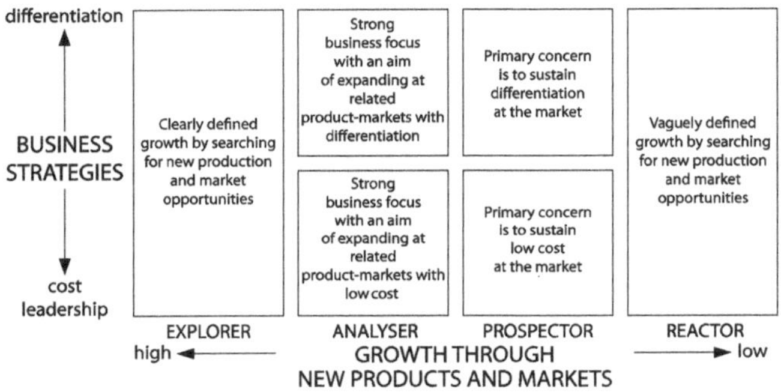

Figure 6.19 Combined typology of generic strategies.

Source: Boyd, Walker, 1999, *10*.

The stuck-in-the-middle position

Companies can combine overall cost leadership with differentiation. When compared with companies following a single generic strategy (overall cost leadership or differentiation), companies following both strategies (overall cost leadership or differentiation) are capable of creating sustainable competitive advantage in a better way.

According to Momcilo Milisavljevic (2012), a company has the two following options to utilise the low-cost advantage in relation to its competition:

1 The first option is to utilise the low and opt for low prices and attract a high number of price-sensitive customers which will lead to profitability
2 The second option is to use the same prices, but use the option of sustaining the current market share and utilise low which will lead to profitability.

The goal is to deliver superior value to customers (offer price lower than that of the competition while keeping the same quality). Competitive advantage of companies delivering superior value to customers includes lower cost for delivering certain perks, which offers a better competitive position compared with competitors whose products have similar appealing perks.

A company following this strategy places itself close to the stuck-in-the-middle position either by low-quality products with prices above the average or by high-quality products with prices equalling the average. Such a business strategy imposes a simultaneous product price reduction and product quality enhancement. As previously seen, following both generic strategies (overall cost leadership and differentiation) simultaneously can be based on four generic blocs (Thompson et al., 2006).

The manner of following generic strategies will vary across industries with activities that need to be conducted to generate the competitive advantage which the company or strategic business unit is after. Michael Porter (1985) highlights the importance of following one strategy for each industry, otherwise there is a risk of ending up stuck in the middle without the generation of competitive advantage. Each of the three generic strategies requires consistency, whether we are discussing the strategies associated with an entire industry (overall cost leadership or differentiation) or generic strategies associated with a particular segment (focus based on overall cost leadership or differentiation). In practice, a company is stuck in the middle when it produces products with perks valued by the customers.

The stuck-in-the-middle position is a situation when a company or a strategic business unit does not have a consistent generic strategy, i.e. neither of the generic strategies mentioned earlier. Such companies do not have a path for their development. Such companies can survive in stable circumstances for a certain period of time. However, as soon as there are changes, companies without a clear concept and a response to the occurring changes are the first ones to vanish. Changes occurring in the environment create developmental problems both for companies with clearly defined generic strategies and to those without them. However, companies with articulated generic strategies will react following the reasoning behind such strategies, whereas other companies will find themselves stuck in the middle and left to the influence of environmental changes, often becoming its victim.

Companies following a particular generic strategy can end up being stuck due to errors made in the selection of the strategic option, inconsistency in its planning and conducting and similar. In addition, companies which have generated profit at their outset, can find themselves in a bad strategic position due to an unsound resource allocation.

If a company wants to avoid the stuck-in-the-middle position, it must make an effort to follow the three generic strategies (overall cost leadership, differentiation and focus) simultaneously. Successful companies following generic strategies need to make sure that they are aligned with a specific generic strategy. In addition, companies need to observe their environment to sustain the sources of competitive advantage in accordance with the opportunities and threats arising in an alternating environment.

The basic features of this position include the following (Porter, 1985):

1. *A company stuck in the middle loses a large number of customers* – The company passes on high-profitable jobs to company focused on targeted segments or differentiation (e.g. if the customers demand lower prices, the company has to give up profit to compete with companies with lower cost)
2. *A company stuck in the middle has got a disordered organisational structure* – The company often encounters conflicts or bad motivation in organisational flows due to problems in the organisational structure (e.g. competitors will quickly erase the generated income from the company which discover a profitable customer)
3. *A company stuck in the middle makes fundamental strategic decisions* – A company needs to take measures needed to establish overall cost leadership or differentiation, i.e. focus orientation (e.g. the cost must be at the level of the cost of competitors including the aggressive investments in modernisation).

That is why a company following each of the three generic strategies without realising neither of them, ends up being stuck in the middle. It is a bad position for a company where competitive advantage is not generated. This position guarantees low profitability. However, it should be pointed out that there are several reasons explaining the reasons why a company which is simultaneously following the generic strategies does not properly apply neither of them (Đuričin et al., 2013):

1. Overall cost leadership requires a simple control system with clear subordination, whereas differentiation requires multi-divisional and cross-functional relations
2. Overall cost leadership focuses on direct cost, whereas differentiation focuses on encouraging creativity
3. Overall cost leadership bases its reward system on cost reduction, whereas differentiation encourages innovation and promotions.

Companies stick in the middle will compete at the market without generating competitive advantage. Unlike them, companies applying a generic strategy (overall cost leadership, differentiation or focus) will have a better position in all segments (Figure 6.20).

The left far end of the U-curve represents differentiation (low share and high profitability), whereas the right far end of the U-curve represents cost leadership (high share and high profitability[9]. However, the U-curve (Đuričin et al., 2013) cannot be applied to all industries. Some industries

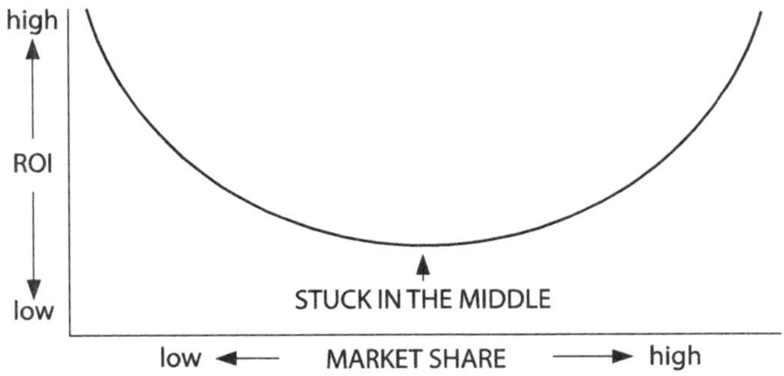

Figure 6.20 The stuck in the middle position.

Source: Porter, 1985, *16*.

do not have the option of neither focus nor differentiation, whereas cost are relatively unimportant in some industries due to the features of customer and buyer. These industries usually follow the rule that the relationship between the market share and profitability is inversely proportional. In other industries, the competition is so intense that companies have to follow either cost leadership or differentiation. A company, once stuck in the middle, needs a lot of time and effort to find an exit from such a position. The most common reason leading to getting stuck in the middle is the constant change of generic strategy. Consequently, this position in some branches means that small companies (using focus or differentiation) and big companies (using overall cost leadership) are the most profitable ones, whereas small and medium companies are the least profitable. According to Michael Porter, there are only two ways to generate profit: (1) differentiation, i.e. realising small market share based on selling products with accepted high value and (2) cost reduction, i.e. realising high market share based on selling low-priced products.

Otherwise, companies attempting some third strategy (medium price range or moderate market share) or simultaneously trying to follow the strategies of overall cost leadership and differentiation are bound to end up stuck in the middle. A company, stuck in the middle, can generate attractive profit only when the structure of the industry where it operates is favourable or if its competitors are stuck in the middle. Nevertheless, such a company is less profitable than competitors following one of the generic strategies. The position of the company is the result of not choosing a way in which it will compete. A company following the strategy of focus is usually highly tempted to jeopardise a generic strategy and end up stuck in the middle due to the restriction of the possible sales volume. Such companies are advised to look for opportunities in other industries rather than jeopardise their position in the current one and end up stuck in the middle.

Each generic strategy represents one way of creating sustainable competitive advantage. In order to achieve its strategic goals, a company must combine different forms of competitive advantages. A company must decide which generic strategy to follow or it will end up stuck in the middle. Sometimes, a company can form one or two separate business units with respective competitive strategies. Hence, if a company fails to clearly separate the strategic business units following different generic strategies, it could wipe out the potential of all the units to create sustainable competitive advantage. It is hard to simultaneously follow overall cost leadership and differentiation since differentiation requires high costs.

Following more than one generic strategy

Cost reduction does not entail differentiation. There are companies which managed to practically reduce cost by simultaneously increasing differentiation. However, cost reduction must not be identified with overall cost leadership (Milisavljević, 2012). Should a company following overall cost leadership encounter a company which does not follow overall cost leadership, it will unconditionally reach a point where further cost reduction is impossible, compared to its serious competitor. By reaching this point, overall cost leadership becomes inconsistent. However, if a company can simultaneously follow overall cost leadership and differentiation, it will reap huge benefits. Namely, overall cost leadership leads to cost reduction, whereas differentiation leads to high prices. A company should aggressively utilise all opportunities to reduce cost which do not undermine differentiation, and it should utilise all opportunities for differentiation which do not lead to cost increase. Numerous practical cases have confuted Michael Porter's attitudes. Influenced by pressure generated from facts, he gave up on the concept of getting stuck in the middle in his later works, stating that the nature of influence of hyper production and globalisation requires companies following differentiation to reduce costs, and companies following overall cost leadership to make an effort towards differentiation. In other words, when the market (segment or niche) is the norm of the competitive game, timing is critical when applying a generic strategy (overall cost leadership or differentiation) (Đuričin et al., 2013). Multiple companies have demonstrated success in following both generic strategies. Namely, it turns out that it is a higher risk to follow a single generic strategy. Even research has gone as far as to demonstrate that it is possible to apply both strategies complementary[10].

A company offers expensive products to its customers which immediately eliminates the possibility of competing with companies offering cheap products, and it is insufficiently differentiated to provide value offered by companies oriented towards the strategy of differentiation (Milisavljević, 2012). According to Michael Porter (1985), there are the following three situations when a company can simultaneously realise both generic strategies: overall cost leadership and differentiation.

The first situation is when *competitors are stuck in the middle.* After ending up in that scenario, sound positioning is not a complete solution for competitors and nobody can force a company to position itself in place where both low costs and differentiation are inconsistent. Such a situation is only temporary. In the end, one of competitors will start to follow a generic strategy in a well-structured manner. Hence, a company must select a form of competitive strategy which is planned as a long-term solution.

The second situation is when *costs are determined by market share*. In this scenario, a company follows overall cost leadership or differentiation due to high market share rather than product design, technology level or service provision and other factors. However, when a company simultaneously strives for overall cost leadership and differentiation, it is always vulnerable towards competitors following a single generic strategy with a realisation of a high market share. This can be realised when there is a notable industry cross-relation which can be utilised by some companies and failed to be utilised by others.

The third situation is when *companies are the main significant innovators*. Introducing significant technological innovation enables the company to reduce costs or enhance differentiation simultaneously and perhaps follow both generic strategies. However, to follow both generic strategies simultaneously, a company must be the sole main significant innovator. When a competitor introduces an innovation, the company is again positioned to balance the use of the innovation for overall cost leadership or differentiation. A company must have some barriers preventing imitation which results in competitive advantage.

It should be noted that some authors advocate following several generic strategies simultaneously, whereas other authors advocate following a single generic strategy.

An analysis of generic strategies can reveal that they focus more on strategic business units while neglecting the company. This mostly concerns diversified companies while neglecting the undiversified. Considering the fact that one of the criticisms of generic strategies is oriented towards the premature dismissal of the portfolio concept, research the possible portfolio concept that can be applied to the strategic business unit level to realise a transfer of cash follows.

Analyse, in any example, the manner in which a company can end up stuck in the industry middle due to the fact that it does not follow any strategy or the manner in which it ended up stuck in the industry middle since it tried to follow both strategies.

Notes

1 *Boston Consulting Group* – BCG is a global private consulting company and a world leader in consultations on management and business strategy. It was founded in 1963 and it has 81 offices in 45 countries worldwide.

2 A recent study on employee practices in small steel plants in the USA indicates that factories tend to have different business strategies using different systems in the practice of employees. Steel plants following overall cost leadership have used systems based on control characterised by strong centralisation, low participation, a low

degree of training, low salaries, low benefits and a highly conditioned pay check, whereas steel plants following differentiation have used a system of employee attachment which is characterised by features opposite the above-mentioned dimensions. A later study of the same factories has shown that the latter steel plants have had higher profitability, lower rate of discarded material and a lower employee fluctuation compared to steel plants following the system of control.

3 A compelling evidence to this is the so-called Enron case (America company ranked 7th in size with assets worth 66 billion dollars). Enron declared bankruptcy because of misuse and unethical behaviour of top management and those responsible for the control of their work and due to overall business results.

4 Top management as function was first developed by Georg Siemens (1839–1901) in Germany in the period between 1870 and 1880 when he founded Deutsche Bank, a universal bank, which shortly after became the leading financial institution, the strongest in continental Europe. The factor that contributed to such success, according to Siemens himself, was top management, the first practical function of that type back then. Siemens pointed out the importance of top management many years before founding the Bank, stating that a bank without effective top management resembles a pile of office furniture ready for a public auction.

5 When Alfred P. Sloan, the president of General Motors back then, invited Peter Drucker, one of the most renowned world experts in management, to offer his solution as a consultant on the way to solve the crisis of thecompany, he asked for a solution without compromises since every board chairman in the company could offer a compromise without his help. This anecdote reveals that, back then, as well as now, the world's biggest companies have used the intuition of consultants and that it is a specific profession based on knowledge.

6 The methodology of creating a strategic plan depends on the planning approach used by the company:: (1) depending on the manner of the planning process conduction, it is possible to differentiate the so-called inside-out and outside-in approach. The inside-out approach focuses on the internal possibilities, i.e. the company strengths. The outside-in approach focuses on external possibilities, i.e. the opportunities of a company, (2) depending on the hierarchical level providing initiative, it is possible to differentiate the top-down and bottom-up approach. The planning begins at highest top-managerial level in the top-down approach. The planning begins at the lowest managerial level in the bottom-up approach. Both approaches (depending on the manner of the process conduction and depending on the hierarchical level providing the initiative) have their advantages and disadvantages. The first approach perceives the company as a whole and some problems can arise due to the lack of interest of the lower managerial levels. The second approach considers the level of interest of lower managerial levels, but problems can arise due to the consideration of the interest of the company as a single entity.

7 *Brainstorming* is such a useful method that everyday tasks and problems are most often solved by its use in modern companies. The participants of the process are usually the members of the board and top managers, i.e. strategic business unit managers participating in the discussion on the strategic plan. The main idea of this criteria is that people with different profiles, i.e. positioned at different levels, do not approach the same problem in the same way. The aim of using this method is to reach a strategic plan of the highest quality by spontaneous thinking and associations coming from all participants. The brainstorming method provides additional stimulation and competitive spirit among participants resulting in quality enhancement of the strategic plan.

8 A coin is a word created by, usually, two other words.

9 If we were, for example, to observe the automotive industry, Mercedes would be positioned at the left, whereas Hyundai would be positioned at the far right end of the U-curve and Fiat, with no competitive advantage based on low cost and

differentiation, would be positioned at the most bottom part of the U-curve, stuck in the middle.

10 For example, many of the biggest producers invest heavily into product differentiation due to market positioning. Their success leads to high market share providing cost reduction and ultimately achieving overall cost leadership.

References

Babić, M., Simić, M., Puljić, M., Šunje A. (2008): *Korporativno upravljanje: principi i mehanizmi*, Revicon: Sarajevo.

Boyd, H., Walker, C. (1999): *A Distance Learning Programe*, London: Financial Time Management.

Buble, M.(Ed.) (1997): *Strategijski Management*, Split: Ekonomski fakultet.

Burns, T., Stalker, G. (1971): *The Management of Innovation*, London: Tavistok.

Chandler, A. (1962): *Strategy and Structure: Chapter in the History of the Industrial Enterprise*, Boston: MIT Press.

Daft, R. (1995): *Organizational Theory and Design*, Mason: South-Western.

Daft, R. (2002): *Management*, Mason: South-Western.

Davies, J. et al. (1997), *Toward a Stewardship Theory of Management*, Academy of Management Journal.

DeNisi, A., Griffin, R. (2008): *Human Resource Management*, Boston: Houghton Mifflin Company.

Drucker, P. (1955): *The Principle of Management*, London: Heineman.

Đuričin, D., Janošević, S., Kaličanin, Đ. (2013): *Menadžment i strategija*, Beograd: Ekonomski fakultet.

Đuričin, D., Janošević, S., Kaličanin, Đ. (2015): *Menadžment i strategija*, Beograd: Ekonomski fakultet.

Erić, D. (2000): *Uvod u menadžment*, Beograd: Čigoja.

Henderson, D. (1981): *The Concept of Strategy*, Boston: The Boston Consulting Group.

Higgins, H. (1994): *The Management Challenge*, New York: Macmillan College Publishing Company.

Hill, C., Jones, G. (1989): *Strategic Management*, Boston: Houghton Mifflin.

Hill, C., Jones, G. (1998): *Strategic Management: An Integrated Approach*, Boston: Houghton Mifflin Company.

Kiechel, W. (2010): *The Lords of Strategy*, Boston: Harvard Business Press.

Kotler, P. (1998): Marketing Management, New Jersey: Prentice Hall.

Kotler, Ph and Keller, K. (2009): *Marketing Management*, London: Pearson/Prentice-Hall.

Kulović, Dž. (2012): *Strategijski menadžment ljudskih resursa*, Sarajevo: Kemigrafika.

Kulović, Dž. (Ed.) (2012): Kompetencije menadžera i uspješnost preduzeća, Sarajevo: Kemigrafika.

Lorsh, J. (1995): Empowering the Board, *Harvard Business Review*, vol. 73, no. 1, 107–117.

Manus, A., Minow, N. (1995): *Corporate Governance*, Cambridge: Blackwell.

Mašić, B. (Ed.) (2008): *Menadžment: principi, koncepti i procesi*, Beograd: Singidunum.

McGee, J., Wilson, D., and Thomas, H. (2005). *Strategy: Analysis and Practice*, Maidenhead: McGraw-Hill.

Miles, C., Snow, C. (1978): *Organizational Strategy, Structure and Process*, New York: McGraw-Hill.

Milisavljević, M. (1999): *Liderstvo u preduzećima*, Beograd: Čigoja.

Milisavljević, M. (2005): *Sstrategijski menadžment*, Beograd: Megatrend univerzitet primijenjih nauka.

Miller, A. (1998): *Strategic Management, Text and Cases*, Boston: McGraw Hill.

Mintzberg, H., Quinn, B., Ghoshal, S. (1995): *The Strategy Process: European Edition*, London: Prentice Hall International.

Montgomery, C., Porter, M. (Eds.) (1999): Strategy, Seeking and Securing Competitive Advantage, Boston: *Harvard Business Review*.

Nankervis, A., Compton, R., Baird, M. (2002): *Strategic Human Resource Management*, Cincinnati: Nelson-Thomson Learning.

Nyberg, A., Fulmer, I. S., Gerhart, B., Carpenter, M. A. (2010): Agency Theory Revisited: CEO Return and Shareholder Interest Alignment, *Academy of Management Journal*, vol. 53, no. 5, 1029–1049.

Ohmae, K. (1982): *The Mind of the Strategist*, London: Penguin Books.

Payne, G. et.al. (2009), Corporate Board Attributes, Team Effectiveness and Financial Performance, *Journal of Management Studies*, June, vol. 46, no. 4, 704–731.

Petković, M., Janćijević, N., Bogičević-Milikić, B. (2002): *Organizacija: teorije, dizajn, ponašanje, promene*, Beograd: Ekonomski fakultet.

Porter, M. (1980): *Competitive Strategy, Techniques for Analysing Industries and Competitors*, New York: The Free Press.

Porter, M. (1985): *Competitive Advantage: Creating and Sustaining Superior Performance*, New York: The Free Press.

Porter, M. (1998): *On Competition*, Boston, Harvard Business School.

Porter, M. (2008): *On Competition: Updated and Expanded Edition*, Boston: Harvard Business Review Press.

Porter, M., Lorsch, J. W. , Nohria, N. (2004): Seven Surprise for New CEO's, *Harvard Business Review*, May, vol. 82, no. 10, 62–72.

Pozen, R. (2011): The Case for Professional Boards, *Harvard Business Review*.

Šehić, Dž., Delić, A. (2012): *Strateški menadžment i organizacijska efektivnost*, Tuzla: Off-Set.

Smith, S. (2003): *Strateg: kako poslovni cilj pretvoriti u uspjeh*, Zagreb: M.E.P. Consult.

Storey, J., Sisson, K. (1990): Limits to Transformation: HRM in British Context, *Industrial Relation Journal*, vol. 20, no. 1, 60–65.

Šunje, A. (2002): *Top-menadžer: vizionar i strateg*, Sarajevo: Tirada.

Thompson, J., Strickland, A. (1998): *Crafting and Implementing Strategy, Text and Readings*, Boston: Irwin McGraw-Hill.

Thompson, A. et al. (2006): *Strategy*, Boston: McGraw-Hill.

Thompson, J., Strickland, A. (1999): *Strategic Management: Concepts and Cases*, Boston: McGraw-Hill.

Tipurić, D. (Ed.) (2010): *Korporativno upravljanje*, Zagreb: Sinergija.

Todorović, J., Đuričin, D., Janošević, S. (2000): *Strategijski menadžment*, Beograd: Institut za tržišna istraživanja.

Whitinghton, R. (1996): S*trategy as a Practice, Long Range Planning*, no. 29, 731–735.

7 Porter's New View on Competitive Advantage: Green and Competitive

Reasons "for" and "against" organisational involvement in social activities

The previous decades have induced a growing awareness of the problems of our social environment caused by irresponsible behaviour of different companies (Harris, 2009). The fundamental theories of social responsibilities were established by Carnegie in *The Gospel of Wealth* which contains the classic statement of corporate social responsibility.[1] His notion is based on two principles: (1) The principle of doing good charity; and (2) the principle of taking over responsibility custody. The principle of doing good charity requires that fortunate members of society to help those less fortunate, unemployed, ill, handicapped, older and similar. The aid can be direct or indirect through different institutions such as churches, movements or societies. The principle of taking over responsibility custody originates from the Bible. It states that more affluent individuals should bear the role of the helper, to take care of things which can contribute to the development of society as a whole.

During the 1960s and 1970s, both of Carnegie's principles were widely accepted. The idea that power creates responsibility (Inić, 2003) was being recognised. The common aspect of both principles was the view on company shareholders as parents in relation to (childish) employees and consumers which was also one of the main critics of *The Gospel of Wealth*, although there are many examples of using this principle today (Kurtić, 2011).

The last several years, perhaps a decade or more, have slowly but consistently changed the definition of business success from how much money a company makes to the way in which the company makes money. That is the reason why numerous companies are taking part in social activities as displayed in Table 7.1.

Company mission were exclusively economical in the early 1990s. However, the paradigm of a company has changed. Accordingly, a company as an economic entity (known as the Friedman approach) has evolved into the social-economic entity (known as the Freeman approach). It shifted the paradigm from dominantly internal orientation (internal groups of interest) and achieved economic benefits to dominantly external

DOI: 10.4324/9781003359173-7

Table 7.1 Reasons for organisational involvement in social activities

Reasons for company involvement in social activities
Public needs have changed, which has led to shifted expectations. It is argued that the society is the factor granting the foundation and business operations of a company; hence, the needs of the society must be met. Creating a better social environment is beneficial to both society and company. Society receives better local communities (living areas) and increased employment opportunities, whereas company benefit from better communities since they are the source of their workforce and the consumer of their products and services. Social involvement of company reduces incentives for additional government regulation and intervention. As a result, company have more freedom and flexibility in decision-making. A company has high power, which, it is believed, should be accompanied by equal responsibility. Contemporary society is a system of inter-relations and internal company activities affect the external environment. Social engagement can be in the interest of shareholders. Problems can be converted into profits. Items viewed as waste in the past (e.g. empty soda cans) can be reused with a profit. Social engagement creates an appealing public image. Company can utilise it to attract customers, employees and investors. Company should try to solve problems other companies could not solve. Finally, the history of companies is a history of finding new ideas. Companies have resources. They should utilise their talented managers and experts as well as their capital resource to solve some of the problems of society. It is better to be safe by preventing social problems through company engagement than to feel sorry afterwards. It can be easier to help those who have been unemployed for long, rather than to cope with social uprisings.
Reasons against company engagement in society
The first task of any company is to maximise profit which shifts its focus to exclusively economic activities. Social engagement could reduce economic efficiency. In the end, society will pay for the social engagement of organisation through higher prices. Social engagement would excessively increase company expenses; they cannot use their resources for social involvement. Social engagement can deteriorate the financial balance. It is argued that the expenses of social programmes increase the product price. Hence, American companies operating on international market would find themselves in an unfortunate position competing against companies form other countries which do not need to bear the same social expenses. Companies have enough power and the increased social engagement would increase their power and influence even further. Businessmen lack social skills for solving social problems. Their education and experience are focused on economics; hence, their skills are not necessarily fine-tuned to deal with social problems. Companies are not obliged to answer to society (unlike other elective government bodies). If such responsibility is not established, companies do not have to take part in social engagement. There is a lack of full support for socially engaging companiess. Accordingly, disagreements among groups with different viewpoints can lead to conflicts.

Source: Adapted from Weihrich and Koontz (1995).

orientation (external groups of interest) and achieved social benefits. The shift is displayed in Figure 7.1.

Nowadays, companies are more widely included into society partly due to inter-relations among different groups in our society. There is certainly the question of what social responsibility of a company actually represents. Moreover, the issue of social responsibility which referred to companies at

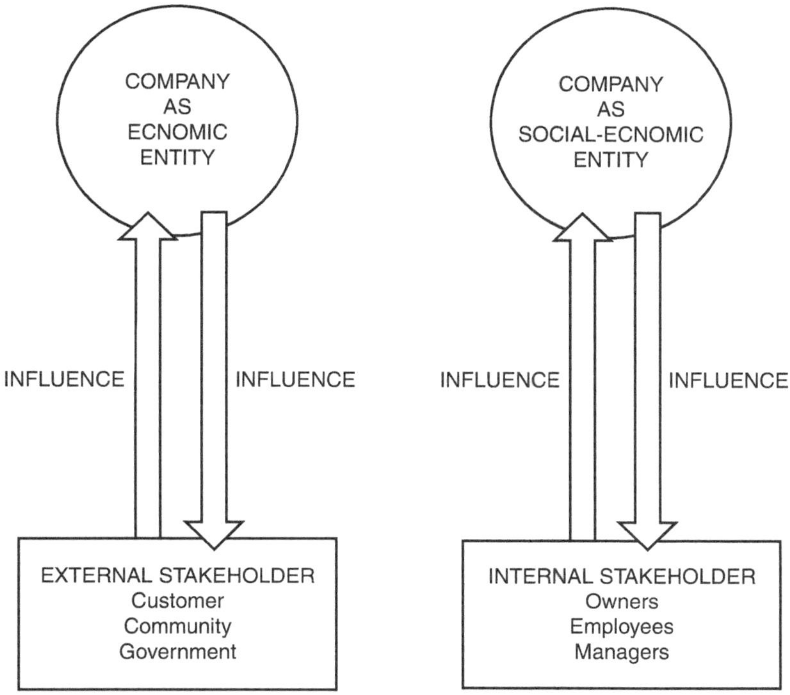

Figure 7.1 Company as an economic and social-economic entity.

the outset, is being presented to different levels of governments, universities, non-profit foundations, charity organisations and similar other organisations. Society, now awaken and loud considering the urgency of social problems, asks managers, top managers in particular, about the actions they are performing to fulfil their social responsibilities and the reasons they are not doing more. Surely, such an approach requires political innovations, a new term advocated by Michael Porter (2020), with the key to unlock politics innovation. Using this competition lens, Gehl and Porter (2020) identify a strategy comprised of a clear set of choices in two key areas: How elections work and how to make laws. Their bracing assessment and practical recommendations cut through the endless debate about various proposed fixes, such as term limits and campaign finance reform. This results true political innovation. Furthermore, they believe that there needs to be a differentiation between two elements of political innovation, as displayed in Figure 7.2.

Hence, powerful innovations address the root causes of dysfunction (not just the symptoms) and are designed to help the political system deliver results in the public interest. Achievable innovations are uncompromisingly non-partisan (no Trojan horses for partisan gain), and success is theoretically possible in years, not decades (constitutional amendments, for example,

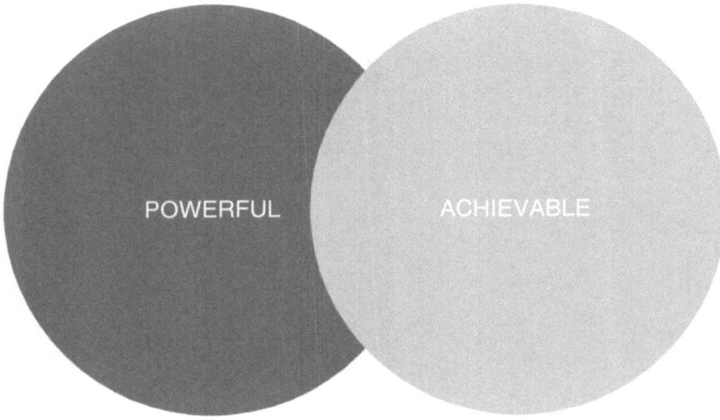

Figure 7.2 Political innovations.

Source: Gehl and Porter (2020).

do not pass this bar). Gehl and Porter (2020) ingeniously apply the tools of business analysis – and five forces framework – to show how the political system functions just as every other competitive industry does, and how the duopoly has led to the devastating outcomes we see today.

That is the reason managers are required to conduct their business operations in a socially responsible manner, i.e. they are expected to function in such a way to represent the well-being of a society as a whole in addition to solely represent the economic interests of the company (Bahtijarević-Šiber et al., 2008).

Levels of corporate social responsibility

The White Paper on Corporate Social Responsibility (2003), published by the European Commission, defines corporate social responsibility as a concept (Kurtić, 2011) which companies use as a guideline to voluntarily integrate their concern of social issues and environmental protection into their business operations and stakeholder relationships (owners, shareholders, employees, consumers, suppliers, government, media and the broader public).

Social responsibility of managers has undergone for stages in its evolution (Table 7.2).

Companies are aware that they must contribute to a sustainable development by managing their business activities in a manner which leads to the increase of economic growth, while simultaneously securing the protection of the environment and promoting social responsibility, including the interests of the consumers. However, it should certainly not result in an *economic benefit increase versus reduction of social benefit* scenario.

Archie Carroll created a model of four criteria of business system social performances, which represents a basis for managerial reactions taking into account their different levels of responsibility (Figure 7.3; Daft, 1994).

Table 7.2 The evolution of the corporate social responsibility concept

Time period	*Phase*	*Essence – managerial focus*
1 From the industrial revolution to the 1930s	Maximising profit	Economic interests: All actions, activities and managerial decisions are focused on meeting the essential goal: maximising the profit of the business system.
2 From the 1930s (period of the Great Depression) to the 1960s	Trust management	Managerial concern for employees, consumers and society as long as they protect the interests of the owner.
3 From the 1960s to the 1990s	Activism	Issues of employment equality, protecting the environment, consumerism[2] and similar.
4 The last decade of the 20th century and the outset of the 21st century	Social sensibility	Ability to effectively and efficiently meet the demands of social responsibility. Managers develop processes of decision-making where the reactions of the environment are anticipated and social and community values are valued (proactive functioning).

Source: Adapted from Kurtić (2011).

1 *Economic responsibility*: The first level of corporate social responsibility is economic responsibility, given that it is, above all, the basic economic unit of society. It is its responsibility to produce the goods and services that society wants and to maximise profits for its owners and shareholders. Economic responsibility, taken to the extreme, is called the profit-maximising view and it is advocated by Nobel laureate economist Friedman. This view shows that a company needs to operate on a profit-oriented basis with its only mission of profit growth, as long as it follows the rules of the game.
2 *Legal responsibility*: All modern societies are based on rules, laws and regulations that business should follow. Legal liability defines what the company considers important, given the appropriate conduct of the company. The company is expected to meet its economic objectives within the laws enacted by the relevant authorities. Therefore, a company that knowingly violates the law is considered a worse performer in this category.
3 *Ethical responsibility*: Ethical responsibility includes behaviours that are not necessarily codified in law and must not serve the direct economic interests of the enterprise. In order to be ethical, a decision-maker in a company should act, as stated earlier, with fairness, honesty and righteousness, respecting the rights of individuals, and ensure different

treatment of individuals only when it is important for the goals and tasks of the company. Unethical behaviour occurs when decisions allow an individual or company to work to the detriment of society.

4 *Discretional responsibility*: Discretional responsibility is exclusively voluntary (non-coercive) and is guided by the wishes of the company to make social contributions without obligations in relation to the economy, law or ethics. Discretionary activities include a generous philanthropic contribution that does not offer a return to the company, nor is it expected. Every company is required to be actively involved in socially responsible activities that result in improving the image of the company as a caregiver of socially responsible activities within society.

However, many managers in different companies and elsewhere have concluded that it is useful for them to take action regarding the intensifying social issues. For example, many companies have profited by filtering matter which pollute the environment through factory chimneys, and selling or reusing the recycled waste. Some companies have gained profit building blocks of flats with low rents in poor neighbourhoods. In other words, contribution to solving social issues does not always produce net expenses. Companies management should be obliged to create, apply and publish harmonisation programmes for internal codices of social responsibility. These codices should be based on domestic norms of the country in

Figure 7.3 Levels of corporate social responsibility.

Source: Daft (1994:163).

question, in accordance with international obligations and should be applied to the company (Šunje and Kulović, 2018).

"How green your business is"

The criteria of "how green your business is" are becoming an increasingly influential factor in product and process quality. In practice, the process of turning a business green is reduced down to the introduction of EMS following the ISO 14001 standard. Green business is a term used for entrepreneurship and production which stem from the principle of sustainable development (Tatić, 2011). Turning a business green is a demand which is becoming an imperative of survival in a market with a host of companies.

There are different levels of green shades of management. In practice, four shades of green are recognised, ranging from light green to dark green, which is in harmony with the level of ecological sensibility of the corporation. The four basic shades are as follows:

1 *Legal approach*: It is most insensitive to environmental problems with a primary focus on compliance. Businesses guided by this approach have a low level of awareness of the importance of environmental management.
2 *Market approach*: It is focused on achieving a competitive advantage of the company taken into account the requirements of consumers; market pressure on consumer awareness that challenges today's businesses.
3 *Stakeholder approach*: It focuses on different stakeholders in an effort to balance a number of stakeholder requirements. The preferences expressed by key stakeholders through their diverse requirements are met.
4 *Activist approach*: It is focused on establishing new paradigms of business based on innovation; creating a business strategy based on environmentally friendly goals within which it creates added value.

The level of the shade of green determines the level of environmental awareness of those companies that advocate the concept of environmental management. Environmental management arises as a result of the increasing awareness of the importance of environmental protection and proactive orientation of the company. The key question companies face is "how green your business is." On this basis, there is a need for "greening of business," which means the level of application of the concept of environmental management in everyday business. Environmental management is defined as the management of all activities in the company that have or may have an impact on the environment. The goal of environmental management is to conduct business activities in a way that will reduce environmental degradation and provide a better environment for future generations. After the integration of the concept of "greening the business" within the business processes, it is important to achieve the integration of all functions within the organisational structure of the company. However, it is very important to distinguish harmful from beneficial relationships.

Good management practice in companies shows how environmental impacts can be controlled, risks reduced, and benefits realised if appropriate management systems and processes are put in place. The practice and experience of companies so far in relation to environmental issues are different. Some companies have made great strides in this regard, and some are just beginning to think about this aspect of their business. Therefore, these recommendations are divided into three groups, and contain the following steps to establish good environmental practice, which is presented in Table 7.3.

Verifying a company potential to meet environmental requirements in terms of "greening of businesses" is important to create a diagnostic approach. Market and non-market environmental assessments are very important and sought after today. It is important to include the scope of

Table 7.3 Recommendations for companies in order to establish good environmental practice

Companies which are beginning to enhance their influence on the environment
Provide active support of the top management of the company which should manage the influence of the company on the environment and society in terms of basic products and services of the company.
Create an initial analysis of company affairs regarding environmental protection.
Ensure that top management receives a task to be responsible for the introduction of improvements on behalf of the executive level.
Companies seeking to create more than just basic conditions.
Create an environmental protection policy and publish it, to employees in particular.
Determine priorities and set goals which will lead to improvements.
Provide sufficient funds needed to achieve the respective goals.
Initiate an employee programme to establish a required level of awareness among them and provide help in the implementation of the programme.
Communicate with other bodies and organisations in society and community, inform them regularly and include them in your programmes.
Companies with a goal of further performance increase.
Take responsibility for constant improvement in this area.
Consider the possible environmental influence when making strategic decisions and in the process of new product and service development.
Formalise the documentation regarding the environmental management system and have it verified by a renowned third party. If possible, formally certify the environmental management system following the ISO 14001 standard or EMAS.
Develop supplier programmes to introduce the improvements to all areas of business process.
Exchange best practices with others and be a leader in your sector and advocate the engagement of other Company and sectors in this area.
Engage in negotiations with the government for creating preconditions and infrastructure needed for a complete transfer to the concept of sustainable development.

Source: Tatić (2011:172).

quality standards that contain valuable concepts that are important to use in the business of the company.

When it comes to environmental impact, an increasing number of companies complies management systems with the requirements of the ISO 14001 standard, which is the basic level of thinking. In terms of the impact on the society in which they operate (local, regional, national, global), companies are increasingly realising that they can build a competitive advantage very well on this basis, and make efforts in various ways to gain market attention and favour.

Porter's modified matrix of business strategies

The concept of building competitive advantage is a very subtle process. Competitive advantage is created quickly, but it erodes quickly, too. The competitive advantage of a company can be determined only in relation to competitors. Competitive advantage exists when a company has a cost-wise more favourable position than competitors, or has some uniqueness that customers are looking for.

Having a competitive advantage means that a company can produce a product with low cost compared with its competitors or may offer a product that its customers value more than a competitor's product.

Companies that implement EMS gain a market advantage over competitors, as we presented earlier, in two basic ways:

1 Through low cost of product with acceptable quality, creating an advantage over other competitors who cannot provide the same to customers. Buyers will stick to such an offer and buy more and thus achieve greater profitability for the manufacturer in turn.
2 Through differentiation of product which is based on the construction of additional values of products which, although they usually lead to a higher price, lead to a higher quality, which is most often protected by the brand. Developing differentiation is a long-term process that requires investment.

In this model, it is only necessary to include the environment and we can create a modified matrix of strategies that are available to companies for achieving competitive advantages, which is shown in Figure 7.4.

The combination of competitive advantage and core competences creates a modified matrix of business strategies for achieving competitive advantage which includes the following strategies:

1 *Eco-efficiency strategy* aims at fulfilling the production needs while consuming less environmental resources in the process.
2 *Eco-branding* strategy based on environmental features of a product is becoming more frequent among consumers with a developed conscious.

3 *Focused differentiation strategy* oriented towards company which aim at both making their products environmentally efficient and informing the public on it, too.
4 *Overall cost leadership strategy* focuses on cost reduction through the identification and elimination of cost drivers.

Standard alone are no longer the only requirement for a company seeking to enhance its performance compared to its competitors. If a corporation seeks to assess the value of the environmental system, ISO 14001 will suffice, but if it wants to check the efficiency of its environmental system, it needs to analyse stakeholder viewpoints, too. It is vital that the environmental strategy of a company is clear, that it motivates consumers to buy its product and that the consumers believe in the advantages of the product. Using its sustainable environmental policy, a company shows that it really is one of the green ones (Porter et al., 1995).

Digital transformation strategy

For companies, in order to grow and develop in the modern environment, it is of utmost importance to radically direct business towards digital technologies. A different view of business means that it is inevitable to change the strategic orientation of the company, that is, to carry out a digital transformation. Competitive advantage in turbulent business conditions is in fact based on the so-called digital platform, which represents the concept of transfer, integration and improvement of digital technologies in modern companies.

The pace of digital transformation depends on industry and area. Companies in the field of information and communication technologies,

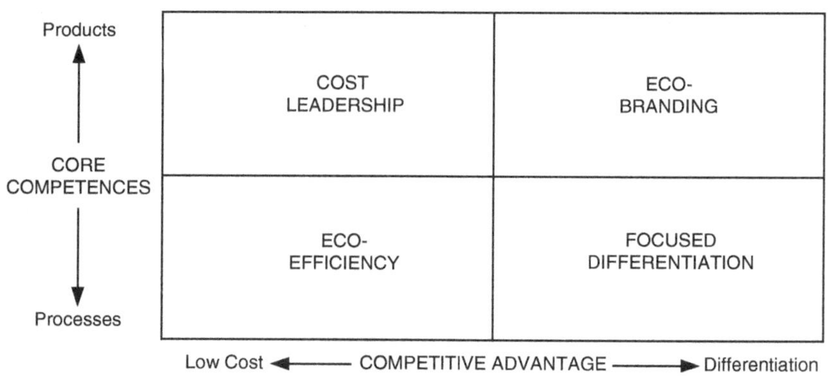

Figure 7.4 Porter's modified matrix of generic strategies for achieving competitive advantage.

Source: Tatić (2011:168).

consulting and PR services are "digitising" the fastest. Due to the complexity of production and the nature of business, digitisation is only carried out in certain segments in the oil and pharmaceutical industry.

The decision on digital transformation should be supported by the top management of the company (Porfirio et al., 2021). It is of utmost importance that decision-makers are aware that digitisation represents a new phase in the life cycle of a company. Digital transformation as a construct has the character of change depending on whether it refers to a business segment or the company as a whole. The transformation is carried out using digital technologies and its purpose may be viewed as something that ought to fully replace certain processes in the organisation, improve the functionality of the processes and in the end ensure an entirely new way in which these processes function (Pihir et al., 2019).

Digital technologies can be considered through three directions in which they operate (Lanzolla et al., 2020; Kitsios and Kamariotou, 2021):

- Increasing the functionality and efficiency of business processes through cloud computing (edge computing, serverless computing, creative algorithms and language modelling, kubernetes and blockchain, secure access service edge and cloud-based disaster recovery), distributed cloud;
- Intensification of connections and trust between people and objects – everything as a service (XaaS), 5G network, data democratisation, customer data platform (CDP), Internet of Things (IoT);
- Increasing automation for business processes and decision-making – augmented reality cloud (AR Cloud), robotic process automation (RPA), low-code platforms, total experience (TE).

Digital technologies are gaining more and more ground in all business segments. Therefore, it is of prime importance to timely recognise that it is possible to select and apply digital technologies in business. We are no longer talking about the digitisation of certain processes in the company, but rather about a change that will alter the vision, mission and strategic framework. Issues of the business area, i.e. business, service and product range, customers, ways of marketing services and products, marketing are raised. The environmental external analysis illustrates that market changes force companies to permanently change the concept of the offer, which indicates that digitisation most often starts from this business segment. Changes in the offer initiate changes in the supporting activities in the value chain, which leads to the reengineering of the business model of the company as a whole.

The competitive environment today consists of companies that are connected with each other, that is, clustered together. This means that it is unlikely that one company will be the main competitor. Multiple companies connected by the same or similar markets, suppliers and digital technologies constitute the modern competitive environment. Therefore, it is necessary to develop additional mechanisms, which will serve the purpose of scanning the environment and identifying competitors, their power and predicting market movements.

Digital transformation is sublimated through a digital transformation strategy. The essence of this strategy is to include and connect all current strategies, to give them homogeneity in the context of adapting to an environment that is constantly and radically changing. The outcome of the digital transformation strategy is the improvement of the performance through an increase in productivity, quality in business processes, sales and customer loyalty.

Porter's competitive strengths represent a strategic framework in which room for manoeuver is created for the company's long-term operations. It is possible to determine with more precision the extent to which the industry is profitable, based on the analysis of rivarly among existing competitors, the threat of new entrants and substitution, as well as the bargaining power of suppliers and buyers. The emphasis is placed on detailed analyses of price trends, costs and investment returns.

It is important to determine the entry barriers before new competitors enter the market. The number of competitors is limited by setting up high barriers. If it is difficult to transfer digital technology (due to high costs, licenses, limited number of software companies, etc.), it means that high market entry costs are in place. Many countries around the world use incentives to subsidise the transfer of digital technologies, and thus affect the increase in the competitiveness of companies.

In practice, there are companies that have been advanced in terms of digital technology from the moment they were founded, and which have not underwent any transformation whatseover, since they were digitised from the start. In this way, an environment is created where digital technologies provide the basis of competitive advantage, which can affect the formation of high entry barriers, especially for the entrants who want to join the market with the help of digital transformation.

Digital transformation tends to give an even greater advantage to the economy of scale because it is easier to establish quality control mechanisms (especially in production processes) and standardisation of business as a whole. Established relations with customers through facilitated or digitised communication can additionally influence the increase in the loyalty rate and thus create an even stronger barrier to new entrants (e.g. online payment services and getting a loan from a bank). In the product distribution segment, a company can have an existing distribution system (if the company is new to the market) or rely on an existing one (if it is a business with a long tradition). Starting a distribution system initiates significant investments, which can threaten the "core" of the company's business to a certain extent.

The threat of substitution in modern business conditions is present in every industry. Depending on the market and technological power of the company, the capacity to notice trends and notice changes of varying intensity depends on the industry to which the company belongs. Digital technologies indicate that the threat of substitution is ubiquitous and "lurks" around every corner. Furthermore, digital technologies can completely alter the business model of a company in a short period of time (e.g. food delivery companies during the COVID-19 pandemic).

The appearance of substitution on the market means that the product and service have better performance and shape a better user experience. Defense against substitutes is almost impossible if the digitisation of business has not been implemented. Digitisation accelerates processes while increasing quality in production, distribution and sales processes. It is crucial for the buyer to know that the substitute will have a better price-quality ratio and almost minimal or no switching costs.

Suppliers can play a significant role in the fight against substitutes. By connecting with suppliers (i.e. by forming alliances, strategic cooperation and in a certain number of cases by purchasing suppliers), the resources needed for production and service provision processes are redefined.

The bargaining power of buyers come to the fore during the COVID-19 pandemic (restricted movement, instability related to job preservation, etc.) and the subsequent economic crisis (the war conflict in Ukraine, the energy crisis). The customer is the main focus of interest of the manufacturer and numerous researches are conducted in order to determine the customer's behaviour as accurately as possible. The customer as the end consumer and consumer of the service and the customer as an intermediary between the producer and the end consumer are at an advantage in the so-called negotiation position. By getting closer to customers in these circumstances, a higher quality of products and services is definitely achieved (user experience), while lowering price is questionable (higher energy costs, inflationary effects).

Digital transformation enables companies to revise the existing business model and approach the customer as an entity in a completely different way. The goal is to establish interaction with customers through digital technologies, which will influence the creation of a completely new user experience. For example, in its research and development department, the Porsche company has obtained detailed information on who makes up the car buyers of this brand. Based on the application of CRM, every interaction (activity) with the customer is recorded and documented, thereby increasing brand loyalty.

Based on their negotiation position, suppliers can significantly influence the competitiveness and performance of companies (McIntyre and Đoković, 2021). If a company is more dependent on suppliers, it means that suppliers are in a better negotiating position. Supplier competitiveness is evaluated on the basis of the following: prices, quality and timely delivery.

The supplier, which has undergone digital transformation, will offer the company it cooperates with a "smart" solution in processes related to product quality, delivery methods and knowledge of the client's business. This means that the digital technologies used by the supplier will affect the performance of its client and as a result the competitiveness of both the supplier and the client will increase.

Digital technologies are used to modify existing products and to create completely new ones. The goal is to achieve long-term competitiveness by making digital products have the "smart" feature. Such products have components that are used to collect a large amount of data and relate to customer behaviour. For example, the company Netflix has partnered with tech giant Microsoft for more efficient management of key resources. Namely, Netflix was looking for a partner to help with the ad delivery process. By using the Microsoft platform, a more affordable subscription plan is enabled, which will have the effect of halting the decline in the number of Netflix subscribers.

Digital transformation has become inevitable for the survival, growth and development of companies in the modern business environment, which is full of sudden changes. The ultimate goal of the transformation is to achieve additional value for all stakeholders in the long term. The market has become digital with its products and services due to the rapid development of digital technologies.

Notes

1 Andrew Carnegie, founder of *Carnegie Steel-King of Steel*. His life is the personification of the American dream – an emigrant who, from misery to wealth, made something out of nothing. He attributed the acquisition of his enormous wealth in the steel industry to people – his associates and the use of the principle of "supreme mind."

2 Consumerism implies the need of managers to constantly listen to the voice of consumers and anticipate their needs.

References

Bahtijarević-Šiber, F., Sikavica, P, Pološki Vokić, N. (2008): *Suvremeni menadžment: vještine, sustavi i izazovi*, Zagreb: Školska knjiga.

Daft, R.L. (1994): *Management*, Fort Worth: The Dryden Press.

Drucker, P. (2005): *Management Essentials*, Zagreb: M.E.P. Consult.

Erić, D. (2000): *Uvod u menadžment*, Beograd: Čigoja.

Gehl, K. M., Porter, M. E. (2020): *The Politics Industry: How Political Innovation Can Break Parisan Garidlock and Save Our Democracy*, Boston: Harvard University Press.

Goodstein, E. S. (2003): *Ekonomika i okoliš*, Zagreb: Mate.

Harris, J. M. (2009): *Environmental Economics and Natural Resources: A Contemporary Approach*, Belgrade: Data status.

Inić, B. P. (2003): *Management 2: Lideri*, Zemun: Birograf.

Kitsios F, Kamariotou M. (2021): "Artificial Intelligence and Business Strategy towards Digital Transformation: A Research Agenda." *Sustainability*, vol. 13, no. 4, 2025. doi:10.3390/su13042025.

Kurtić, A. (2011): *Menadžment poslovnih sistema: sistemi, procesi, funkcije*, Sarajevo: Centar za napredne studije.

Lanzolla, G., Lorenz, A., Miron-Spektor, E., Schilling, M., Solinas, G., Tucci, C. L. (2020): "Digital Transformation: What Is New If Anything?" *Emerging Patterns and Management Research, Academy of Management Discoveries*, vol. 6, no. 3, 341–350.

McIntyre, J., Đoković, F. (2021): *Strategijski menadžment*, Univerzitet Singidunum.

Müller, H. (2004): *Turizam i ekologija*, Zagreb: Masmedia.

Pihir, K. T.-P., and Tomičić Furjan, M. (2019): "Digital Transformation Playground - Literature Review and Framework of Concepts." *Journal of Information and Organizational Sciences*, vol. 43, no. 1, 33–48.

Porfirio, J. A., Carrilho, T., Felicio, J. A., Jardim, J. (2021). "Leadership Characteristics and Digital Transformation." *Journal of Business Research*, vol. 124, 610–619.

Porter, M., Kramer, M. (2002): "The Competitive Advantage of Corporate Philanthropy." *Harvard Business Review*, November, vol. 80, no. 12, 56–68.

Porter, M., Van der Linde, C. (1995): "Green and Competitive: Ending the Stalemate." *Harvard Business Review*, September, vol. 73, no. 5, 120–134.

Šunje, A., Kulović, D. (2018): *Necessity of Business Restructuring of State and Public Enterprises in Bosnia and Herzegovina*, Pale: Zbornik radova Ekonomskog fakulteta u Istočnom Sarajevu.

Tatić, K. (2011): *Menadžerska Ekonomija*, Sarajevo: Ekonomski fakultet.

Weihrich, H, Koontz, H. (1995): *Menedžment*, Zagreb: Mate.

Index

Note: **Bold** page numbers refer to tables and *italic* page numbers refer to figures.